Sikkim's Tryst with Nathu La

What Awaits India's East and Northeast?

Sikkim's Tryst with Nathu La

What Awaits India's East and Northeast?

Edited by

Jayanta Kumar Ray

Rakhee Bhattacharya

Kausik Bandyopadhyay

Maulana Abul Kalam Azad Institute of Asian Studies, Kolkata

ANSHAH Anshah Publishing House

ISBN: 978-81-8364-050-3

First Published in India in 2009

Sikkim's Tryst with Nathu La

Published by:
ANSHAH PUBLISHING HOUSE
Delhi
Sales Office : 115-A, Vikas Marg, Shakarpur, Delhi-110 092
Phone: 9810522367, 22500954

Foreword

The Indian Northeast region, comprising about 5 per cent of the land area and 8 per cent of the population of the country, is one of the most complex in Asia, with about 200 ethnic groups, languages and dialects. These societies have lived in isolation not only from the rest of the country but also from each other, and both legal and illegal migrations have created new fault-lines in traditional societies. The whole area, where parochialism transcends nationalism and regionalism, is in painful transition, trying to learn tolerance of other ethnic groups and adjust to the concept of planned development.

There is a tendency to assert that thc Northeast is not 'integrated' with the rest of India because of ethnicity and insurgency, but this is only partially true. Arunachal Pradesh, which has the biggest number of tribes, is peaceful, while Manipur, which is prey to secessionist groups, is otherwise well integrated in terms of art, culture and sports. Nagaland is the only state where militants are not reconciled to their tribal space being a part of the Indian Union, though, even there, many people see benefits when compared to neighbours like Myanmar and Bangladesh.

There is another aspect to human integration: 90 journalists from Assam alone work in Delhi, 10 per cent of the information technology sector people in Bangalore are from the Northeast, hospitality sectors all over India look for and employ young people from the Northeast because they speak good English. Five thousand young persons from the region each year go to other states to find employment.

The Northeast comprises eight states with only one per cent bordering India – the rest of the borders are with Myanmar, China, Nepal, Bhutan and Bangladesh. India's trade with the countries bordering the Northeast has gone up by five times, but no impact is seen in that region because this commerce is through the seaports. The five-nation BIMSTEC was supposed to help the Northeast, but there is a lack of connectivity that precludes the opportunities leading to results.

Our import substitution economy after 1947 deprived the Northeast of its natural markets, as did the 1971 Bangladesh war. There are massive imports into the region, and Chinese consumer goods are to be seen in every marketplace. The exchange rate is unreasonably low for Chinese imports, and these goods have obviously not come through established channels. Illegal trade and smuggling exist because there is no trade facilitation.

There are three points for border trade with China at places where there is no dispute regarding the boundary; Lipulekh in Uttaranchal opened in 1993 and Shipkila in Himachal Pradesh in 1994. The Indian delegation to Beijing in 1994 proposed the opening of Nathu-la to the Chinese. It then took nine years for the memorandum to be signed, and a further three for the border point to be opened for trade.

For 58 years after the Younghusband expedition of 1904, Nathu-la had been the main artery between India and China and made possible 80 per cent of the trade between the two countries. The expectation at the reopening of Nathu-la was that by 2010 trade at Nathu-la would represent 10 per cent of the total Indo-Chinese trade, namely $1 billion. Why 2010? Because the Border Roads Organization said it would take as long as that for the one-track road to be made into two lanes. Considering that India and China are two fastest growing world economies, and with Tibet itself growing at 12 per cent, Nathu-la should improve prospects for the whole Northeast, which has been left behind at about half of India's growth rate.

However, the optimistic prospects envisaged for Nathu-la trade and its beneficial effects have not materialized, and do not look as if they ever will. If the Northeast opens up, would it be primarily for our exports or only for imports of cheaper Chinese goods? This question seems to obsess the decision-makers in New Delhi, who always want to play safe.

Progress in the Northeast depends on the creation of assets in power, infrastructure and opportunities. India may be looking East but evidently not to our own Northeast. The shocking fact is that 97 per cent of the natural resources in the Northeast, such as hydroelectricity, biodiversity and minerals, is not exploited. There is practically no private sector involvement. The entrepreneur does not need tax breaks and incentives from the state. What he looks for are raw materials sources, the potential market and logistics.

Tourism could transform the Northeast. Ethnologically and linguistically, the Northeast has historic links with South-West China and the Mon-Khmer peoples in Myanmar and Thailand. The structures for tourism are poor, but infrastructure is equally poor in South-West China, Tibet, Nepal and Bhutan, which are all also landlocked. Yet those countries and regions attract manifold numbers of tourists; Bhutan, Nepal, Tibet and Myanmar surpass by far the tourist numbers to the Northeast. No use has been made of specialized promotion, such as adventure, veterans of World War II, wildlife, spiritual or other nostalgia (for tea planters and missionaries) or eco-tourism. Air connectivity to the neighbouring countries does not exist, and in the permit *raj* of the inner line, restricted area, and protected area, permits constitute a serious obstacle.

The Northeastern Council was set up as long ago as 1971 and has been revamped many times since. Health and education are identified as priorities, along with employment, good governance and food security. The public's interest in participating in development is high. But while multiple recommendations are drawn up, little or nothing is seen on the ground.

The centre's response has characteristically been, as in Kashmir, to throw money at the problem with no consideration of outcomes or accountability. In addition to the allocations in the state plans, there are funds from the NEC, and Central ministries, since 1998 have allocated a non-lapsable 10 per cent of their budgets for the Northeast. There is reimbursement of expenditure incurred by Northeastern states on security-related issues, funds for the modernization of the police, border areas' development grants and other sources of funding—too numerous to mention. Yet the minimum identified needs have not been met despite the massive funds poured into the region. With this cornucopia of funds, there has been great seepage and massive corruption. Effective measures to prevent this have neither been devised nor executed. Pumping in funds leads to distortions in the economy unless there are investments in real assets. The shift from agriculture to industry and services is going at a snail's pace even compared to the rest of India.

There are legitimate fears of loss of identity, and the demand by various ethnic groups for increasingly more autonomy continues and has to be addressed. The need to protect the socio-cultural and religious practices of the various ethnic groups and to give them an effective say in running their own institutions has often been underlined. But there is no adequate devolution to the minority tribes in the autonomous areas, and funds are not released directly to the autonomous councils.

The various ethnic fractures prevent cooperation in anti-militancy drives. The Union government has to deal with combating the 30-odd active militant groups both because of the state's reluctance to get involved owing to the alleged lack of financial and human resources, and the Centre's suspicion of the state governments' ability to keep intelligence reports confidential. Even to resist illegal migration, HIV-AIDS and drug trafficking, there is little cooperation between the states. In other words, there is a lack of trust and faith all around.

This is the reason that so many aspects of governance in the region have been left to the supervision of the army, and the prolonged deployment of the military, which is unfamiliar with the local terrain, language, culture and social ethos, has led to serious recriminations and has alienated local people. After 50 years of existence in the Northeast, the Armed Forces Act is viewed as tyrannical, and it inspires hatred.

The Union government might want to look East but most of its bureaucrats in the region look West. Admittedly, life is difficult, and education facilities are limited. There are restrictions on the acquisition of property by 'outsiders'. The result is that there is no long-term commitment on the part of the civil service. An administrative and police service for the region composed exclusively of officers from the Northeast is long overdue.

It is in this context that I would appreciate the efforts of the present volume to bring together diverse perspectives on the issues of development of Sikkim in the wider context of the reopening of Nathu–la and the perceived Indo-China economic cooperation. The way it includes the voices of the locals, and gets those compared and contrasted with the scholars from outside, should inspire future forays into the subject more intrinsically.

Krishnan Srinivasan
Former Foreign Secretary, Government of India
& Hony. Fellow, MAKAIAS

Preface

Maulana Abul Kalam Azad Institute of Asian Studies (MAKAIAS), Kolkata, took up the initiative to pursue a long-term Northeast India Research Programme to understand and address the dynamics and issues of development in Northeast India in the late 1990s. Since then, it carried out a number of projects, organised conferences and symposiums, and brought out publications in this process. The aim of such initiatives was not only to pursue academic research and promote intellectual awareness on the subject, but also to provide viable suggestions and policy inputs for the central as well as the regional governments. The first phase of initiatives came to fruition in 2006, when the Institute, at the initiative of Prof. Jayanta Kumar Ray, our Chairman, undertook a Northeast India Research Programme, with a core group of Fellows working on the subject. Eminent experts like Prof. B.B. Bhattacharyya, Hon'ble Vice Chancellor, Jawaharlal Nehru University, have been our advisors in the effort.

Since the beginning of the second phase, we have already organised two national conferences – one in Aizawl on 19-20 April 2007 and the other in Shillong on 11 July 2007. These seminars covered many of the macro issues of the regions, concerned with development as the overarching factor. The seminars gave us tremendous feedback from the speakers, both from within and outside the States. Scholars participated extensively, dealing with many pertinent issues that underline the challenges today in Northeast India. Proceedings of these conferences, being published by the Institute, will serve as a valuable input to the researchers as well as to the policy makers.

While holding this kind of seminars, we work on the assumption that, going to that remotest part of the country and doing this academic exercise along with the participation of the local people, there could develop a mutual sense of trust, friendship and cooperation. The people there were over-enthusiastic to discuss their problems. So, such academic exercises, stressing participation by the local people, can probably be one way to eliminate their sense of alienation and isolation that always prevails amongst the people in the region. The people of such remote areas of India have a feeling that it is only the Delhi bureaucracy, which works on the policies of the Government of India. But we tried to argue that, academic interactions could also be an extremely useful and powerful tool to deal with the issues of Northeast India. Grievances were ventilated vigorously by the local scholars both in their presentations and in the interactive sessions of the seminar. Many respected senior citizens of the civil society, young energetic scholars, students and professionals took part in both the above-noted seminars.

So, as a learning experience through these seminars, it was realized that, it is very important to establish a strong academic forum in the region by holding seminars, dialogues, etc. and most importantly by doing ground level/action research in collaboration with the participation of the local scholars. Thus, the reason for holding seminars in these Northeastern states is to search for a team of young and committed scholars, who can jointly take up some micro issues of development in the region, which are location-specific, and make an in-depth ground level research, using local resources and catering to the local needs and demands. This is an important dimension of the research initiative of MAKAIAS on Northeast India. With this in mind, it has been planned to organize seminars/seminar series in all the eight States of Northeast India over a long span of time, covering one State at a time, dealing with both their local problems as well as the issues arising out of relations with countries across the international border. This is because, unless local issues are understood deeply, one cannot design policies to cope with the bewildering heterogeneity and complexity of Northeast India. Also, since the region shares long boundaries with India's neighbouring countries, all economic, strategic and cultural aspects of relations with neighbours have to be given necessary attention. Only then, possibly, a degree of peace, prosperity and self-sufficiency can prevail within this region, and lasting solutions to existing problems can be found.

With all this in mind, a third conference was organised on *Sikkim in the Perspective of the Development Dynamics of East and Northeast India* in Sikkim, the most prosperous State of Northeast India. It was organised in collaboration with the Ecotourism and Conservation Society of Sikkim (ECOSS) in Gangtok on 19-20 November 2007. This conference may also be regarded as a follow-up of an earlier one-day seminar on *Perspective of Economic Development in the Teesta-Eco Region* organised by MAKAIAS in collaboration with the Sikkim Development Foundation in Gangtok on 4 November 2003. It envisaged many of the issues taken up for academic and policy considerations after the reopening of the Nathu–la.

Jayanta Kumar Ray
Rakhee Bhattacharya
Kausik Bandyopadhyay

Acknowledgements

This volume is an outcome of the Northeast India Research Programme of Maulana Abul Kalam Azad Institute of Asian Studies (MAKAIAS), Kolkata. We take the privilege to thank all, who have remained involved and supportive in this research endeavour over the years. We extend our deep gratitude to Prof. B. B. Bhattacharya, Vice Chancellor, Jawaharlal Nehru University, New Delhi, who is the Advisor of the Northeast India Research Programme of MAKAIAS. Our thanks go to Prof. H.S. Vasudevan, Ambassador Krishnan Srinivasan, Dr. Amiya Chaudhuri, Dr. P.K. Sengupta, Dr. Binoda Kumar Mishra, Mr. Soumya Kanti Mitra and Mr. Mainak Sen for their persistent academic as well as logistic supports in this ambitious programme. We owe a special debt to Mr. P.D. Rai, without whose enthusiasm and guidance, the conference in Sikkim would have been difficult to organise. We are thankful to the staff of the Ecotourism and Conservation Society of Sikkim, Gangtok, especially its Executive Secretary Mr. Renzino Lepcha, for his unfailing cooperation in this regard. Mr. M.G Kiran deserves a special thanks for his cooperation in collating the documents and photographs for this volume. We are indebted to the distinguished authors of this volume, who, despite their pressing commitments, have enriched the volume with their insightful contributions. Finally, we thank all our friends and well wishers, who worked silently but steadily to make this venture a reality.

Contents

List of Tables

Introduction

This volume comprises nine essays focussing on Sikkim's development based on its own resources, on resources generated by interactions with a neighbouring country through Nathu La, and by integration with the whole of Northeast and east India, along with a few important documents, speeches and reports, relating to the reopening of Nathu La for Indo-China trade, relevant maps and photographs.

In the first essay, Amiya K. Chaudhuri casts a close look at the nature of politics and good governance in Sikkim in a development perspective. He does this by considering the stage of economic development, distributive justice, availability of economic resources actual and potential, the governing structure, competitive politics and interplay of the political parties within the state. The historical background, geographic location, demographic and cultural attributes also come out as important determinants in this context. Emphasizing the uniqueness of the Sikkimese political culture, where the question of Sikkimese identity plays a crucial role, he argues that a latecomer, small land-locked, state of India like Sikkim, even with weak communication networks and an ethnically divided society, could achieve visible economic advance because of its stable inclusive political structure and a proper socio-political vision backed by good governance. Chaudhuri rightly concludes that Sikkim can even prove itself as a model of good governance that helps in building a vibrant economy. However, when it comes to the possible impact of Nathu La's reopening on Sikkim's economy, he remains a little bit circumspect, and shows concern about Sikkim's economic security in such a context.

P.D. Rai, in his essay "Economic Achievements and Future Challenges of Sikkim", examines Sikkim's economic development in rapid transition and ponders whether the State is becoming a key model for the Northeastern States. He attributes Sikkim's economic development to a number of important factors – a modern form of federal government, the central government's consistent policy of providing funds to accelerate the development of infrastructure and social transformation, private capital formation, growth of tourism and its associated services, recent upsurge in industrial activity, establishment of higher educational institutions, transformation in the banking sector and setting up hydropower projects. However, in the context of the reopening of Nathu La, which is sure to change Sikkim's future outlook forever, Rai cautions us about the geographical, environmental, societal, geopolitical and demographical challenges Sikkim has begun to face. Along with two most important internal assets of Sikkim – heritage and biodiversity – he draws attention to a key externality: the politico-socio-economic instability of Darjeeling district. To make Sikkim's economic transformation sustainable, Rai concludes, human resources and managerial capacities have to strongly complement the financial and infrastructural resources.

M.G. Kiran's contribution gives us a government's perspective on the true significance of the reopening of Nathu La. Outlining the potentials of this trade route, he informs how the State Government plans gradually to convert this shortest and easiest overland access to China as one of the resilient means of commodity and service exchanges in the next few years. Despite the problems of trade that remain to be resolved on both sides of the border, Kiran believes, Sikkim, with huge tourism and economic potentials, has much more to gain out of this economic tie-up, and hopes that, if India could match the Chinese infrastructure on her side of the border, Nathu La should witness free trade by 2010.

The realities of trade through Nathu La after its reopening have found illustrative elaboration in K. Elumalai's essay "India-China Border Trade through Nathu La: Prospects for Growth and Investment in Sikkim". The essay discusses the issues related to border trade between India and China through Nathu La, and its implications for Sikkim's economy through a small field survey in the form of stakeholder consultations, conducted in Sikkim and Nathu La between October 2006 and January 2007. Elumalai casts his eye on various dimensions of the trade in this context: growth of bilateral trade between India and China, the nature of border trade through various land routes, the performance of border trade through Nathu La, major problems reported by traders, the scope of expanding border trade and its impact on Sikkim's economy. For Elumalai, the opening of Nathu La provides a window of opportunities for generating various economic activities in Sikkim, thereby leading to the general welfare of the local people of the State. He therefore suggests that Nathu La should be a regular trading point between India and China now for furthering the economic and security interests of not only Sikkim but also east and Northeast India as a whole.

Binoda K. Mishra, in his paper, "Looking at Nathu La through the Security Prism", however, approaches the matter from a somewhat different perspective and argues that while there are promises of absolute gains from border trade arrangements between Northeast India and Southwest China, the security concerns, defined in terms of relative gains, make India cautious and her policies ambivalent. Quite naturally, the calculation of benefits from the opening of this pass is just not economic but also strategic vis-à-vis a country with which India does not share a predictable action-reaction relationship. Mishra, therefore, suggests that the question of opening this pass and using it for economic prosperity of the border areas of both the countries have to be considered in the context of the overall political and strategic relationship the countries have shared in the past and expect to share in the future. Yet, he remains optimistic in his assertion that border trade, particularly through Nathu La, can be viewed as a confidence building measure, and be pursued with a positive approach, keeping it outside the relative gain calculus.

Another significant dimension of Sikkim's development in the context of reopening Nathu La has been the formidable growth potential of its tourism sector. Renzino Lepcha, in his paper "Travel and Tourism: Economic and Cultural Ties and Buoyancy", delves into the problems and prospects of tourism in the Northeast in general and Sikkim in particular in the wider context of contemporary global movement of tourism. He underlines the importance of rich religious and cultural heritage of Sikkim in developing its tourism sector to an international standard. The process of cultural revitalisation needs to go hand in hand with economic buoyancy to achieve this end. In such a perspective, the Nathu La Pass can easily become one of the most important tourism circuits in the world, thereby giving a tremendous boost to the region's economy. Despite outlining the tourism possibilities through this route by 2012, Lepcha laments that the current cautious attitude of India makes Nathu La seem far from being a viable proposition for expanding tourism between India and China. He urges the Indian Government to take positive initiatives to unlock the real value of the route.

Going beyond the issues of Sikkim's development and the implications of Nathu La, Shubhrajeet Konwer brings into focus more general concerns of security and border management with regard to the immediate international neighbours of Northeast India – China, Bhutan,

Bangladesh and Myanmar. There are serious obstacles and troubles such as the proliferation of small arms, drug trafficking, illegal migration, shelter to terrorists in Myanmar, Bhutan and Bangladesh, border disputes with China and border skirmishes with Bangladesh's army – which have multiplied Northeast India's vulnerability in recent years. Konwer's essay identifies the nature and problems of cross border terror linkages and the security challenges that the Indian state faces. In an age of growing trade and investment with the ASEAN countries, unless the issues of security are properly addressed, urges Konwer, the Northeastern States are not likely to benefit from the same, and the Indian government's avowed policy of development of the region through 'Look East' will remain very much a mirage.

Taking into consideration the rich biodiversity of the Teesta-Eco region, J.P. Tamang, in his essay "Teesta Eco-Region and Bio-Resources: An Awaited Future", discusses the future potentials of the Darjeeling hills and Sikkim as well as Northeast India as a whole in the context of the reopening of Nathu La. Being an active centre of evolution of many new gene pools, this region is possessed with such valuable components as indigenous food crops, ethnic fermented foods, edible wild plants and their fruits, wild honey, medicinal herbs, orchids, and ornamental and wild flower plants, which, if utilized properly, may lead to the region's sustainable development. Tamang also highlights the opportunity for big investment in the agro-processing sectors in the Teesta Eco-region by way of value-addition to region's food/bio resources. To him, the ample bio resources of the region can be explored by establishing a *prima facie* good bio-resources management.

The last essay by Sohel Firdos focusses on Nathu La's potential contribution to the growth of tea trade between India and China and the development of Sikkim in that process. Examining the linkages between the tea industry of West Bengal and the development of Sikkim, he explores the challenges and prospects of marketing, investment and trade in tea in the State. If good connectivity and proper infrastructure are established, Sikkim may emerge as a hub of collection, distribution and marketing of tea grown in West Bengal and Assam, since tea industry in India is facing a renewed challenge of competition to compete in the export market, both in terms of quality and quantity. In the context of the reopening of Nathu La, which can always become a vital point of tea export to Tibet, argues Firdos, Sikkim may act as a collection point and blending centre of tea from China and eastern India for re-export, thereby generating foreign exchange for the State.

Sikkim's economy has been performing brilliantly in recent years with a strong political vision and leadership, and seems to have a bright chance to catch up with many other prosperous states of India. In this sense, it can be the role model for other Northeastern states. So it is urgent to find all the economic viabilities of this state, as development is the ultimate aim and goal of this research mission. This economic viability cannot be gauged without the perspective of Nathu La, which experienced a historic reopening for trans-border trade on 6 July 2006 after 44 years with profound hope and vision for Sikkim-China relations. Nathu La has become one of the most vibrant issues for Sikkim in terms of its socio-political and economic ambience. People's dreams and despairs with Nathu La are now debated at various forums. The optimists believe that if this pass is optimally utilized, prosperity will definitely go beyond Sikkim and will have a spillover effect in the whole of east and Northeast India. So Sikkim's destiny today can no longer be envisioned without Nathu La and its related issues.

Overall, with an aim to prove that Nathu La can provide a lesson that borders should become the meeting point for people to exchange and share transnational ideas, wealth and culture for a better world, rather than dividing them with a narrow political vision, the volume is expected to draw attention to, and generate interest in, not only the problems and prospects of Sikkim, but of other Northeastern states, who also have been the victims of the closed borders with their neighbouring nations for a very long period of time.

Chapter 1

Sikkim: Politics and Good Governance in Development Perspective

Amiya K. Chaudhuri

Some Theoretical Considerations

India as a federal state with certain unique features of its own, *sui generis* as it may be defined, has been constitutionally so designed as to maintain a proper balance between the Centre and the states on the one hand, and among the states on the other in regard to legislative, administrative and financial powers. Besides, there are federal compulsions and systemic necessities pertaining to modernisation of politico-electoral processes and economic development. Specific Centre-state relationship in the recent era of intense political party competitions that has been affecting economic development is also a major concern. The role of political parties, whether national, state or local, inside or outside legislative institutions, both in the state and local levels, is an important determinant everywhere. The Constitution in its several Articles aims at providing good governance both at the central and state levels. It is a matter of conjecture whether the central administration during the past half a century has been able to achieve good governance *per se*, or at least to a minimum attainable degree. In several of the states the idea of good governance may broadly be defined as contextualized[1] in regard to contour and contents, politics and government, and the political processes. It appears therefore that the features and internal characteristics of the politics and governance of the states of India, more or less, indicate some commonalities. But on deeper examination it also reflects the micro dimensions of the proposition.

The state politics of India is a constitutionally crafted structure, but the processes following there and affecting the governance are unique, and the combination of a complex social economic, religious, linguistic and ethnic baggage, sometimes severally but more often individually.

We are to miss these complexities if the politics of the state is seen in a simple descriptive format. In this sense we find "hardly serious efforts linking the structural characteristics with broader sociological context in which the former are articulated or meaningfully explained."[2] The stages of economic development, distributive justice and economic resources available and potential, the governing structure, competitive politics and interplay of the political parties within the states are also to be considered to study the nature of the politics and governance of an individual state. The historical background, geographic location, demographic and cultural attributes and the legacy of the political economy of the state are important determinants in this context. In this situation "what is thus critical in any understanding of the political" in the Indian state scenarios is societal and economic underpinning of the politics and governance whereby "one can construct a framework of analysis which is plausible and theoretically refreshing."[3] The observations in this regard of an expert in the study of state politics are theoretically sound and relevant. He recognized in the mid 1970s that "no discussion of the operative dimension will be complete without a passing reference to the question of style, vocabulary and language of the state politics"[4] in India. He further noted that the recent exposition of state politics was "an analytical framework for the study of state politics in India, which has a built-in bias towards systemic approach but with a difference in so far as it insists on an application with a developmental and hence essentially dynamic perspective."[5] Keeping in mind the outlines given above, the politics and economic development that result from the process of governance in the Himalayan state of Sikkim are to be traced in the following pages.

Sikkim as the tiniest and 22nd state of India is unique in senses more than one. It was a protectorate, and the process of integration with the mainstream politics of India had an inherent problem because it had its own socio-cultural and politico-economic system and a traditional paradigm of development[6] with a political culture perceptibly different from what we are familiar with. Its democratic transition from an associated feudal existence to a full-fledged unit of federal India is quite unlike more than 550 princely states of the Union as existed before the adoption of Indian Constitution on 26 January 1950. It is a latecomer in its democratic orientation but quick enough to follow the process of political modernisation as far as possible in an ethnically defined society. When many of the Indian states including the smaller ones of the Northeastern region suffered from socio-political and electoral fragmentation, and more often than not having to adjust to fractured social verdict in government making, Sikkim stands a bit apart. Wholesale political defection of individual members of the legislative bodies, sometimes changing of side by the legislature party itself, which has been found elsewhere in north Indian states including some of the Northeastern states, is rarely found in Sikkim.

The Sikkimese people are to a large extent of Mongoloid origin. It is a tribally divided society but the number of tribes, tribal divisions and consequent tensions among them are not as intense and conflicting in respect of their own identities as found in most of the other eastern Himalayan states. During a period of rapid socio-economic changes all over the country, the original inhabitants of Sikkim were very much anxious and afraid of losing their exclusive control over the state's resources and power. Therefore, the identity as Sikkimese of the locals in present day Sikkim became a crucial determinant to keep away non-Sikkimese who were supposed to be far above their local counterparts in terms of political consciousness, socio-economic status, resource position, education and "manipulative qualities."[7]

Regarding the socio-anthropological dimension, the following quote is very relevant. "The first tribe which entered this inhospitable land was the *Magar* who migrated from central Tibet. Another Mongoloid tribe-the *Lepchas*-who called themselves *Rangpo* (the ravine dwellers) entered this land via Burma and Assam. The Lepchas drove the Magars westward into the country of Limbo (presently eastern part of Nepal) and further west."[8] The present day Sikkim society is not as it was in the later half of the 19th and the 2nd half of the twentieth century. Political calculations of the British regime in India, focussed on permitting sufficient latitude of maneuverability of the Sikkimese rulers, led to a large number of Nepalese people being allowed in Nepal to counterbalance the population structures both internally and extra territorially. Now the Nepalese settlers are the largest population components of Sikkim. Bhutias and Lepchas are the two other main tribes besides a few other miniscule shifting tribal people. The Nepalese settlement in the state brought about a significant change in the demography, and in fact exerted considerable pressure on the "land settlement pattern". Consequently, "agricultural technique"[9] had to keep pace with emerging pattern of cultivation practiced by the other two ethnic groups, viz., Lepchas and Bhutias.

The professionals, business classes, traders and other middle levels of service sector people from other Indian states are also part of the social hierarchy, though not socially important enough. The communitarian lifestyle of the Lepchas, feudalistic order and Lamaistic way of life, Tibetan

Buddhist socio-religious mores and Nepalese social practices and work culture were all woven into a transitional political culture. Later on after a democratic movement in Sikkim, which imbibed the spirit of nationalist Indian political movement, a democratic political culture – a mix of tribal political outlook and political modernisation under the influences of political party dynamics – began to grow in Sikkim. "After Sikkim emerged as a constituent state of India, all the basic instruments of development were geared into action. This needed to be done to give an Indian identity to the Sikkimese economy, which primarily had been a feudal state with aristocracy usurping the cream of development. Since the mid-1970s, the entire fulcrum of development in Sikkim has undergone a metamorphosis in social, economic and ecological fronts."[10]

The present day Sikkim has traversed a long way economically, socially and politically. Sikkim before 1975 was sparsely populated. People used to live in far-flung areas. Educational, health, transport and communication facilities were almost nonexistent. Literacy rate was less than 15 per cent, and female literacy was not more than 4 per cent. But in the mid 1990s, and particularly since 2000, the socio-economic scenario of Sikkim appears to be brightening. Table 1.1 points to the comparison with the Indian average:

Table 1.1: Literacy in Sikkim (%)

Census Year	*India*	*Sikkim*
1951	18.33	6.59
1961	28.31	12.30
1971	34.45	17.74
1981	43.67	34.05
1991	52.2	56.94
2001	65.38	68.80

Source: Census of India 2001.

Table 1.1 shows almost a jump in literacy rate in 1981- the time when Sikkim already came to join the mainstream of Indian state system, so much so that it surpassed the Indian average by 3.42 per cent. It appears from the scenario as seen in Sikkim that literacy as in other advanced Indian states, is a major determinant of political modernisation and economic development.

Another important indicator of development is as to how the state tries to reduce the number of people living below poverty line. Table 1.2 shows the picture clearly.

Ranking is important, and by 2007 available data might show much more improvement.

Table 1.2 : People Below Poverty Line (%)

Years	*All India*	*Sikkim*	*Ranking*
1973-74	54.88	50.86	16th
1977-78	51.32	55.89	9th
1983	44.48	39.71	15th
1987-88	38.86	36.06	14th
1993-94	35.97	41.43	5th
1999-2000	26.10	36.55	4th

Source: Figures at a Glance Sikkim Vis-a-Vis India, Govt. of Sikkim.

A recent document indicates, "Twenty-five years back, when Sikkim became the twenty second State of India it had very limited development space both in economic and political sense. The onset of democracy and building of economic structures changed the entire profile of Sikkim. From a traditional economy with a feudal slant, Sikkim has emerged as a modern and robust State of today."[11] Actually pertinent decisions in respect of its inter-ethnic harmony and launching of major economic regeneration programmes are being taken by the political establishment headed by a forward looking chief minister Pawan K. Chamling, who is unlike his flamboyant predecessors for whom politics overshadowed economic consideration. The state is severely land–locked and its economy was mostly dependent on external considerations. Integrated and all-inclusive policy of economic development was conspicuous by its total absence. The situations remained as it was from the late 1970s to the 1990s. Development efforts have been concentrated in urban areas, and the state has witnessed a high rate of migration from the villages to the urban and periurban conglomerations. Rapid urbanisation has far outpaced the existing infrastructure and civic amenities. Although the census data show a decline in urban population from 16.65 per cent to 9.15 per cent in 1991, urban population according to the annual plan, 1998-99, was closer to 20 per cent. Lower urban population figures in the census data are a result of the re-demarcation of some of the revenue blocks surrounding Gangtok as a rural land. Earlier these blocks were part of the Gangtok Municipal Corporation[12]; apparently this conclusion does not contradict the argument above.

Institutional politics and unpolluted process of the same can only set in motion what one understands as good governance. Good governance, defined at least contextually – politically honest decision-making, proper implementation of the decisions as far as practicable, and transparency in the process – is the essential minimum for the success of development initiatives. Misgovernance and corruption lower the revenues of the state exchequer and increase the fragility of the financial base of the revenue system of the government. "Key institutional capacity elements are a comprehensive legal framework defended by an impartial competent judicial system, accountable, open and transparent executive decision-making, coupled with a capable, flexible and efficient bureaucracy and strong civil society participation. Opportunities for corruption increase with the number and complexity of rules and regulations, licenses, taxes and subsidies, which set up conflicting property rights, investment proposals and many other things that require complicated resolutions. An efficient, uncorrupt bureaucracy is a key factor and it tends to encourage investments in different fields of economic and related activities. Efficiency of public services is particularly important for the poor, who depend on public services, such as primary education and health, to improve their lot and mitigate the risks they face. Non-transparent budgeting and spending, widespread subsidies, and corruption are likely to lower the efficiency and equity of public spending."[13] In the Indian context the Government of Maharashtra set up a committee to make a report on how within the limitations of a constituent state, the government could take some positive steps to achieve at least what is possible. Good government as a concept belongs to the realm of an ideal. Sometimes it may be judged as what is contextually achievable. It also "needs to be appreciated that the concept of good governance is much larger than mere administrative reforms in the conventional sense of the term. In fact, it covers much more ground and substance than administrative reforms. Good governance has much to do with the ethical grounding of governance and must be evaluated with reference to specific norms and objectives … it must have firm moorings to certain moral values,"[14] like fair play, individual and collective freedom, equity and justice—social and political. It could be approximated but next to impossible to reach. But on the other hand, without a modicum of good governance, social changes and economic development become almost elusive. It is more difficult to achieve in a democratic society like ours where intense party politics and fragile governing structures and unstable electoral coalitions, quite unlike in developed West European and some Scandinavian countries, stand as stumbling blocks. The Marxist pundits once used to claim that Soviet Russia achieved economic prosperity quite enormously, but this claim did not take long to fall apart. In this context, we are to bring into a larger focus the high economic growth rate of modern day China following a neo-liberal approach in terms of liberalisation and globalisation. But it is to be admitted that what is possible in a monolithic party state, may not be possible in any democratic state with many demerits but with the exceptional virtue of freedom of expression and individual choice. Therefore, China achieved what once the Soviet Union did because of its uncompromising Marxist socio-economic culture and a monolithic political structure. Unlike the Soviet regime, China neither adopted *Glasnost*, i.e, a baggage of freedom of expression nor *Perestroika* or economic reforms. The Chinese system survives possibly because even adopting the latter it did not fail to realize the explosiveness of the former.[15] In the name of good governance and principle of equity, even with its state and party machinery as also its absolute control over societal spaces, the Soviet system could not survive. What is to happen in China may be in some distant future or so, may be any body's guess or perception, because good governance includes harmonious relations among most sections of the people in society, responsive government and above all freedom of choice within the parameters of the constitution of the state.

Judging from the points raised above, it is really a matter to be seriously considered as to how a latecomer small land-locked state in India like Sikkim, with weak communication networks and ethnically divided society can achieve such visible economic advance. Stable political structure and governmental initiatives are obviously very necessary factors. Despite ethnic manipulation by the larger community and the negative political influence and intrigues from outside the state, Sikkim may be shown almost as a model to the other states of India particularly the Northeastern ones. The governance in Sikkim at this point of tortuous time probably does not falter in the ongoing process of political and economic modernisation and development. As the Sikkim government increasingly moves out of many of its traditional spheres and moorings, it has already begun a serious governmental down-sizing process. It will surely allow it to focus on better delivery system of goods and public services. Since the successive governments of the state have to play a very vital role in boosting up and sustaining development, one way to reduce corruption is to "ensure the broad-based participation of people in the process. Development should involve all government branches, civil society and the business community, and ensure their commitment to an anti-corruption agenda. Planned schemes have been reviewed and prioritised, as over the years several plans have been continued and expanded incrementally. All the schemes should be thoroughly reviewed and prioritised. New schemes should be made contingent on the availability of resources."[16]

The above points are to be dilated further while discussing the political process and administration, the political economy and the political will of the governments of Sikkim over the years. The initial argument is that many of the potentially able state governments of India are lagging behind Sikkim, which, under the inclusive politics of the present regime, has been working with the right type of socio-political vision backed by administrative efficiency. The state politics of Sikkim and the leadership of a few politicians at the helm of the state administration appear to be moving in the right direction, and possibly this is the uniqueness of the Sikkimese people. Although their political achievements are still incomplete, yet this movement in the right direction is a positive step.

Geographical Location, Demographic, Cultural Attributes and Historical Perspective

It is very necessary to take into consideration the geographical location, demographic characteristics, cultural attributes and the legacies of past history and its contemporary dynamics to understand the politics and the evolving system of democratic governance and the direction the political economy of the state is heading towards. Sikkim is no different on this hypothesis; rather the state may grow to be a model as indicated earlier.[17] This Himalayan state of Sikkim is situated between Nepal in the west and Bhutan in the east. It is a small stretch of ruggedly greenish land of just 115 by 65 kilometres. On the northern border, the gradient rises to the Tibetan plateau and its southern border runs along West Bengal. It is one of the beautiful tourist spots in India, and often found to be teeming with foreign tourists and Himalaya watchers. It is a small speck of territory, the latitude being 27 degree north and 88 degree east in the map of Asia, but to the observers its size cannot shroud its richness of culture, customs and heritage. Sikkim demonstrates that small is beautiful. It is smart and marching forward. The state of Sikkim is the inner part of the ranges of the Himalayas and has no open valley or plains. Besides, the following facts are very important to make an assessment of the prevailing development perspective of Sikkim.[18] Within a distance of 80 kilometres the elevation rises from 200 metres in the Teesta river valley to nearly 8598 metres at the Kanchenjunga peak. The geo-physical area of the state comprises 7095 sq.km. The total population is 5,40493, the male and female divisions being 2,88217 and 2,52276, that is 0.5 per cent of the

Indian population (Census 2001). And the density of population is only 76 per sq.km, remarkably low as compared to any of the Indian states. According to the Census Report of 2001, the sex ratio is 986 females/ 1000 males – considerably above the Indian average (see also Table 1.3 and Table 1.4). This is a very important point to be noted when considering the development perspective and the work culture of the segments of the population structure as also the government of the day having the objective of sustained development. The government is to chalk out a plan taking into account the demography of the state and the nature, specific needs and divisions of the people living in each of the areas. Table 1.3 and Table 1.4 show Sikkim's position in contrast with India as a whole..

Table 1.3 : Further Geographic Statistics (Sikkim and India)

Items	*Unit*	*Sikkim*	*India*
Area	Sq.Km	7095	3287263
Urbanization	%	11.10	27.80
Districts	No.	4	593
Divisions	No.	9	5470
Villages/Revenue Blocks	No.	453	638588
No. of Towns	No.	9	5161
Total Households	No.	114223	19357995
Average Household Size	No.	4.70	5.30
Per Capita Outlay on Housing	Rs.	463 (2nd highest among states)	27

Source: Census 2001 & Figures at a Glance Sikkim vis-à-vis India. Govt. of Sikkim

Table 1.4 indicates important per capita GSDP, BPL, HDI data that are quite high in comparison with other Indian states.

The entire state has been divided into four districts having land and population structures of its own. Table 1.5 shows the demographic details of the four districts of the state.

The State of Sikkim, that we find today, is rapidly accelerating its economic development in terms of building industrial infrastructures, centres for business expansion. The economic indices point to that direction (Table 1.5). And if one looks at the human development index one will get some idea as to the level of living standard of the people of Sikkim.[19] In this regard, Sikkim, which started almost from the scratch in 1975, is presently far ahead of many of the larger and smaller states of

Table 1.4: Population Structure and Human Development Index

Total	*No.*	*540851*	*1028610328*	*2001 Census*
Male	No.	288484	532156772	2001
Female	No.	252367	496453556	2001
SC	%	5.00	16.20	2001
ST	%	20.60	8.20	2001
Main Workers	%	39.31	30.54	2001
Per Capita GSDP at Current Prices	Rs.	23786	23492	2003-04
People Below Poverty Line	%	36.55	26.10	1999-2000
Human Development Index	No.	0.532	0.602	1998 (SKM) 2005 (IND)
Per Capita Outlay on Health	Rs.	296 (2nd Highest among states)	11969	2002-03

Source: Figures at a Glance, Govt. of Sikkim.

Table 1.5: Population and Area-wise Break-up of the state of Sikkim

District	*Area (sq.km)*	*Population*	*Headquarters*
East	954.0	244790	Gangtok
North	4226.0	41023	Mangan
South	750.0	131506	Namchi
West	1166.0	123174	Gylshing

Source: Report, Government of Sikkim

India. The present chief minister of the state, in releasing an authentic and valuable report, stated, "My Government has been successful in restoring people's faith in democratic ethos and a democratically elected government. Every Sikkimese can now participate in the democratic elections at all levels and political development process in a fearless and free manner. As a result, we have perhaps an unparalleled distinction of being a State with very high degree of political stability and well-established tradition of social harmony."[20]

Political culture of Sikkim is unlike many other states. It is a non-confrontational mix of tribal ways of life among the Nepalese settlers, dominant tribal communities, e.g. Lepchas, Bhutias, and the minor ones like Magar, Gurung, Tamang, Sherpas etc. But to ensure this, the Constitution of India makes a special provision for the Governor of the State. For the purpose of promoting cordial relations, peace and communal harmony among the ethnic communities in the State, the Governor of Sikkim has been empowered under *Article* 371F(9) [Special Power]. These result from historical inheritance, rituals, that mostly reflect people's agricultural occupations, modes of family life, community choice, rituals and religious practices. The state, finally, had to adopt a politico-electoral process in a newly emerging democratic system of governance, political party dynamics, and adjust to the extra-regional influences brought in by the societal classes like the teachers, professionals and the modern business practitioners that gradually began opening up the closed Sikkimese societies.[21]

Like in all the other states in India, the government has always been viewed as an authority in Sikkim in its socio-political sphere. This means that the development role has to be played by the government alone. It has severely affected the resources that could otherwise be tapped from sources other than that of the government. "This is why we are trying to revive that bond of volunteerism that used to traditionally characterise Sikkimese society. It has been widely felt that there is ample space for non-governmental organisations (NGO) to work in the area of development in Sikkim."[22]

The Political Economy

Before examining the emphatic views of the present chief executive of the state regarding the role of non-government organizations (NGO) as also existing capacity utilisation of the state, a few more data are to be noted. The four districts of the state are divided into nine divisions.

This is necessary to organise and activate the local governments and the local governing processes both rural and urban. These nine divisions are Gangtok, Pakyong, Namchi, Soreng, Gylshing, Rabongla, Mangan and Chunthang. Numbers of Zila Parishad wards are 100, while the Gram Panchayat units are 166 and the Revenue Blocks are 454. The main occupation profiles of the people are varied. They are mostly farmers, small-time artisans, cardamom growers, contractors, service holders, cab owners and taxi drivers. It is a multi-lingual state where Nepali, Bhutia, Lepcha, Limbo, Magar, Rai, Gurung, Sherpa, Tamang, Newari and Sunuwar languages and dialects are spoken. Surprisingly the per capita income amounts to Rs.29, 808 at current prices as in 2005-06. The income of the urban population (numbering 11.10 per cent) is naturally comparatively higher than its rural counterpart. However, the below poverty line people's percentage point is 19.20 in 2005-2006. The gross domestic product (GDP) increased to Rs. 1717 crores in 2005-06 at current prices. Table 1.6 gives an idea of the work force in perspective since 1971.

Table 1.6: Gradual Increase of the Work Force (1971-2001)[23]

Item *Population*	*1971* *209843*	*1981* *316385*	*1991* *406457*	*2001* *540851*
Total Workers:	111609	147436	164392	212904
Cultivators	NA	88610	97834	101200
Agricultural Labourers	–	4887	13793	9081
Workers in Household Industry	–	1586	1309	3168
Other Workers	–	52353	55785	99455
Marginal Workers	–	5378	4329	50139
Non Workers	98236	163571	237736	277808

Source: Figures at a Glance, Govt. of Sikkim.

Table 1.7 is a comparative study of the small mountainous states of India's Northeast, including Tripura. Sikkim was fairly ahead of all the states in respect of Human Development Index in and around 1994, and has been gradually improving since 2001.

The politico-economic development and political modernisation of the state have been brightened up. Several factors are responsible for it. Invitation of outside investments, serious efforts to build up modern infrastructures in terms of opening up of a closed economy in the land-locked hilly areas, boosting up of business opportunities, and prospect of opening up of trade route to Tibetan China through Nathu La pass and people's free access to mainland India and neighbouring Nepal and Bhutan, making new power plants, conservation of water resources and permission to build up a few barrages over Sikkim's main rivers, above all designing the Teesta barrage project in spite of stray protest movements by citizens fearing displacement and environmental hazards – are some outstanding achievements of Sikkim's political economy. "The Teesta Hydel Power project promises development in the long neglected region of north Sikkim. However, the region's indigenous inhabitants, largely the Lepchas and the Bhutias, along with the Buddhist community, have been engaged in a sustained campaign against the project. Such protests are not merely on grounds of displacement but that it will affect the region's cultural and ethnic traditions in the river Teesta and its environ."[24] But there is no denying that in a period of development in a massive way

Table 1.7: Ranking of the Hill States (out of 25 states) in Terms of Per capita Net Domestic Product (at currents prices) and Poverty

State	*1983-84*		*1987-88*		*1993-94*	
	Per capita Rank	*Poverty Rank*	*Per capita Rank*	*Poverty Rank*	*Per capita Rank*	*Poverty Rank*
Arunachal	6	8	8	8	7	7
Assam	19	9	19	9	19	5
Himachal	8	25	15	23	14	15
Manipur	16	16	12	17	18	13
Meghalaya	18	14	16	14	17	9
Mizoram	22	17	6	18	11	17
Nagaland	9	13	10	13	9	9
Sikkim	12	12	7	10	10	4
Tripura	24	11	22	11	24	8

Source: *Sikkim Human Development Report 2001.*

some sort of a teething trouble is inevitable although the authorities spearheading the development projects need to be careful about the affected people and the totality of societal, human and ecological and environmental concerns.

Table 1.8 shows Human Development Index and its components that have been increasing since 1991.

Table 1.8: Sikkim's Human Development Index and its Components

Year	*Life Ratio*	*Literacy*	*Enrolment Expectancy*	*Educational Attainment*	*Per capita Income*	*HDI*
1991	0.625	0.569	0.436	0.525	0.274	0.454
1995	0.650	0.674	0.476	0.608	0.253	0.504
1995	0.663	0.738	0.448	0.641	0.292	0.532

Source: Compiled from Mahendra P. Lama, Sikkim Human Development Report, 2001

**Note:* Latest data are still not available as on February 2008. It is learnt that another volume of Sikkim's Human Development Report 2007 is to be brought out in mid-2008.

The figures given in Table 1.8 are laid out taking into account the figures of each of the four districts of the state. To a great extent the rising trends indicate the development and the improving life profiles of the people of Sikkim. Earlier in Table 1.7, important differentials of the Northeastern states including Sikkim and its development perspective were shown as against the whole of India. In respect of literacy, particularly female literacy rate, Sikkim is ahead of the Indian average. It is a fact, which can be empirically shown, that female literacy may check the excessive birth rate, which is a stumbling block for income generation in all underdeveloped areas.[25] From this hypothesis the question that may arise as to why all other north-east states having a high degree of literacy are lagging behind Sikkim in their economic development objectives. There might be several reasons as diagnosed in many of the northeastern states like Mizoram, Meghalaya, Manipur, Arunachal, Assam, and Tripura. The most important of them are corruption at different levels, leakages of central funds sent by the Centre for various development projects, funds for rural employment guarantee and literacy programmes and insufficient utilisation of central funds for specific purposes, etc. It appears from available records (possibly the development index indicates so in the present day Sikkim) that the government of Sikkim is sufficiently aware about these negatives.

Table 1.9: India and the North East: Population and Literacy: A Comparative Estimate

Literacy Rate (%)

States	*Total*	*Persons*	*Males*	*Females*
India	**1027015247**	**65.38**	**75.85**	**54.16**
Arunachal	1091117	54.74	64.07	44.24
Assam	26638407	64.28	71.93	56.03
Manipur	2388634	68.87	77.87	59.70
Meghalaya	2306069	63.31	66.14	60.41
Mizoram	891058	88.49	90.69	86.13
Nagaland	1988636	67.11	71.77	61.92
Sikkim	**540493**	**69.68**	**76.73**	**61.46**
Tripura	3191168	73.66	81.47	65.41

Source: Compiled, Sikkim Human Development Report, 2001.

According to the analysis based on the human development perspective, Sikkim entered an era of economic development since the historic constitutional change of April 1975, when the state had joined the mainstream of national political life, becoming the 22nd State of the Union. The fact is that Sikkim, having switched over from a monarchical system to a democratic government, naturally generated great enthusiasm, and rising expectations in the minds of the people. The backlog of development that had to be made up in order to reach the level of other similarly placed states in the Union rendered the task of planned development extremely difficult and challenging but at the same time an exciting adventure. Nevertheless, the rural population of Sikkim, who fought bravely for changing the old order and those who had sacrificed in the past, have to be provided with, at least, the national minimum of their needs.[26]

The present political establishment, because of its stability, has been pursuing genuinely the path of economic development since 1994. Table 1.10 conclusively shows the level of development in comparative perspective, which indicates the growth trajectory that Sikkim proposes to follow in the years to come.

Table 1.10: Growth Rate of GSDP at Constant 1993-94 Prices in the IHR (1996-97to 1999-2000)

States	*Growth Rate (%)*
Jammu & Kashmir	5.50
Himachal Pradesh	6.50
Sikkim	**9.60**
Meghalaya	6.30
Tripura	8.40
Mizoram	NA
Manipur	6.80
Nagaland	NA
Arunachal Pradesh	5.10
India GDP	**5.80**

Source: Lok Sabha Unstarred Question No. 557,17/07/02.

Recent documents indicate that the growth rate of India exceeds a little more than 8 per cent, and still lags behind what it was in Sikkim seven years back in 2000.

To conclude, the economy of the state, the political structure and environmental concerns are to be brought into their legitimate focus. Without political will of the concerned regime as well as the effort and the vision of a balanced development perspective, the political economy of development of state cannot be pursued to its logical conclusion. Sikkim is predominantly an agricultural state that requires to be modernised. The effort may come to be fruitful only when the existing demographic structures and the possibility of any shift in foreseeable future, and proper planning in different parts of the territory, are seriously considered. Industrially, the state is still backward because of its difficult terrain, and its isolated geographic regions and locations. Exploitation of existing mineral resources, surface water and building necessary network of communications and laying up of industrial bases are very challenging.[27]

People's participation in the development process and their influence on decision making process in the government are important for an effective delivery system. The decentralisation of power to local bodies increases the efficiency and transparency, which makes the bureaucracy really accountable to the people.[28] This is not impossible if the political leadership is determined and the whole territory of the state is ruled not only from a centre but the governing process is spilled over from the grassroots upward. In this discourse of political economy it transpires that the political leadership, both at the centre and the periphery, tries to ensure that rural governments in the shape of Panchayati Raj system are capable enough to undertake what exactly is required of them.

A Brief Perspective of Historical and Political Regimes

Sikkim today, as it appears from the discussion above, has appeared all the time since its merger as a vibrant democracy. But its transition from feudal autocracy with religious fervour was tortuous. It was ruled by the Namgyal dynasty till 1975. The last monarchical ruler, Chogyal, was unwilling to accede to India even in the late 1960s. Feudal by inheritance, he was intriguing and made a last moment attempt to thwart a democratic transition by influencing the border states of China, Nepal and Bhutan. As the monarch married an American woman, he tried to utilise her to win over the USA also. But Chogyal's last-ditch effort failed, and Sikkim was merged with the federal India. The monarchical system of more than 300 years came to an end. Twelve generations of the institution of Chogyal that ruled over Sikkim was abolished in 1975, and a transitional democratic process followed. China eventually recognised Sikkim as an integral part of Indian Territory in 2003, that led to the thaw in Sino-Indian relations as far as that part of Indian state was concerned (China till date has not clarified its position in respect of the Indian state Arunachal). In return India had to declare Tibet as a part of China. Subsequently, on a joint declaration by the two prime ministers Dr. Manmohan Singh of India and Wen Jiabao of China, the Himalayan pass of Nathu La was opened to cross border trade.

The Indian National Congress, along with a few state level political parties began working for the consolidation of the nascent democracy in Sikkim. After a gap of a few years a genuine politico-electoral system came to play the real role of establishing good governance, contextualised or whatever, where people have participated enthusiastically to determine their politico-economic future. It was a period of rising popular aspirations that are to be mobilised only through a relook at the political economy of the state as understood by the political leadership. The steps were taken by stages, and the sea change that began since the mid-1990s explain the paradigm shift in the thinking and execution of the economic development projects that we find in Sikkim today. It is sufficiently appreciated by the politicians that an almost universal participation of people at central and peripheral levels was necessary.

Table 1.11: Election of Legislative Assembly of Sikkim (1979-2004)

Year	*Total Voters*	*No. of Valid Votes Polled*	*No. of Polled Votes Rejected*	*Total Votes Polled*	*% of Votes Polled*	*% of Polled Votes Rejected*
1979	117157	72339	3960	76299	65.13	5.19
1985	155041	97057	2378	99435	64.13	2.39
1989	192619	133619	5608	139227	72.28	4.03
1994	217743	173457	4566	178023	81.76	2.56
1999	255377	204927	4056	208983	81.83	1.94
2004	248959	196465	781	197246	79.23	0.40

Source: Report, Election Commission

Average of voters during 1979 to 2004 (6 Terms) : 197816

Average of votes polled during 1979 to 2004 (6 Terms) : 149869

% of average votes polled during 1997 to 2004 (6 Terms) : 75.76

Table 1.11 shows the percentage points of votes that have been increasing in the Legislative Assembly elections in Sikkim since 1979. Such a large percentage of votes (75.76%) polled is found only in West Bengal and Tripura for reasons of their own while the all India average is 59 per cent only. In the transitional period, Kazi Lendup Dorji played a very important part. The political groups that sprang up during the past to serve the interests of the then ruling establishment apart from a few national and known Indian political parties, were converted into local and regional parties. Shree Nar Bahadur Bhandari of the Congress Party also played an important role in the democratic process of the state, and initiated the development process. It was really easier for him, particularly during his first stints, because of his closer association with the central Congress leadership under Rajiv Gandhi. In the on-going political development process, relooking the political economy based on the rising aspirations of the state as a whole as also to serve the universal interest of the people across the spectrum of original tribes and settlers, every chief minister more or less played some constructive role despite a little corruption then and now. Table 1.12 shows the successive periods that were under the chief ministers of the state.

Table 1.12: Chief Ministers & President's Rule

Period	*Name*
16 May 1975 – 17 August 1979	Kazi Lendup Dorji
17 August-1979 – 18 October 1979	President's Rule
18 October 1979 – 11 May 1984	Nar Bahadur Bhandari (1st term)
11 May 1984 – 25 May 1984	Bhim Bahadur Gurung
25 May 1984 – 8 March 1985	President's Rule
8 March 1985 – 17 June 1994	Nar Bhahadur Bhandari (2nd term)
17 June 1994 – 12 December 1994	Sanchman Limboo
12 December 1994 – continuing	Pawan Kumar Chamling

Source: Records, Government of Sikkim

Table 1.12 shows two terms of President's rule indicating factionalism in the Indian National Congress Party. But Nar Bahadur Bhandari came in for the 2nd term and served the governments for full two terms. There were stray corruption charges against him. He tided over the difficulty but finally had to give up to Pawan Chamling of Sikkim Democratic Front (SDF) – a state party only. The point must be noted here and as shown in Table 1.13 that no national party after Nar Bahadur Bhandari managed to have any political hold over the state to form the government either singly or collectively as coalition.

But it would be less than just if anyone ignores the initiative Bhandari took in the process of political modernisation and economic development.

The Sikkim Legislative Assembly has only 32 Members. In all, 12 seats are reserved for the Scheduled Tribes and 2 seats for the Scheduled Castes, indicating more or less a harmonious representation of the Sikkimese people. The house reflects the existing composition with different groups of the people, ethnic and otherwise. Table 1.13 shows very interesting details. There are a number of political parties, their votes are shared and the majority party forms the government. The Assembly upholds the decisions of the council of ministers led by the chief minister. Therefore the chief minister – the leader, be it of a single party or a ramshackle coalition government – directs the socio-economic vision of development of the state. It has been almost always found in Sikkim since early 1980s that the chief minister found a strong party initially, the Congress and then the state level party, backing him. As a result, the political establishment and the bureaucracy at tandem were able to carry on its economic development projects and programmes to a moderately desired level.

Table 1.13: Sikkim Legislative Assembly Election Results (1979-2004): Seats won, Valid Votes Polled and % of Vote Polled by Party.

Party	*Year: 1979*			*1985*			*1989*			*1994*			*1999*				*2004*		
	Seat Won	*No. of valid vote polled*	*% Votes Polled by parties*	*Seat Won*	*No. of valid vote polled*	*% Votes Polled by parties*		*Seat won*	*No. of valid vote polled*	*% Votes Polled by parties*	*Seat Won*	*No. of valid vote polled*	*% Votes Polled by parties*	*Seat Won*	*No. of valid vote polled*	*% Votes Polled by parties*	*Seat Won*	*No. of valid vote polled*	*% votes Polled by parties*
CPM	0	241	0.33	0	336	0.35					0	270	0.16	0	398	0.19	0	144	0.07
CPI	-	-	-	0	25	0.03													
INC	0	1476	2.04	1	23440	24.15		0	24121	18.05	2	26045	15.02	0	7512	3.67	1	51329	26.13
JP	0	9534	13.18	0	913	0.94													
SSCL	0	85	0.12																
SC(R)	4	11889	15.76																
SJP	16	22776	31.49																
SPC	4	11400	15.76	0	438	0.45													
SSP				30	60371	62.20		32	94078	70.41	10	60851	35.08	7	85827	41.88	0	90	0.05
RSP								0	11472	8.59									
DPC								0	298	0.22									
BJP											0	274	0.16				0	667	0.34
RSP (I)											0	2906	1.68						
SDF											19	72856	42.00	24	107214		31	139662	71.09
SHRP																	0	1123	0.57
IND	1	11938	16.50		111534	11.88		0	3650	2.73	1	10255	5.91	1	3976	1.94	0	3450	1.76
Total	32	72339	100	32	133619	100		32	133619	100	32	173457	100	32	204927	100	32	196465	100

Source: Election Commission of India

Note: CPM=Communist Party of India(M), CPI= Communist Party of India, INC=Indian National Congress, JP=Janata Party,SSCL=Sikkim Scheduled Caste League, Sikkim Congress (Revolutionary), SJP=Sikkim Janata Parishad, SPC=Sikkim Prajatantra Congress, SSP= Sikkim Sangram Parishad, RSP=Rising Sun Party, RSP(I)=Revolutionary Socialist Party, DPC= Denzong Peoples Chogpi, BJP= Bharatiya Janata Party, SDF= Sikkim Democratic Front, SHRP= Sikkim Himali Rajya Parishad, IND= Independent.

Concluding Observations

Sikkim is a very small Himalayan state but with sufficient economic development potential. The transition of the state from its feudal ethos to democratic values was not easy, but not extremely tortuous either. The people are ethnically divided but the divisions are not as intense as elsewhere in India's Northeastern states in respect of identity politics. The people are peace loving and responsive to the cause of development. The political parties are competitive but not confrontational always. The chief ministers of the state have mostly enjoyed a stable government. The political tensions between the Centre at Delhi and the states that are observed in different regions due to several factors are hardly found in Sikkim. The politics of the state never takes precedence over economics. That is one of the major factors that help a new look political economy of development in Sikkim. The governmental decisions are carried on not only from the capital at the Centre but from the peripheries as well through the constitutionally adopted policy of decentralised governance. All these arguments made above are to show that Sikkim, although very small in comparison, can prove itself as a model of good governance that helps in building a vibrant economy of development.

But the government of Sikkim as well as the Central government should bear in mind that the opening up of Nathu La pass for mutual trade expansion may not be that advantageous for Sikkim. The Chinese side of the Nathu La is absolutely fortified.[29] The roadways and other communication channels are very well connected with Mainland China, whereas the Indian sides are still to be properly laid out and developed. Apart from India's external security concerns, the cheaper Chinese goods pumped into this side of the border at the peril of Sikkim's handicrafts and smaller manufacturing items might stand as a threat to Sikkim's economic security.

REFERENCES

1. Subrata K. Mitra, *The Puzzle of India's Governance: Culture, Context, and Comparative Theory*, New York: Routledge, 2005.
2. "Politics of India", available at http://www.du.ac/du/stc/politics.pdf.
3. Ibid.
4. Iqbal Narain, *State Politics in India,* Meerut: Meenakshi Prakashan, 1976, p.xl.
5. Ibid, p.xl.
6. Mahendra P. Lama (ed), *Sikkim: Society, Polity, Economy, Environment*, New Delhi: Indus Publishing company, Second Print, 2000.
7. Amal Datta, "Ethnicity and Resource Management in Sikkim", in Lama, *Sikkim*, pp. 68-81.

8. J.D. Hooker, *Himalyan Journal*, Vol. I, London (1854), quoted in R.S. Chauhan, "Sikkim Politics of Immigrant", in Narain, *State Politics in India*, p. 545.
9. Datta, "Ethnicity and Resource Management in Sikkim", p. 73.
10. Mahendra P Lama, "Editor's Note", in Lama, *Sikkim*, p. 14.
11. "Forword", *Sikkim Human Development Report 2001*, Government of Sikkim, Delhi: Social Science Press, 2001.
12. "Managing Urban Growth", Sikkim: The people's voice, available at http:/ /Sikkim.gov.in/ASP/Visiondocument?Managing.urban.htm.
13. *India: Policy to reduce Poverty and accelerate Sustainable Development,* 2000, World Bank.
14. Madhav Godbole, Report of the One Man Committee on Good Governance, July 2001, http://www.maharasthra.gov.in
15. In the events of uprooting the peasants from land, while making way for establishing Special Economic Zones (SEZ) China had to suppress more than 87000 popular protests in the year 2005 only. See Srikanth Kondapalli, "China's Strategic & Security Policies in 2006: An Assessment", *South Asia Defence and Strategic Year Book 2007,* New Delhi: Panchsheel, 2006, p. 116.
16. Op cit, http:// www.sikkim.gov.in
17. *Sikkim Human Development Report 2001.*
18. "Facts and figures", available at http://www.sikkim.gov.in/ASP/Miscc/ SG_FACTS.htm.
19. *Sikkim Human Development Report 2001.*
20. "Foreword", in ibid.
21. Ibid
22. Ibid.
23. Data after 2001 are not available. As reported in the 19-20 November 2007 Seminar at Sikkim by the present Education Minister, the next *Human Development Report of Sikkim* is expected to come out sometime in the mid 2008.
24. Vibha Arora, "Unheard Voices of Protest in Sikkim", *Economic and Political Weekly*, 25 August 2007.
25. A.R. Kamath of Poona Institute of Economics and Politics wrote a series of articles in the *Mainstream,* New Delhi, during late 1960s on the basis of his empirical studies on the relation between women's illiteracy and the growth of population in India.
26. *Sikkim Human Development Report 2001*, p. 16.
27. "Report", *Forest Environment and Wildlife Management Department, Government of Sikkim*, p.112.
28. For details, see http://sikkim.gov.in/ASP/Visiondocument decentralization.htm.
29. As observed by the team of researchers from the Maulana Abul Kalam Azad Institute of Asian Studies, which visited the Nathu La pass during 17-19 November 2007.

Chapter 2

Economic Achievements and Future Challenges of Sikkim

P. D. Rai

Sikkim is, geopolitically, highly strategic even though it is so small an area in the Eastern Himalayas. The mountain passes of Jelep La and Nathu La make it prized in terms of access to the Tibetan Plateau and to the economic, social and political exchanges. It offers the shortest route to Lhasa, the capital of Tibet, from Kolkata and its sea ports – a mere 1350 Km or so. The British conquered Sikkim by the late 1800s and Sikkim became part of India in 1975. Always a bone of contention with China, Sikkim is now acknowledged as part of India by that country but not before extracting some major concessions. Tibet has been recognised by India as part of China.

A key question is "Have the people of Sikkim benefitted by becoming a State of India?"

Another way to put this question is "Did the policy of Government of India to totally overwhelm the Sikkimese people with funds for development really work?"

In 1975 Sikkim was ushered into the Indian Union as the 22nd State. The historic May 8 agreement of 1973, which literally oversaw the overthrow of the king of Sikkim also known as the Chogyal, translated into Article 371F of the Constitution, a form of protection which safeguarded old laws and perhaps local customs as well[1] . So far nothing has been tested in the Supreme Court.

Today Article 371F has become a much used and touted constitutional provision for safeguarding Sikkimese from onslaughts, be it in demography or in terms of non compliance with the Income Tax Act. Half a million people can actually be overwhelmed by the 1.1 billion in the rest of India!

Who is Sikkimese anyway? The closest definition identifies Sikkimese with all those who were given Sikkim subject certificates by the erstwhile King (Chogyal) when a kind of census was done in the 1960's. There is a register, which lists those who were registered as Sikkimese. Today many find that their names are not there. Many were left out then. Many say they were left out. Some controversy is there but this is perhaps the most credible list of 'Sikkimese'. Today there is another way to give legitimacy by giving, after due verification, the Certificate of Identity (COI). This is given to those who are offsprings and those who have been 'left out'.

Economic Performance Indicators and Data:

If we go by indicators like the GSDP, then we find the following:

Table 2.1: Sikkim: Estimates of Gross Domestic Product and Per Capita Income at Current Prices

Year	*GSDP (Rs. Cr)*	*% Change over previous year*	*Per Capita GSDP (Rs)*	*% Change over previous year*
1993-94	403		8457	
1994-95	440	9.18	8714	3.03
1995-96	520	18.18	10056	35.40
1996-97	592	13.85	11141	10.78
1997-98	680	14.86	12644	13.49
1998-99	787	15.74	14652	15.88
1999-00	844	7.24	16343	11.54
2000-01	971	15.04	18261	11.73
2001-02	1080	11.22	19568	7.16
2002-03	1234	14.26	22239	13.65
2003-04 (PE)	1386	12.31	24621	10.71
2004-05 (QE)	1531	10.46	26851	9.05
2005-06 (AE)	1717	12.15	29808	11.01

Source: Economic Survey of Sikkim 2006-07, Government of Sikkim[2]

Sikkim has shown double-digit growth in terms of GSDP. This is fuelled mainly by serviced sector which now constitutes close to 50 per cent in terms of contribution. The primary sector has stagnated, showing a decline in contribution. From about 51.59 per cent in 1980-81 it is now about 20 per cent. Does this also indicate rapid urbanisation? In fact it is not at all surprising to go into villages and see only old people working in the fields and also to see large tracts of land, which are not worked on today. Government handouts are enough of a disincentive together with high cost and low availability.

Table 2.2: Shares of Contribution in the Total GSDP of the Sikkim Economy

Sectors	*1980-81*	*1985-86*	*1990-91*	*1995-96*	*1999-00*	*2004-05 QE*
Primary	51.59	50.96	46.49	39.41	25.52	20.54
Secondary	18.11	16.46	12.97	18.80	19.73	30.22
Tertiary	30.30	32.58	40.54	41.79	54.75	49.24

Source: Economic Survey of Sikkim 2006-07, Government of Sikkim[3]

Add to these outlays the centrally sponsored schemes (CSS) and the allocation from the non lapsable pool which is given by the Ministry of Development of Northeastern Region (MDONER) and NEC, then it will become amply clear how much funds are actually coming into the State.

Annual outlays are much larger if we consider non plan and other incomes – anywhere in the order of Rs. 1,000 crores plus.

This is a lot of Central Government funds for a small state like Sikkim. This also explains the overwhelming domination of the Union Government in calling the shots in all the sectors of the economy. It is pertinent that there should be a paragraph of this kind written in an official document:

The perennial dependence for resources on the Central Government and a patronising attitude towards the region has created a culture of dependence, a subsidy syndrome and rent-seeking behaviour associated with government contracts. The public investment in the region has low productivity as a significant part of the investment spills over the jurisdiction due to very weak backward and forward linkages.[5]

Sikkim in Rapid Transition – Is it transforming into a key model Northeast state?

Sikkim is transforming rapidly in all the sectors – economic, social and demographic. This is happening on account of the following reasons:

1. GOI has had a consistent policy of giving a large amount of funds to accelerate the development of infrastructure and social transformation after Sikkim became a part of India in 1975. This was also to quell any kind of building of resistance to the merger. It has worked. The net result is that Gangtok today has urbanised to an extent that it is not quite recognisable. Furthermore roads (1773 km) and connectivity, electrification and dispersal of schools and primary health centres would be the envy of most states. Government has fanned out its

Table 2.3: Sectoral Allocations of 5 yr Plans

	7th Plan AE 1985-90		*8th Plan AE 1992-97*		*9th Plan AE 1997-2002*		*10th Plan PE 2002-07*	
Outlay in Rs. Crores	***% age***	***Rs. Cr. 216.67***	***% age***	***Rs. Cr. 770.36***	***% age***	***Rs. Cr. 1091.32***	***% age***	***Rs. Cr. 1655.74***
Agriculture and Forests	18.29	39.63	16.72	128.80	9.60	104.77	12.37	204.82
Rural Development	1.81	3.92	3.34	25.73	4.05	44.20	3.30	54.64
Irrigation	3.55	7.69	1.85	14.25	2.10	22.92	1.23	20.37
Power	9.64	20.89	13.4	103.23	12.00	130.96	21.71	359.46
Village industries	1.34	2.90	1.48	11.40	1.32	14.41	1.24	20.53
Other industries	2.04	4.42	2	15.41	1.16	12.66	0.56	9.27
Roads and Bridges	16.68	36.14	11.74	90.44	12.50	136.42	8.66	143.39
Road transport	3.13	6.78	1.3	10.01	0.68	7.42	0.48	7.95
Science and Tech	0.08	0.17	0.03	0.23	0.31	3.38	0.40	6.62
Ecology and Environment	0.15	0.33	0.22	1.69	0.12	1.31	0.12	1.99
Tourism	0.75	1.63	0.97	7.47	1.27	13.86	1.20	19.87
Civil Supplies	0.18	0.39	0.38	2.93	0.18	1.96	0.23	3.81
General Education	13.17	28.54	10.82	83.35	17.20	187.71	13.00	215.25
Sports and Youth Affairs	0.51	1.11	0.33	2.54	0.60	6.55	1.46	24.17
Art and culture	0.93	2.02	0.51	3.93	1.00	10.91	1.70	28.15
Medical and Public Health	1.93	4.18	9.2	70.87	5.60	61.11	4.84	80.14
Water supply and Sanitation	6.41	13.89	8.16	62.86	2.80	30.56	6.45	106.80
Housing	1.43	3.10	5.11	39.37	9.30	101.49	4.00	66.23
Urban Development	0.88	1.91	1.33	10.25	1.80	19.64	6.00	99.34
Information and publicity	0.4	0.87	0.37	2.85	0.50	5.46	0.45	7.45
Nutrition, Women & CW	0.78	1.69	1.13	8.71	1.75	19.10	2.52	41.72
Public Works	2.14	4.64	2.87	22.11	2.00	21.83	2.00	33.11
Others	13.78	29.86	6.74	51.92	12.16	132.70	6.08	100.67
TOTAL	**100**	**216.67**	**100.00**	**770.36**	**100.00**	**1,091.32**	**100.00**	**1,655.74**

Source: Economic Survey of Sikkim 2006-07, Government of Sikkim[4]

administration and other institutions to most parts of the state. The Panchayati Raj institutions are functioning in all districts. In the North District there are traditional institutions, known as the Dzumsas. All this has led to the burgeoning of the bureaucracy, and now more than 35,000 people are engaged as Government servants. It is fair to say that one in almost every household is a Government servant.

2. A second reason has been that due to the prevalent feudal system people recognise only one set of rulers. We can characterise this as feudal baggage. It was first the Chogyal Palden Thondup Namgyal, then Kazi Lhendup Dorji, then Nar Bahadur Bhandari and now Pawan Chamling. Willy-nilly the people of Sikkim have had a very stable and peaceful time to develop its human capital. The Human Development Index Report does speak of many gains in education, social transformation and increased life span[6] . So in line with point number one, many young people have been able to get fairly good higher education and have been able to come back and man the many new departments that have been created since 1975. Sikkimese people reflect the opposite of what goes on in Bengal. There, *dharnas*, agitations and *bandhs* are a daily happening. Here it is socially shunned. People have a plain dislike for violence and are always keen to see society being in a state of peace. Of course with growing disparities and education the key question is for how long?
3. Furthermore, there have been huge leakages from the Government system, through contracts and other Government funding mechanism. This has led to capital formation, which has resulted in the building of many large private buildings and other infrastructure. This continues unabated. Due to the constraints on land in Gangtok, this building activity has now moved to other parts of the State. A case in point is the district headquarters of Namchi, which is currently witnessing unprecedented urbanisation. This also happens to be the constituency of the incumbent chief minister. So it has received favoured treatment in the devolution of resources from the Government and its programmes.
4. Since 1990 Sikkim has opened up its tourism sector. This got a fillip due to the closing down or slowing down of Kashmir as a tourist attraction and Darjeeling becoming too congested for tourist comfort. Sikkim was a fresh destination and, with its

pristine magic, very alluring indeed. Thus, Pelling and Gangtok have become major tourist destinations. Today, North Sikkim has begun to draw huge numbers of tourists. Sikkim records annually over 2.8 lakh tourist arrivals, roughly ten per cent of them being foreigners. It is growing at above 15 per cent per annum. Tourism has spawned a major sub sector in our economy, leading in transportation, hotel services and other tourist-led services. Local businessmen have the luxury of catering to both the local demand and tourist-led demand.

5. More recently, after the year 2000, and after Sikkim became a part of the Northeast Council (2002), pharmaceutical majors have been making a beeline for Sikkim. Most of them are setting up manufacturing units and are supposedly doing well. Rangpo to Singtam and Rangpo to Rorathang have become virtual industrial corridors. Thus there is an upsurge of industrial activity which in many ways is a result of the GOI incentives given in the form of tax breaks as well as the peace and tranquility of Sikkim, non enforcement of labour laws and shunning of violence by the Sikkimese people.
6. Setting up of higher educational institutions in the State has been another major reason for accelerated change. Manipal Institute of Technological Sciences and Manipal University have been around for over seven years now. Furthermore, more recently, Sikkim University has been set up as a National University. This will further enhance the access to higher learning in the State. Sikkimese students had to go to other States on scholarships to pursue higher education. Now with these institutions more and more students can pursue their higher education in Sikkim itself. This will give a boost to access issues.
7. Another very interesting transformation has been witnessed in the banking sector in Sikkim. Sikkim has its own bank – the State Bank of Sikkim which was set up by a Durbar proclamation. Today all the major public sector, 17 in number, and private sector banks, 4 in number, have their branches in Gangtok if not in other parts of the State. The CD ratio has also improved over the years and is now at about 40 per cent. It used to be less than 20 per cent about 7 years ago. This is an indicator of improved credit ratings of businesses and people of the state. Total credit flow from banks is at Rs. 160 crores in 2005-06. This was a meager Rs. 12 crores in 1999-00. (Source:

NABARD)[7]. Obviously the largest benefits went to the service sector – 87 per cent.

8. The setting up of hydropower projects is also now an immediate key driver of change. It is, on the one hand, creating awareness of the dangers of development, and on the other raising the hopes of the local population that progressively better times are ahead. Recent developments in this sector are worrisome. There has been some protest about hydropower projects and notable among them is the one in Dzongu, in North Sikkim. Hunger strikes and other measures have been resorted to by the Affected Citizens of Teesta (ACT) to put the Government on notice[8].

Add to this the strong macroeconomic picture of the India growth story. India is growing at over 9 per cent, and the economic outlook for the next decade is extremely promising. This fact alone creates the feeling that there are great opportunities in the making for Sikkim. This buoyancy is being felt in all sectors of the economy.

Hence, these are the major causes for the rapid change that are overtaking Sikkim at present but simultaneously pose major challenges. Nathu La reopening further adds to the list. On 6th July 2006 and after 44 years, Nathu La was opened for border trade. A mere 15 items can be imported and 25 items exported. These are all traditional in content.

Nathu La reopening, under the present globalisation trend and geopolitical scenario, will alter Sikkim's future outlook forever.

Economic transformation of Sikkim has both its good and bad points. It creates major structural and other challenges. These will play out in the coming decade.

So, to put it succinctly, the following are indications of rapid transformation as observed

1. Rapid urbanisation has taken place. Gangtok today is a metropolis, and all indicators of a modern city are evident. Retail outlets have flourished. Traffic snarls, albeit still manageable, are the order of the day. Lots of eating out joints, discotheques and clubs, bars are doing good business. This is limited not only to Gangtok. It is happening in at least four other towns.
2. Gangtok and Pelling are increasingly looking like tourist driven towns with lots of travel agents and hotels donning the urban landscape. One can therefore gauge that tourism is fast becoming a mega drive for the private sector. It is definitely responsible

for the soaking up of much of the educated youth of the state – either as first generation entrepreneurs or as providers' livelihoods.

3. Loss of green and forest cover in most of the urbanising centres is evident even as more dust hits us on the roads.
4. It is important to note that the demographics have changed dramatically in the urban areas. Gangtok, from quick estimates, has a population of over 50 per cent who have moved into Sikkim in the last 10 years.
5. Social tensions are now palpable and many drawing room discussions are about the changes that are taking place, unchecked. Drug and substance abuse is on the rise and so is the incidence of HIV AIDs.
6. Pollution in the State has increased manifold. This is evident from changes in horticultural patterns as well as indicators like dirty shirt collars at the end of the day.
7. Land is a very scarce commodity and it is now even scarcer with prices hitting record levels. Typically land in Tadong area is going at a market value of Rs. 2,500 per sq ft!

Focus group studies and discussions have indicated that all this is happening at an accelerated pace. Government response to this has been knee jerk at best. The big question always is "Can the local population cope with this pace of change?"

The Vision Document of the State has articulated a high growth strategy with emphasis on equity and ecological soundness, leading to sustainability[9] .

Whether the present development process will lead to the achievement of the Vision of the State as articulated in the State's Vision Document is highly questionable. It is rapid no doubt, but whether it is inclusive and ecologically friendly are moot points to ponder. In my opinion, we are steering clearly away from the path of sustainable development and mindlessly traveling on the path of ecological and fiscal disaster. There is still time to correct this and this will need both structural and policy mechanism paradigm shifts.

1. Demographic Change – the Real Time Bomb

Consistent with rapid economic activity and rise in the purchasing power of the people there has been a quiet and rapid flow of people from outside the state. Bihar, Bengal and Nepal have been the main contributors. This is a key externality. That there is a massive change in demography in the high growth areas of each of the districts is discernible to the naked eye. Muslim population in the State has increased several folds. This is evident as now we see signs of cultural transformation in the last few years, which was absent as recently as a decade ago.

A recent report of a local Tadong area Panchayat Ward Vision report points to a population of over 40 per cent of people from outside the State. Gangtok town has more than 50 per cent of people from outside the State.

ACT has reported in its memorandum to the State Government about the problems related to labour import and the social ills that come along with this.[10] A pristine place like Dzongu will be threatened by health and social problems.

There are discussions within civil society about the growing alienation of local people. This is not a healthy sign and can lead to major social unrest in times to come. Many young people are articulating this openly in different forums.

No report or study has been conducted by the State Government or any other agency on the quantum of demographic change and the effects or likely effects of the same.

Though Sikkim is protected to some extent by 'Old Laws' which are held as sacrosanct within the framework of the 371F of the Constitution, there are no other guarantees to maintain a separate 'identity'. Thus an 'identity' crisis to my mind is looming large like the fabled 'Damocles' sword'.

The next set of elections for the municipalities will be a watershed to bring these sets of issues to the table, requiring political and intellectual debates.

2. Biodiversity Tangle

Sikkim is very small. The area is 7096 square kilometers. More than 80 per cent of the area is under forests, though only 39 per cent or so is under forest cover. People, the forest, the natural capital and heritage have long lived in perfect harmony. They promoted sustainable lifestyles till 1975.

However, severe fissures are beginning to be seen. The city of Gangtok is a typical hill station of India. Fully loaded with concrete and not much of maneuvering room for easy movement and logistics are the properties. Somehow it continues to run in part, thanks to the discipline of the local people. Traffic is orderly. Many tourists and visitors have remarked on this. The city appears to be clean. Relatively, perhaps! However, many urban issues are thrown up like waste management, water and power distribution. Planning for a modern hill town is conspicuous by its absence. Match boxes for buildings are the norm without as much as a gesture toward imparting an architectural uniqueness.

However, Sikkim is indeed endowed with plenty of glaciers and mountain biodiversity. Plenty of microclimates, from the tropical to the alpine, ensure habits of all kinds leading to a mega-diversity in so small an area. This is fascinating. The water rich State of Sikkim is the envy of everyone. The over 750 square kilometers of glaciers ensure plenty of water in the rivers of Rangit and Teesta that flow out as one– the Teesta, and enters the Brahamaputra in Bangladesh. Furthermore, nature endowed Sikkim with several low level passes which connect the Tibetan Plateau and all its glory to the plains of India! How strategic is that! Only now Indian thinkers and planners are finding out the possibilities. The Chinese have already built up a rail link to Lhasa from Beijing!

This is a blessing. It is full of promise for socio-economic advancement. However, if not handled right, it can be disastrous.

We have a key externality here, Climate Change. In year, 2007, there have been more landslides along the NH 31A (national highway) than ever before in the history of Sikkim. There were over 63 breaches and five of them were major. Sikkim was cut off for about a month during September-October. It created problems of shortages. Gas cylinder lines became longer and longer in every part of the state. This also resulted in some violence, which was unprecedented. These are worrisome signals and indicators. That we are going to have more changes in weather pattern is a forgone conclusion as these are systemic changes we can do little about. So vulnerabilities are being exposed here.

Due to climate change all glaciers in the Himalayas are receding.[11] This is now a proven fact. 'Receding glaciers' mean that mountain lakes are formed. We have over 400 such lakes. Outbursts in these lakes are not uncommon. So we need to understand this as one of the vulnerabilities even as we take on more and more load by building dams for hydropower generation. Another area of vulnerability is the runoffs and the erosion that is taking place. Most of it is man made.

Can we go a bit slow?

Moreover, we need to be concerned about our water supply in times to come. Since Gangtok depends on mountain water, glacier fed, there will be issues in the future about supply.

3. Nathu La – the Bugbear

The opening of the Nathu La trade route in July 2006 has ushered in a new externality into the economic system of the State. It is a known, yet, inexperienced scenario. After 44 years the world has undergone huge transformation, and it is not the same. Sikkim was a sovereign entity in 1962. The Chinese were not as embedded in Tibet as now. So it has changed parameters drastically. India probably is worried about its strategic significance and implications for geopolitical security. China on the other hand looks at Nathu La as the gateway to the Kolkata port! So is Nathu La being played out as a deaf man's dialogue? This is a key question that needs to be, at least, debated.

The Chinese want full-scale trade. They have gone on record to say that they would like a short list of banned items. That is all. The rest can flow. India insists on going slow; continues with the list of 30 'traditional' items or so to be 'locally' traded. According to credible reports, China has built its entire infrastructure leading up to Nathu La. A railway linking Beijing to Lhasa is already operational. India, on the other hand, has just got a small mart at Sherathang and that too as tin sheds! The national highway 31A is in a mess, and can hardly be the kind of link one would expect of an international trade centre. The NH 31A has not been strengthened to date. In fact it is weaker and slower than ever before as has been explained in the earlier section.

This is the story till date. Two-year trade data show very little has actually happened in real terms. The traders in Sikkim are not at all happy as they are investing a lot but getting little returns. They are hanging in there for the long run, perhaps.

To date, Sikkim has not presented any cogent argument to the Centre as to how it is going to benefit directly from this trade. It is high time that the Sikkim policy makers start putting their minds together to formulate solid arguments to somehow garner some fiscal mileage out of the trading system. This could be in the form of cess or a direct devolution on the quantum of trade. This has to be done in order to pay for clearing the environmental mess that this trade will surely make in the years to come. Social issues will also further be accentuated. Of this there is little doubt. Another important issue – how will the capacity of the local people to trade be increased. Furthermore, we need to increase the capacity to deal with the ills of unknown outcomes which will come in due to the serious vulnerabilities of local people. How are these going to be addressed is a moot question.

4. Darjeeling – The Political Tango

The political, social and economic development of the Darjeeling District is of great importance and relevance to the overall economic prosperity of Sikkim and this region. This is by itself a key externality. That we have many people who hail from that District serving in Sikkim, both in the private and public sector, is well known. Darjeeling has been a major educational centre in the past. Till about a decade ago perhaps. However, sadly, it has degenerated. Many of our top bureaucrats serving today and other intellectuals have had their basic and higher education in Darjeeling.

Many major businessmen who have made it big in Sikkim have their roots in Kalimpong, Darjeeling and Siliguri. It is said that Sikkim has made Siliguri, what it is today – a great trading town is flourishing, not on account of West Bengal's policy, but because it happens to be the centre of trade for Sikkim, Eastern Nepal, North Bengal, North Bangladesh and the Northeast of India, the chicken's neck, as it is famously called. Siliguri is definitely the gateway to Sikkim. It is only 100 km from Gangtok.

However, stability of this part of the country has been dependent on what happens to Kamtapuris and the Gorkhaland movement. Bandhs and road blockages are a key feature of protest by these groups. This has a major effect on the movement of people, goods and services to and from Sikkim. More recently the people of the Darjeeling hill district have been agitating against the Gorkha Hill Council supremo, Subhash Ghisingh.[12] This has again ushered in a disquiet which, as some experts opine, is the end game for Ghisingh. Or is it?

That very little development has happened in remote districts is itself damning of the development paradigm of West Bengal. Tea gardens are closing and more recently the Centre has had to step in to get them reopened and refinanced. These are ominous signs. Moreover, the per capita economic gap between Darjeeling and Sikkim has widened further over the last two decades. This has raised major social tensions and political temperatures in recent times. That our Chief Minister and Mr. Ghisingh do not get along is a well known phenomenon.

With the onset of trading with China via Nathu La becoming a reality, there is now concern about the role the region of Darjeeling district will play in this all-important economic agenda. How much it will prosper and how it will play out is also dependent on how the relations with the Hill district evolve.

It must evolve on the basis of equal stakeholders in this whole game of development in the region. Geographical contiguity as well as ethnic similarity are key features on which synergy is possible. However, this might take some time to play out. This is on account of the fact that intellectuals and civil society voices have been effectively gagged since the ascendancy of Subhash Ghisingh.

So it will be a while before some kind of balance sets in between Sikkim and Darjeeling Gorkha Hills. But this is important for Sikkim's growth and development.

5. Sikkim and Northeast Council

Sikkim is the 8th member of the NE Council, having been admitted to the council in the year 2002.

What is interesting is that there is no geographical contiguity. However, since the people find that they have more in common with the mountain people of the hill and mountain tribes of the Northeast, it made sense for the Government of India to try to integrate Sikkim with the rest of the Northeast. Mountainous people have been generally been left out in terms of developmental focus. Mountain specificities are now acknowledged, which render mountain people more vulnerable.

Sikkim has economic indicators that are better than most of the other States.

Sikkim continues to shine amongst the Northeastern States. It also receives benefits by way of devolution from NEC projects and non lapsable pool of resources controlled by the Ministry of DONER.

Sikkim is exporting to the other NE States its success story in the fields of tourism, especially eco-tourism. It has also been helping other states understand peace, and what peace and harmony can do to bring some amount of prosperity. It can find answers to problems of demographic changes from states like Assam and Meghalaya.

More than anything else, Sikkim can combine some of its firepower to effectively deal with regional and national issues, especially in Parliament. Its voice can be heard through the NE track as well.

There is growing evidence to show that Sikkim shares greater biodiversity space and richness with the Northeast. It is within the framework of being a biodiversity hotspot of the world. Furthermore, Sikkim shares some very interesting heritage agricultural practices. This will enable Sikkim to tackle such and other biodiversity issues and its economic outcomes more effectively in the future.[13]

Can Economic transformation happen along with peace, equity and sustainability?

Since the clock of history cannot be turned back, this perhaps is the key question that we as a people have to answer. Much of the framework of development is already in place. We have plenty of financial resources as is amply demonstrated. However, the challenge lies in the human and the managerial capability. Can we make it sustainable? Mountains and their people have their own sets of issues.[14] These must be taken into account. Our ancestors led sustainable lifestyles but there were problems of equity. There were major governance issues as is historically recorded. Today we have been catapulted to another world where we are seeing major gains in equity and equality of opportunities. However, these are increasingly confronted by all aforementioned externalities and attended challenges.

Earlier, in another paper, I had talked of Stewardship. It is more important now. It is just not about visionary leadership but also respecting the land and its resources so that we ensure that there will be no reduction in the choices for the future generations – a key ingredient of sustainable development.

Our leadership, at this time, along with all stakeholders, needs to revisit the entire gamut of developmental policies. Among them are some which are highly extractive and invasive. For example, the whole question of building mega hydro electricity projects. We need to work out the cost benefit ratio looking at the triple bottom line rather than just the economic. The political rhetoric at this time is just on the economic.

Furthermore, we need to seriously consider and perhaps adopt for action the following:

1. Demographic challenges – a holistic approach to understand the dynamics of demography is the need of the hour. It must be said that no real thought has been given to this since we have some form of protection. This is perhaps not enough. We need to bite the bullet. It is best to start with understanding the big picture and drill down to finding specific mechanisms to cope with this all-important change. If we are unable to do this then the future is going to see an eruption of social tension, which is building up constantly. It would help to learn from Meghalaya and other NE states about this.
2. Human capital formation – taking on the challenge of preparing the next generations in alignment with priorities. This is very closely related to the point above. In fact, it is part of the solution. More and more of our young generation, who are weaned away from the rural areas, are finding it extremely hard to become employable. This is on account of the poor inputs that they have received from schools and colleges. Furthermore, they do not get lateral inputs from any other credible source. This makes life difficult, and many then resort to use of drugs. Already this is a

major issue. A key area of intervention is in raising standards at the primary school level.

3. Access to livelihoods and markets – agricultural, horticultural, floricultural, non farm activities and services. In order to create diversification in the mountain economy, it is worthwhile exploring more ways of linkages to major markets. One key driver in this is the tourism industry. Today, it is easier to get cabbage cheaper from Siliguri than from Lachung in North Sikkim! This I call the cabbage conundrum. Similar news from the milk front. Aggregation is a possibility and the real answer. This again is a managerial issue. It needs careful identification of the stakeholders and communities involved. It is possible, as already there are indications of small *'hats'* being set up in high traffic junctions. A case in point is the *'Kanchi Bazaar'* at the 9th mile – about 12 km before Gangtok. A key intervention here can be through micro finance and micro insurance. These can be used to promote many more livelihoods.
4. Change in energy usage pattern – this is a crying need. This can be done by using hybrid inputs like electricity, biomass and gas. A long term energy policy on the use and mix needs to be articulated forthwith.
5. Change in transportation systems – a systemic change is necessary.
6. Reducing cost and carbon content in products of consumption by innovative changes – localisation of produce and markets.
7. Concentrating on ecotourism to replace mass tourism – even though there is rhetoric to this effect, more needs to be done at the level of policy to be able to drive home this change. This is a good example of point No. 6.
8. Strengthening of Panchayati Raj institutions – this really holds the key to devolution of powers and upliftment of the rural poor. Working in harmony with local level NGOs and other civil society groups.
9. Cleaning up the bureaucracy and enhancing its capacity to deliver – this is a key concern which has been flagged in the NER Vision 2020 document as well.
10. Promoting greater transparency – this is really a governance issue.
11. Media and press – strengthening these institutions to instill a proper picture in the national consciousness. Furthermore, to play a role as watch dogs. Also to funnel the thoughts and ideas of intellectuals and thinkers of the state in matters that need to be debated.

12. Judiciary – strengthening this institution.
13. Mitigating public sector corruption – recently the Governor of Sikkim has flagged this issue as perhaps the most important one facing Sikkim.
14. Reducing vulnerabilities of mountain folks – mountains, because of their very nature and properties, cast immense vulnerabilities on the people who inhabit them.
15. Reduction in dependence on borrowings and central aid.
16. Continue to secure greater access for our people to health care and especially super specialist care. Rely on a robust plan for preventive health care, public health care systems and health insurance in the long run. This necessarily must reach the grassroots through the Panchayati Raj institutions. We already have a good health care system. We need to make it more effective and accessible to the poor.

REFERENCES

1. B.S. Das, *The Sikkim Saga*, Appendix 7
2. Mahendra P. Lama, *Economic Survey 2006-07 Sikkim*, Government of Sikkim, 2007.
3. Ibid.
4. Ibid.
5. Quoted from *DONER, NER Vision 2020 draft*, New Delhi: NIPFP, 2007.
6. Mahendra P. Lama, *Sikkim Human Development Report 2001*, Government of Sikkim, New Delhi: Social Science Press, 2001.
7. "NABARD Sikkim Focus Paper", 2007.
8. Centre For Inter Disciplinary Studies of Mountain & Hill Environment, Delhi University, Carrying Capacity of Teesta Region.
9. Ashok K. Lahiri et al, *Sikkim: The People's Vision*, Government of Sikkim, New Delhi: Indus Publishing Company, 2001.
10. Vibha Arora, "Unheard Voices of Protest in Sikkim", *Economic and Political Weekly*, 25 August 2007, p. 3451.
11. Xu Jianchu et al, "The Melting Himalayas", ICIMOD Technical Paper (2007), Kathmandu.
12. "Gorkhaland, Fragile Social Fabric", *Economic and Political Weekly*, 20 October 2007, p. 4196.
13. Eklabya Sharma et al., "The Landscape Approach in Biodiversity Conservation", ICIMOD Framework Paper (2007), Kathmandu.
14. Narpat S. Jodha, "Adaptation Strategies against growing environmental and social vulnerabilities in mountain areas", *Himalayan Journal of Sciences*, Vol. 3, Issue 5 (Jan – June 2005).

Chapter 3

Realities of Reopening: The State Government's Perspective of Nathu La

M.G. Kiran

Nathu La – the pass of listening ear in Tibetan – is an international border of two Asian giants, India and China. Barely 52 kms away from the state capital, Gangtok, it is situated at an altitude of 4310 ft. above sea level. History was created at this very place on the 6th of July 2006, when the Nathu La Trade Route to TAR of China was re-opened, re-establishing the historical-cultural-commercial linkages between the two great civilisations—India and China. It was a historic occasion for the people of India in general and of Sikkim in particular. It was not only a confidence building measure but brought pride, joy and credit to Sikkim for providing India and China a space of reiterating and promoting "Panchasheel", the five principles of coexistence that govern the relationship between the two powers. Although it took some time for Beijing to realise the importance of "Hindi Chini Bhai Bhai", China has finally recognised India's sovereignty over Sikkim. Beijing took a long time to accept the ground reality that Sikkim is part of the Indian Union.

The reopening of this historic trade route after a gap of 44 years has been appreciated as well as received with mixed reactions. Looking back at the history of the trade through Nathu La, the initiation of formal trade linkages between British India and Tibet through Nathu La Pass dates back to the late 18th century. It was the report of John Edgar, the then Deputy Commissioner of Darjeeling in 1873, which first captured the attention of the British Indian Government about the great commercial potentials of this route. The trade route was active for almost a century but ended abruptly after the 1962 war between India and China. Afterwards, Nathu La was always looked upon as a hostile zone by both sides and no one had ever thought that this route would one day reopen and regain its lost glory. We have been lucky enough to have witnessed this historic reopening, the credit of which goes entirely to the Sikkim Democratic Front Government led by Shri Pawan Chamling.

It may be recalled here that during the visit of the then Prime Minister of India, Atal Behari Vajpayee, to the state in April 2003, the Chief Minister, Pawan Chamling submitted a memorandum, which also included the demand for an early reopening of Nathu La Trade Route among others. Subsequently, in June 2003, Vajpayee visited China, where a historic Agreement was signed between the two nations at Beijing expanding border trade. This Agreement proved significant as China formally recognised Sikkim as a constituent state of India.

After the signing of this Agreement, there has been no looking back. The state Government, in consultation with the Central Government, put in every effort to see the Agreement turn into a reality. The State Government needed a comprehensive report dealing with all aspects of reopening of the trade route. Accordingly, a high level Nathu La Trade Study Group led by Mahendra P. Lama, a well-known development economist and the Chairman of the Centre for South, Central, South East and South West Pacific Studies, School of International Studies, Jawaharlal Nehru University, New Delhi, was constituted. The group examined a major portion of the historical documents and manuscripts, conducted interviews with people and stakeholders in various parts of India, Nepal and Tibet Autonomous Region (TAR) in China, made field visits, held discussions with the high level officials of TAR on various aspects of trade, infrastructure and tourism. The group submitted its report in 2005.

Two days before the great event, the Indian delegation led by Christy Fernandes, the then Additional Secretary in the Ministry of Commerce and Industry, Government of India, visited Lhasa and reached an agreement with the Chinese Government to finally reopen the historic route on 6 July 2006. As per the Agreement reached between the two delegations in Lhasa:

1. Border trade through Nathu La would resume from 6 July 2006.
2. The border trade mart would remain open from 1 June to 30 September every year from Monday to Thursday from 7.30 am to 3.30 pm Indian time, and 10 am to 6 pm Chinese time.
3. A permit fee of Rs.50 each would be levied for every vehicle entering Sikkim from China. Similarly, 5 Yuans would be levied on every vehicle crossing over to the Chinese side up to the trade mart at Renquinggang.

And the twenty nine items exportable to China are agricultural implements, blankets, copper products, clothes, cycles, coffee, tea, barley, rice, flour, dry fruit, dry and fresh vegetables, vegetable oil, gur and misri, tobacco, snuff, spices, shoes, kerosene oil, stationery, utensils, wheat, liquor, milk processed product, canned food, cigarettes, local herb, palm oil and hardware. And the 15 items importable from China are goat skin, sheep skin, wool, raw silk, yak tail, yak hair, china clay, borax, seaibelyipe, butter, Kashmiri goat, common salt, horse, goat and sheep.

However, there is no denying the fact that there is a huge trade potential and in order to tap this, the State Government plans to gradually convert this shortest and easiest overland access to China as one of the resilient means of commodity and service exchanges in the next few years. Though this trade is at its nascent stage, it would, once developed, generate a whole range of benefits to the otherwise land–locked state of Sikkim and the neighbouring states as well, including the Northeast region and West Bengal. Indian traders, investors and service sector operators can easily and extensively access TAR, while their counterparts in China can also access both India and entire South Asia Growth Quadrangle (SAGQ) markets. The Confederation of Indian Industries (CII) calls it a likely "economic re-emergence of Eastern India". Morever, the trade exchanges will definitely trigger employment generation and other trade related activities in the region, thereby increasing the economic growth of the state.

Just as there are opportunities, there will be as many problems. The first three months of border trade faced a lot of teething problems, and the trade in true sense could not take off smoothly. The Indian traders faced the problems of low CIF value of single consignment ceiling, Import Export Code requirement, short duration of trading period and above all the 29 and 15 items that were on the list for export and import, respectively, were outdated and not feasible as the value of some of the items was comparatively too little. However, there is a need to regularly review the list of exportable and importable commodities because the present list is only symbolic and does not carry any trading weight and potentials. It also has to match the market realities on both sides of the border.

Nevertheless, with the timely intervention of the State Government, several of the creases were ironed out in order to make this trade route a major avenue for both economic and multifaceted development. From the current year, the duration of trade has been extended from 1 May to 30 November, the CIF value of a single consignment ceiling has been raised from Rs. 25, 000 to Rs.1 lakh, and further in case of applicants for importer and exporter code number, who are ordinary residents of Sikkim, trade tax/sales tax regulation number issued by the Government of Sikkim is accepted as a substitute to permanent account number (PAN).

Another immediate requirement is the need to transform and improve the present trade related infrastructures to a robust and modern system that can handle a burgeoning bilateral trade between the two countries. The Union Government has already decided to lay a two-lane highway up to Nathu La and a railway line up to Rangpo. The Ministry of Commerce, Government of India, had even entrusted RITES with the preparation of a project report for the creation of better infrastructure facilities, taking into consideration the prospect of free trade.

However, the State Government worked on a war footing during the inauguration of the reopening, and completed the basic infrastructure required for the initial level of trading. With limited resources at hand and minimum time, the State Government has been able to provide over 30 structures in the trading mart complex at Sherathang to house all important offices and residence including warehouses, customs office, post office, banks, immigration posts, BSNL and ITBT posts. Offices for information technology, health officials, cafeteria, waiting sheds have also been allotted. Potable drinking water has also been provided to the entire complex which is being fed by a nearby stream through source tapping. Power supply is being made through two Gensets with an installed capacity of 320 KVA. Regular power connectivity will be made by the concerned department soon. The Border Roads Organisation has undertaken the work of further improvement, strengthening an expansion of the existing road connectivity.

Considering the fact that this is just the second year of the trade, many hiccups have been put at end, but there is a need for reexamination. Every area of the trade has to be looked into - from the problems faced by Indian traders to infrastructure development to Border Trade Acts. It may be mentioned that a total of 696 Indian traders visited TAR and 1,253 Chinese Tibetan traders crossed over to India for trade while India imported goods worth Rs. 10,83,150 and exported goods worth Rs. 8,87,285, besides rice, atta, maida, tea and clothes.

Adding further impetus to this trade relation, a four member Chinese delegation led by Ms. Bu Jiamguo, Minister Councillor, Chinese Embassy paid a two day visit to Sikkim and even crossed over to TAR from Nathu La Pass. The team held discussion with the Chief Minister of Sikkim, Pawan Chamling, and Minister for Commerce and Industry, R.B. Subba, in June 2007. Among various issues discussed during the meeting, the inclusion of new items in the list of trade, tourism and a Gangtok-Lhasa Bus service also figured.

Another boon for Sikkim emerging out of this trade route is tourism, and the State Government is determined to fully avail of this opportunity. The Chief Minister has been constantly trying to integrate trade and tourism keeping in view the Buddhist Circuit. He has also been fervently proposing a Sikkim-Lhasa bus service as a pilgrimage tour. Fortunately, the Government of India has also now identified the Buddhist Circuit as one of the priority areas in tourism development policy. The Chief Minister has also been time and again emphasizing the need for connecting Sikkim to all the major Buddhist destinations in India and neighbouring countries, eg. Bodh Gaya in Bihar, Rumtek in Sikkim, Tawang in Arunachal Pradesh, Lumbini in Nepal, Taktsang in Bhutan, Jokhang and Potala in Lhasa. The Nathu La would serve as a gateway to the Roof of the World, and Jalpaiguri and Siliguri would be the main hubs of trade. There would be immense opportunities and benefits to both sides, if tourism as hoped by the State Government flourishes. Tourism has always been Sikkim's forte, and the Nathu La route being the shortest route to Tibet, Sikkim could tap its tourism potential to its best. The Nathu La by itself has been a major tourist attraction with hundreds of tourists travelling to the border to see and enjoy the border.

This landlocked state, with huge economic and tourism potential, has much more to gain out of this economic tie-up. The only hitch is that trade should not be limited to border trade only. The State Government has also laid special emphasis on setting up a Special Economic Zone of its own in Sikkim.

However, it is hoped that border trade would one day evolve into successful international trade based on the Most Favoured Nation Treatment (MFN) principle rather than the existing restrictive border trading. There are indications that China is working for its infrastructural development on a war footing, e.g. the construction of four airports at Shigatse, laying of pipelines, railway link till Yatung, etc. The infrastructure development in TAR is 12 times more than in India. The present scenario clearly highlights that much more has been done on the other side of the border as compared to the Indian side. Known for their resoluteness in work, China's Beijing-Lhasa Express connecting Lhasa to the rest of China has been lauded by all as an engineering marvel.

Therefore, keeping in mind the rapid development strategy adopted by the Chinese, India should also not lag behind. Every effort should be put to match their energy and potential so that, hopefully, by the year 2010 there would be free trade at Nathu La.

Chapter 4

Indo-China Border Trade through Nathu La: Prospects for Growth and Investment in Sikkim

K. Elumalai

India and China, the fastest growing economies in the world, witnessed sustained GDP growth rate of about 10 per cent and 6 per cent, respectively, during 1980-2005.[1] Both the countries have increasingly been integrated with global economy but in varying degrees. Despite the lacklustre performance of these two economies till the late seventies, the economic behaviour has changed dramatically in the last two decades.[2] The economic reforms introduced in 1978 in China have ushered the country into a new era of economic growth. India had started with limited liberalisation during the mid-eighties followed by significant reforms since the early nineties to overcome external economic problems. Despite temporal differences in the opening up of economies, both India and China have set the stage for market forces to play a greater role in the economic decision making process.

The emergence of India and China as important economic power centres, and their influence in the world economy, are being recognised through their rapid growths. In 2005, Gross Domestic Product (GDP) at Purchasing Power Parity for China was about US$ 8.6 trillion, the second largest in the world after the USA (US$ 12.4 trillion). India, with the GDP of US$ 3.8 trillion, ranks fourth largest economy after Japan with GDP of US$3.9 trillion, i.e. only slightly above that of India (World Bank, 2007). As the size of these two economies grew, their share in global GDP growth increased substantially over time. During 1995-2003, India accounted for about 6 per cent of world output, contributing about 11 per cent to the latter's growth. China accounted for about 11 per cent of global GDP, contributing about 23 per cent to its growth.[3] Thus, these two economies, combined together, account for about a third of global output growth. There are predictions that if the current growth momentum continues, India's economy will become larger than Japan's and China's economy could be larger than that of the USA by 2032 and 2041, respectively.[4]

Meanwhile, at the bilateral level, political relations between India and China had strengthened during early eighties. This had led to a rapid increase in bilateral trade. Further, to strengthen trade relations between the two countries, a trade agreement was signed, providing Most Favoured Nation (MFN) status during 1984. Since then, a series of agreements covering the Joint Economic Group, Joint Working Group, Double Taxation Avoidance and Border Trade have been signed to enhance trade and economic co-operation.

The essay organised in seven sections, discusses the issues related to border trade between India and China through Nathu La, and their implications for Sikkim's economy. A small field survey in the form of stakeholder consultations was conducted in Sikkim and Nathu La during October 2006 and January 2007. Both quantitative and qualitative information were collected from different stakeholders, including senior officials of the Government of India, Government of Sikkim, Customs officials, traders, transporters, tourists, Indo-Tibetan Border Police (ITBP) and Border Roads Organisation (BRO). Secondary published information pertaining to Sikkim and Nathu La was also collected from various sources including 1) the Directorate of Economics, Statistics, Monitoring & Evaluation, Government of Sikkim, 2) the Department of Sikkim Tourism, 3) North Eastern Development Finance Corporation Ltd., 4) Sikkim Industrial Development and Investment Corporation Ltd., and 5) National Accounts Statistics.

INDIA-CHINA BILATERAL TRADE

The total volume of bilateral trade between India and China has increased rapidly during the last decade. Bilateral trade between India and China increased from US$ 1.2 billion in 1995-96 to US$ 25.7 billion during 2006-07 (Table 4.1). The whopping increase in trade volume is mainly due to the existence of trade complementarities and relative comparative advantage in each of the two countries. However, the balance of trade has been in favour of China.

Table 4.1: India's Trade with China (US$ Million)

Year	*Exports*	*Imports*	*Trade Balance*
1995-96	333.2	813.2	– 480.0
1996-97	615.3	757.6	– 142.2
1997-98	718.9	1120.7	– 401.8
1998-99	427.1	1096.5	– 669.4
1999-00	539.4	1288.3	– 748.9
2000-01	830.0	1494.9	– 664.9
2001-02	954.8	2042.5	– 1087.7
2002-03	1979.4	2797.6	– 818.2
2003-04	2957.1	4056.0	– 1098.9
2004-05	5613.6	7095.1	– 1481.5
2005-06	6758.1	10866.5	– 4108.4
2006-07	8285.1	17387.3	– 9102.2

Source: India Trades, CMIE

Table 4.2: Per cent share of India's Exports of Top 10 Principal Commodities to China

Commodity Name	*2001-02*	*2002-03*	*2003-04*	*2004-05*	*2005-06*	*2006-07*
Iron ore	21.7	20.7	27.9	47.8	48.4	40.1
Cotton raw including waste	0.0	0.0	1.2	0.4	6.1	7.9
Processed minerals	2.4	4.4	3.4	4.4	5.2	4.3
Primary & semi-finished iron & steel	1.2	24.8	19.5	10.5	5.1	4.3
Plastic & linoleum products	14.9	9.0	10.3	8.0	5.0	6.1
Other ores & minerals	11.9	7.8	4.3	6.4	4.7	8.0
Inorganic/organic/agro chemicals	5.1	4.5	2.8	4.0	3.1	2.2
Drugs, pharmaceuticals & fine chemicals	8.4	4.7	3.5	2.2	2.6	1.7
Oil meals	0.4	0.2	0.6	0.6	2.1	0.8
Machinery & instruments	1.2	1.6	2.5	1.9	2.0	1.9

Source: India Trades, CMIE

It may be observed from Table 4.2 that the composition of India's export basket is not quite diversified. The major export items include basic and intermediate goods. In 2006-07, iron ore constituted about 40 per cent of total exports to China. Though, the export share of primary and semi-finished iron and steel declined in recent years, yet it was the second largest exported commodity until 2004-05. A notable feature of India's exports to China has been that the export of raw cotton (including waste) has increased from an insignificant amount till 2003-04 to about 8 per cent of total exports in 2006-07. Plastic and linoleum products and ores and minerals constitute about 6 per cent and 8 per cent of total exports, respectively. The export of drugs and pharmaceuticals showed a fluctuating trend.

Table 4.3: Per cent share of India's Imports of Top 10 Principal Commodities from China

Commodity Name	*2001-02*	*2002-03*	*2003-04*	*2004-05*	*2005-06*	*2006-07*
Electronic goods	18.9	29.0	34.1	29.9	32.1	28.7
Non-electrical machinery	3.5	3.8	4.5	6.4	9.3	10.6
Organic chemicals	11.9	11.7	11.7	8.9	8.9	7.4
Coal, coke & briquettes	12.9	6.3	5.5	12.7	6.6	6.3
Other commodities	4.6	4.2	4.2	3.6	4.1	4.0
Electrical machinery	2.9	2.6	2.5	3.1	3.3	3.1
Medicinal & pharmaceutical products	5.2	5.4	4.6	2.8	3.3	2.7
Other textile yarn, fabrics, made up articles	2.3	2.7	2.6	2.6	3.1	2.3
Iron & steel	0.7	0.3	0.8	2.0	3.1	8.5
Silk yarn & fabrics	1.6	1.9	2.6	2.4	1.9	1.1

Source: India Trades, CMIE

Contrary to the trend observed for India's exports, composition of China's exports to India is relatively diversified (Table 4.3). Exports are dominated by electronic goods. During 2006-07, China's export of electronic goods to India constituted about 29 per cent of total exports. The export share of non-electrical machinery and organic chemicals were about 11 per cent and 7 per cent, respectively. Export of coal, coke and briquettes, by and large, showed a fluctuating trend. The continued availability of good quality coal, coke and briquettes is important for India's metallurgical industry. The export share of electrical machinery and textile yarn, fabrics, made up articles, remained almost constant during the study period. However, the export of iron and steel has showed an increasing trend, constituting about 9 per cent of total exports.

INDO-CHINA BORDER TRADE

1. Border Trade through Lipulekh

For centuries, border trade between India and China flourished before it was closed in 1962 following the Indo-China War. Building up on political relations initiated in the eighties, it was agreed to resume border trade. Consequently, in December 1991, the Government of India and the Government of People's Republic of China, being desirous of promoting trade relations and through friendly consultations, signed a Memorandum of Understanding to resume border trade, on the basis of equality and mutual benefit.[5] The agreement referred to border trade as overland trade and the exchange of commodities by the residents along the border area of the two countries. It was decided to allow border trade between the Tibet Autonomous Region (TAR) of China and the State of Uttar Pradesh of India. Border trade markets were established at Pulan in TAR of China and Gunji in the Pithoragarh district in the State of Uttar Pradesh (presently, Uttaranchal) of India. Border markets are open from 1 June to 30 September of every year. However, concerned authorities on mutual agreements can extend or reduce the trade period depending upon exigencies like weather conditions. Lipulekh (Qiangla) is the border pass for the entry and exit of persons engaged in border trade and the exchange of commodities and means of transportation from both the sides. Traders carry travel passes issued by the competent authorities of the respective countries. The agreement further specifies that border security and cross-border management personnel will enter into liaison arrangements to ensure a smooth operation of border trade, to curb smuggling and illegal entry and exit.[6]

Trade takes place on the commodities approved by Directorate General of Foreign Trade (DGFT), Government of India. There are 29 commodities allowed to be exported from India and 15 commodities permitted to be imported from China. The commodities exported and imported outside the approved list may attract duty.

2. Border Trade through Shipkila

As agreed in the Memorandum signed in 1991, trade can be permitted in other border points as may be mutually agreed upon between two countries from time to time. Accordingly, India and China decided to extend border trade through another point between the State of Himachal Pradesh and TAR of China during 1993. Namgya in Kinnaur district of Himachal Pradesh and Jiuba in Zada County in TAR of China were designated as the border trade markets. Shipkila is the border pass for the entry and exit of persons engaged in border trade and the exchange of commodities and means of transportation from two sides. Namgya is located 8 km away from Shipkila.

As in Lipulekh, border trade through Shipkila also takes place on the commodities approved by DGFT, Government of India. During 2005-06, Lipulekh Pass witnessed a trade flow of Rs. 16 million (Rs. 4 million of exports and Rs.12 million of imports). Shipkila registered a total trade of Rs. 32 million of which exports and imports constituted Rs. 1 million and Rs. 31 million respectively. However, through both of these border routes one way barter system prevailed. Only Indian traders used to cross the border and engage in trading. Lama (2005) reported that there were no proper structure and procedures established by China to guide Tibetan traders to participate in the trade. Further, the movement of Indian traders was highly restricted in TAR, and at times they were allowed to travel during night time only. Though Jiuba in TAR was officially designated as the border trade mart, access to Indian traders up to the mart was highly restricted.

3. Border Trade through Nathu La

India and China signed a Memorandum to open the third point for border trade through Nathu La on 23 June 2003. The final agreement was clinched on 18 June 2006. Both the countries agreed to use Nathu La as the point for entry and exit of persons, exchange of commodities and means of transport. On the Indian side, Sherathang, located 47 Km away from Gangtok and 5 Km from Nathu La, and in TAR, Donquingang, located 17 Km away from Nathu La, were designated as border trade marts. All the provisions of the Memorandum on the Resumption of Border Trade signed between the two governments on 13 December 1991 and the Protocol on Entry and Exit Procedures for Border Trade signed on 1 July 2002 shall also be applicable to the border trade through Nathu La. Officially, border trade began on 6 July 2006. Opening of Nathu La for trade, after 44 years of its closure, has generated great interest among people, academics, researchers and policy makers. In fact, a proposal for opening of Nathu La and Jelep La for trade was put forward by both the countries after resolving a long pending dispute over recognition of Tibet by India and Sikkim by China.

PERFORMANCE OF BORDER TRADE THROUGH NATHU LA

1. Nathu La Trade Policy Initiatives

The Central and Sikkim Governments have initiated various measures towards operationalisation and smooth conduct of the border trade through Nathu La. Some of these measures are outlined below.

(i) Constitution of Nathu La Trade Study Group

During 2004, the Government of Sikkim commissioned a high-level study group to explore all the issues related to making Nathu La route operational for border trade between Sikkim and TAR regions. It conducted surveys in Tibet, Sikkim and other parts of India. The study group submitted its report on "Sikkim-Tibet Trade via Nathu La: A Policy Study on Prospects, Opportunities and Requisite Preparedness" for the consideration of Sikkim government in August 2005. The major recommendations of the study groups are as follows.

- Phasing of actions
  - 2005-2010: Initiation of trading on both sides backed by existing and some additional infrastructures. Meanwhile, start building wider and deeper infrastructure facilities.
  - 2010: Trading on a larger scale starts taking place, based on upgraded and more developed infrastructure.
  - 2012: Integration of trade with tourism for which a fresh bilateral legal basis needs to be concluded to facilitate the movement of tourists across the border. During 2012-15, only Indian and Chinese tourists shall be permitted to cross the border through Nathu La on a package tour basis. Open tourism should be allowed from 2015.
  - 2015: Inclusion of movement of freights to and from the neighbouring countries, including Bangladesh, Bhutan and Nepal.
  - 2018: SAARC tourism (tourists from all SAARC countries) should be allowed.
- Travel passes should be given only to the Sikkimese subjects for the initial five years (2005-2010) of trading.
- All the activities related to trade facilitation and promotion should be given to the Sikkim public sector units like the State Bank of Sikkim, Sikkim Nationalized Transport (SNT), Sikkim Trading Corporation (STC) and Sikkim Industrial Development and Investment Corporation Ltd. (SIDICO) for the initial five years of trading. These units can collaborate with the private sector.
- All tourism related activities should be entrusted to public and private agencies of Sikkim for the initial five years (2012-2017)
- In order to promote the commodities exclusively produced in Sikkim, at least 20 per cent of total shops should be earmarked for small and medium entrepreneurs of Sikkim.
- Sikkim should effectively participate in developing its own facilities in Siliguri by acquiring land in strategic places for the facilitation of trade.
- A widely represented and strong Centre-State Border Trade Coordination Committee should be constituted with the

representatives of various ministries, professionals and experts.

- Given the extent of infrastructure required and the likely gains in the long run it would be prudent to put in place a one time Infrastructure Development Package of Rs. 1650-1700 crores to be used in a phased manner by 2012.
- India-China Joint Action Team (ICJAT) and Nathu La Trade Coordination Group, comprising experts from Sikkim and West Bengal should be constituted

The Government of Sikkim considered the recommendations of the study group seriously in shaping State-level policy decisions pertaining to Sikkim-Tibet Trade. In fact, most of these recommendations had already been implemented during the 2006 trading season.

(ii) Construction of Trade Mart

A temporary trade mart was developed at Sherathang for exchange of goods between Sikkimese and Chinese traders. Basically, army horse stables were converted into shopping malls/sheds. These sheds were developed to provide various trading facilities. These facilities comprised Custom check post, State Bank of India, telecommunications (MTNL), administrative block, warehouse, Indo-Tibetan Border Police (ITBP) post, canteen, and trade mart. A structure called "trade mart" was used for display and sale of goods. These sheds were considered to be makeshift arrangements.

(iii) Issuance of Travel Pass

Travel Pass is a legal document issued by a competent authority of the respective countries. The holders of travel pass are permitted to engage in border trade. Travel pass, like a "Passport", is a sure means of establishing the holder's identity and should, therefore, be carried personally. The Pass is valid for trade purposes only but not for tourism. On the Indian side, the travel pass is issued by the Collector-cum-Magistrate, East District of Sikkim. At present, the issuance of travel pass is only restricted to Sikkim traders who are residents of Sikkim. The pass is issued to traders who pass through security clearance for character and antecedents.

(iv) Permissible Commodities for Trade

The Government of India maintains the same list of commodities approved for trading through Lipulekh and Shipkila passes. A fresh notification issued by Department of Commerce, Government of India, on 13 June 2006 reiterated that 15 commodities were allowed to be imported and 29 commodities permitted to be exported through all the three border trading posts. Border trade is basically meant for meeting local demands of the people living in border areas. It is supposed that approved commodities are locally produced by the people living along both sides of the Indo-China border.

Further, according to the Foreign Trade (Development and Regulation) Act, 1992, any exporter or importer, on the importation into or exportation out of any Custom port of any goods, should state Importer-Exporter Code (IEC) Number allotted by the competent authority. However, in Foreign Trade Policy (2004-2009) persons engaged in trading from/to Nepal and from/to Myanmar through Indo-Myanmar border areas are exempted from stating IEC number provided the CIF value of a single consignment does not exceed Rs. 25,000. Considering a similar provision, the Government of India has allowed traders to import/export permissible items from/to China through designated border posts up to CIF value of Rs. 25,000 per day.

2. Performance of Border Trade

The data pertaining to Sikkim-Tibet trade through Nathu La conducted during 7 July-28 September 2006 are presented here. Export and import of goods were allowed four days in a week through Monday to Thursday. As mentioned elsewhere, only Sikkim residents were given travel pass to participate in trading. Traders mostly based in Gangtok engaged in trading. Only a few traders from the border areas of Nathu La and Sherathang had participated. However, traders from different parts of the country showed interest in exports and imports through the Nathu La route. It was reported that traders from West Bengal and Uttar Pradesh approached the travel pass issuing authority in Gangtok for approval.

As against the observations for Lipulekh and Shipkila, the frequency of Chinese traders visiting the Sherathang trade mart was relatively high, when compared to Indian traders visiting the Donquingang trade mart. The number of times Chinese traders made visits to the Indian trade mart had increased dramatically from July to August and then August to September. But, the number of visits made by Indian traders over months was not equally high (Table 4.4).

Among commodities exported from India, Non-Basmati rice was the major item accounting for about 78 per cent of total value of exports (Table 4.5). A small quantity of blankets and clothes were also exported. During repeated visits to the Chinese trade mart, the Sikkim traders learnt that Tibetans were fond of Indian bidi and cigarettes. As a result, snuffs

Table 4.4: Frequency of Indian and Chinese Traders who visited Trade Mart

Month	*Indian traders visits to Donquingang*	*Chinese traders visits to Sherathang*
July	110	175
August	155	289
September	456	772

Source: Customs Office, Gangtok

found place in the export basket amounting to about Rs. 146,400 during September. Since Tibetans prefer green tea to black tea, the Indian traders could not find many buyers for the latter. It was reported that several packs of black tea returned unsold to Sikkim. Only about 55 kg of black tea was sold during August.

Table 4.5: Composition of Export of Permitted Commodities from India

Items	*Quantity (Kg)*	*CIF value (Rs)*
July		
Non Basmati Rice	7020	115710
Flour	630	8150
August		
Non Basmati Rice	11840	331375
Black Tea	55	6050
Blanket (Nos)	30	3900
September		
Non Basmati Rice	6910	239810
Blanket (Nos)	83	16150
Clothes (mts)	608	18240
Snuffs	1200	146400
Total Value		**885785**

Source: Customs Office, Gangtok

The Government of India permitted 15 commodities for import from China. Wool was the only commodity that had import demand from Sikkim traders (Table 4.6.). In the month of August, a few Tibetan traders brought Yak tail worth Rs. 5600. Yak tail is mainly used for decorative purposes, but did not have a considerable import demand. It is interesting to observe from CIF value declared by traders that trade balance is in favour of China.

Table 4.6: Composition of Import of Permitted Commodities from TAR of China

Items	*Quantity (Kg)*	*CIF value (Rs)*
July		
Wool (sheep)	198	29250
August		
Yak tail (Nos)	7	5600
September		
Wool (sheep)	11610	1047600
Total value		**1082450**

Source: Customs Office, Gangtok

3. Problems Faced by Traders

The general problems reported by traders and other stakeholders in conducting trade are summarised below.

- Restricted list of commodities for trade: The Government of India approved duty free export and import of commodities, which did not have much local demand either in Sikkim or in Tibet. The traders from Sikkim had very little idea about the demand pattern of Tibet. However, they could gauge the local demand of Tibet through repeated visits to the Chinese trade mart, but they could not export many commodities due to restrictions.
- Ceiling on trade volume: Presently, a trader is permitted to export or import a consignment worth Rs. 25,000 per day. Accordingly, the State Bank of India provides a trader US$ 500 per day for trading purposes and meeting other expenses. Traders feel that the ceiling value is insignificant given the potential of trade.
- Trading time: Border trade markets were open from 7.30 am to 3.30 pm (Indian time) and 10.00 am to 6.00 pm (corresponding Chinese time) only on four days during a week. Given the distance between Gangtok and Nathu La and poor road conditions, Indian traders could do business for about two hours only in the Chinese trade mart within the current time limit. Even if the traders start at 5.30 am from Gangtok, they can reach the Chinese trade mart by 12 noon after completing all the formalities. There are no provisions for traders to stay overnight to enable them to continue to do business during the following day. Even though China has constructed 7 bedrooms for accommodation, which can house 21 persons, the present guidelines do not allow traders to stay overnight at the Chinese trade mart.

- Facilitation at trade mart: Some of the Indian traders felt that it was difficult to transact business with incoming Tibetan traders due to the language problem. There were no volunteers available to help Indian/Chinese traders at the Sherathang trade mart. However, China has employed volunteers/officials of Border Trade Management Committee to provide guidance to Indian traders to engage in business and to access various facilities at the Donquingang trade mart. The volunteers also helped Indian traders to load or unload goods at the Chinese Custom station.
- Cross border movement of trucks: During the last trading season, goods were generally carried by traders' own jeeps, which were allowed to enter into either side of the border. A Sikkim trader carried rice by his own truck to Donquingang. Those who did not own jeeps or trucks hired Tibetan vehicles from Nathu La to reach the Chinese trade mart. Tibetan vehicles were not of high capacity and charged a high amount of Rs. 2000/truck load of goods and Rs. 500 per passenger for two-way travel.
- Quarantine and quality certification: A quarantine officer deputed by the Government of Sikkim was posted at the Sherathang trade mart. But, testing facilities were not established on the Indian side. During the last trading season, certain commodities like wool and Yak tail, which require quarantine control, were approved based on the certificate issued by Government of China. However, there are some listed commodities like silk, sheep and goat skins, which warrant strict quality control before importation. Such quality certification facilities should be established.

Scope of Expanding Indo-China Trade through Nathu La

The opening of Nathu La for trade after a long period of time was considered to be a big indicator of warming bilateral relations between India and China. Some of the traders recounted that Indian goods used to move up to Lhasa (490 km from Nathu La) through Yatong (37 km from Nathu La) before closure of border in 1962. The Chinese goods were imported through the same route to Kalimpong from where goods were distributed to different parts of India. There exists a vast potential to be exploited for India and China through overland trade. This will benefit people living in Sikkim and TAR of China through various secondary effects. This Section explores the potential for expanding Indo-China border trade through Nathu La. An attempt is also made to find out possibilities of converting border trade into regular overland or Most

Favoured Nation (MFN) trade between India and China. These assessments are based on the indicators like anticipated volume of trade, economic opportunities in TAR, transhipment distance and informal trade through Nepal.

1. Anticipated Volume of Trade

Bilateral trade between India and China has increased dramatically over time. The volume of trade is expected to reach US$ 40 billion by the end of 2010.[7] Presently, most of the trade between India and China takes place through the sea route. Given the pace of infrastructure development including road and rail network linking Tibet with main land China, there could be a huge potential for bilateral trade in future through Nathu La. Considering the cost advantage, it might be possible to divert the movement of goods from the sea route to the overland route through Nathu La. India has also geared up chalking out various plans to upgrade the road and other infrastructure facilities to meet the increased trade volume.

Through a small field survey, the present study found that traders in Sikkim are optimistic about prospects of trade in the coming years. Under the assumption that trade on MFN basis, restricted to traders of Sikkim only, is allowed to take place, the total trade volume through Nathu La is expected to reach about US$ 22 million during 2007. The trading period is assumed to be April to November. The increased volume of trade will drive towards a diversification of India's export basket.

2. Economic Opportunities in TAR

Economic changes in Tibet have attracted the world's attention in recent years. These changes provide ample scope to explore the opportunities available to expand trade. It would also be interesting to critically analyse the new development paradigm, which China is promoting to link Tibet with other parts of China. This will have huge implications in the long run for the Indian economy in general and Sikkim and West Bengal economies in particular, if large scale trade is allowed through Nathu La.

Tibet with a population of 2.5 million has witnessed a volley of aid programmes pouring from the Central Government of China during recent times. With special financial and technological support, there has been a noticeable restructuring of the Tibetan economy. Tibet has registered a GDP growth rate of 12 per cent, which is higher than China's national average of 9.8 per cent during 2005.[8] Among different sectors, tertiary industries constituting tourism, communications, posts and tele-communications, contributed about 57 per cent of the total state-level

GDP. Tourism has been one of the fastest developing sectors, with the total income of 1.93 billion yuan in 2005. With increase in per capita income, the life style and the consumption pattern has considerably changed over time. The traditional consumption basket consisting of Chatthu (mixture of wheat and barley flour) and yak meat has changed to modern-day ready-to-cook food.

To give fillip to the ongoing developments and to link the land-locked TAR with the mainland of China and to the rest of the world, China launched the world's highest railway line during early July 2006. The railway line has been built at the cost of 24 billion yuan (US$ 2.96 billion). The Qinghai-Tibet railway, covering the distance of 1,956 Km, connects the capital city of Xining in northwest Qinghai province to Lhasa of TAR. China plans to extend the rail link from Lhasa to Shigatse (250 Km from Lhasa) and Nyingch (400 Km from Lhasa) and finally to Yadong, which is closer to Nathu La, by 2010. With the completion of this rail link, access to five major Chinese cities viz., Beijing, Shanghai, Xining, Chengdu and Guangzhou will become easier.[9]

It is proposed that this railway will carry 75 per cent of all the inbound cargo into Tibet, cutting transportation cost and boosting local economy.[10] Travel from Beijing to Lhasa is expected to be covered in 48 hours through this rail line. China also plans to develop flight connectivity to TAR. Presently, there are two airports in Tibet: one in Lhasa and another in Qamdo. There is a proposal to open a third airport in Nyingchi, based in Southeast Tibet bordering India and Myanmar.

Compared to the other two land routes, China is keen to make use of Nathu La route for promoting trade relations with India and other neighbouring countries. Most of the requirements of Tibet are met by goods imported from Nepal. It was reported that about 400-500 truckloads of goods are transported daily from Kathmandu to Lhasa.[11] For India, it opens a window of opportunities to meet the emerging demand for basic and intermediate goods in Tibet. Though Tibet is now connected with Mainland China through a proper road and rail network, yet it could be cheaper to import goods from India. Further, it would be possible to divert a substantial volume of goods that are traded bilaterally from the sea route to the overland route via Nathu La. However, it will largely depend on the comparative cost of transport by the sea and land routes.

3. Trans-Shipment Distance and Time

Nathu La provides a strategic advantage for India and China as the point of entry and exit for movement of goods. Presently, most of exports and imports between India and China take place through ports of Kolkata and Shanghai. It takes almost one month from the date of dispatch to arrival at the respective port city. The freight charges are relatively high. In this regard, land route through Nathu La may provide an option for faster transhipment at lower cost. The geographical proximity and presence of motorable roads between Gangtok and Lhasa, all goods including heavy items can be transported in 2 days whereas through Shipkila and Lipulekh passes, it might take at least 5 and 10 days, respectively, to reach Lhasa.

The distance between Nathu La and Lhasa is 490 km. China has already constructed highways connecting Lhasa with Yadong. The 17 km two lane approach road from Donquningang trade mart in Yadong to Nathu La is under construction, and is likely to be completed by 2007. The Kolkata port is located about 772 km from Nathu La. Kolkata and Nathu La are connected by the National Highway (NH) 34 and 31 and state highway Jawaharlal Nehru Marg. The existing transport facilities can be strengthened and used for freight movement through Kolkata port, which can act as a major hub for large volume trading. Further, there is an offshoot road from NH 31A leading to Assam and other northeastern states. By this route, it could be possible to connect the landlocked northeastern states with TAR of China and to exploit trade potentials to benefit the local people. Besides, the Kolkata-Gangtok-Nathu La route, there exists another viable route, namely Kolkata-Kalimpong-Nathu La route. This alternative route was the traditional and major route used by India-Tibet traders before 1962 through Jelep La. Kalimpong, which is located 92 km from Nathu La, was the major hub for assembling and transport of goods to/from Tibet.

India may have some trade-offs in opening Nathu La for trading with China. Presently, about 90 per cent of Tibet's international trade (US$ 200 million) is shipped through Tianjin port city, which is located about 4400 km from Lhasa.[12] But, the distance between Kolkata and Lhasa is about 1200 km only. With the Nathu La pass opened, it is likely to involve less cost and time to trans-ship goods from Tibet to Kolkata. The well-established rail network will also help China to move goods from different interior parts of China to Asian countries through the Kolkata port. This might benefit India by generating economic activities for various segments of labour force and by bringing additional income from a large movement of goods.

Besides India and China, the move is likely to benefit other neighbouring countries like Nepal, Bhutan and Bangladesh. Presently, Tibet-Nepal trade takes place through the Kathmandu-Lhasa route, which covers a distance of 1,000 km. Kodari in Nepal and Lhasa in Tibet are the major trading centres where goods are assembled and transported. It is found that most of the goods imported from Lhasa to Kathmandu finally find their way to Indian markets.[13] The exports from Kathmandu to Tibet and other parts of China are of Indian origin. Traders reported that trade route through Nathu La is about one third shorter than Kathmandu-Lhasa route. Thus, for traders based in the Tarai region of Nepal, Gangtok-Lhasa or Kalimpong-Lhasa route will be much shorter for export and import of goods from China. Bangladesh and Bhutan are also likely to get benefitted by their geographical proximity and road connectivity.

4. Nepal Factor

With a weak industrial and agricultural base, the people in Sikkim procure their essential commodities from different parts of the country. Siliguri (114 Km from Gangtok) is the nearest major commercial centre, from where most of the Sikkim traders purchase goods and transport to Gangtok and other parts. Due to its strategic location, Chinese goods transported from Nepal through various points like Dhulabari and Pasupathi find their way into Siliguri easily. From Siliguri in Darjeeling district, Chinese goods are distributed into different parts of India including Sikkim.

An attempt was made to capture the nature and quantum of informal trade particularly in Chinese goods with Sikkim during the course of field survey in Gangtok, and to understand its implications for Indo-China trade through Nathu La. The derived estimates are indicative. It was reported that every month about 50-80 Sikkim traders visit Dhulabari and other border points in Nepal to purchase goods (Table 4.7). The wholesale and retail traders based in Siliguri also bring in Chinese goods based on orders placed by Sikkim traders. At times, hawkers bring goods in small bags and sell from door to door in Gangtok. It is estimated that a retail trader journeys 2-3 times per month from Siliguri to Gangtok. A

Table 4.7: Some Characteristics of Informal Trade through Nepal-Sikkim

Particulars	
Number of Sikkim traders visiting Nepal border per month	50-80
Annual value of goods smuggled into Sikkim (Rs. Crore)	3.3
Number of textile shops selling Chinese garments in Gangtok	200
Number of visits made per month by a retail trader from Siliguri to Gangtok	2-3

Source: Traders and Experts Survey.

conservative value of Chinese goods entering into Sikkim through this channel was estimated at Rs. 3.3 crores during 2006.

The informally traded goods mostly comprise low value consumer items. Among the goods entering into Sikkim, the share of readymade garments was the highest (Table 4.8). Readymade garments constituted about 70 per cent of the total value of Chinese goods brought in. Surprisingly, electronic goods accounted for 15 per cent only. Other items included shoes, gift items, crockery and chocolates. It was reported that goods imported directly from China through the Nepal route are of good quality. But, items imported from Lhasa (Tibet) are duplicates and are poor in quality.

Table 4.8: Chinese Goods that come to Sikkim through Nepal-Siliguri Route

Items	% share
Readymade garments (including bedsheets, blankets, socks)	70.0
Gift items	2.0
Crockery (clay cups, water mugs, tea cups etc)	2.0
Photo frame	1.0
Flower vase, artificial flower	2.0
Electronic goods	15.0
Umbrella	1.0
Shoes	5.0
Stationery	1.0
Chocolates	1.0
All	100

Source: Traders and Experts Survey

Traders feel that informal trade through Nepal should be discouraged. Opening of Nathu La for trade may provide enough incentives for diversion of goods coming through the Nepal route informally to the formal Nathu La route. Further, about 10-15 per cent of cost is incurred on transportation of goods from the Nepal border to Gangtok and other parts of Sikkim. Since proper billing is not available, it is likely to lead to corrupt practices adopted by some of the traders Thus, the Nathu La route may act as "safety valve" against the informal movement of Chinese goods into India. In fact, most of the goods might cost cheaper if they are imported directly from China. For instance, the original cost of Chinese umbrella at Dhulabari ranges from Rs. 40-50, but when it reaches Gangtok it costs about Rs. 90-100. Similarly, a pair of shoes cost Rs. 350 at Dhulabari, and the same pair will be sold at Rs. 600 in Gangtok.

Border trade requires the physical movement of people across the borders. In the long run, it may create some uneasiness in the border in the form of nefarious and illegal trade activities. It would be better from the economic and security point of view to make Nathu La a regular trading point between India and China. To make this happen, essential facilities such as a modern custom check post and other physical infrastructure need to be put in place.

Impact of Indo-China Border Trade on Sikkim Economy

The motive behind the opening of Nathu La border post was to facilitate the exchange of goods among people living in border areas of India and China. However, in course of time, export and import of goods might transcend the border areas of Sikkim and TAR of China, and move into the mainland of the respective countries. Given the state of optimism, the expected economic gains from Indo-China trade through Nathu La are likely to be enormous. There are no reliable assessments available on the potential impact of Nathu La trade on the state of Sikkim. An attempt has been made in the present study to explore the likely impacts on the state economy.

(i) Agricultural Diversification

In Sikkim, about 15 per cent of total geographical area (7096 sq. km) is utilised for crop production activities. Over 60 per cent of population is involved in agriculture. A low input-output based subsistence mixed farming system is widely practised. The major crops grown include rice, maize, cardamom, vegetables and fruits.

In comparison to Sikkim, agriculture is not so well developed in Tibet. Most of the areas fall under an arid climate.[14] Being closer to Tibet, Sikkim will witness a demand driven agricultural growth. It was learnt during field surveys in Sikkim that the Tibetans have a special desire for some of Sikkim grown produce like rice and tea. It is possible that the farmers in Sikkim may shift areas from existing crops, or increase the cultivated area, to grow high value commodities in future due to increased demand pressure and profitability. Such high-value commodities may include horticulture and floriculture products including vegetables, oranges, orchids, cardamom, and herbs and medicinal plants. As proposed in the Sikkim New Industrial Policy 1996, the setting up of Agri Export Zones (AEZ) and Food Park will add a new dimension to the development of agricultural and allied sectors in Sikkim.

(ii) Manufacturing

The industrial base of Sikkim is not very strong. There are a few small or medium sized industries located in different parts of Sikkim. Most of these industrial units are state owned with little private participation. In addition to strengthening of existing industries, new industrial units are likely to come up in Sikkim and adjoining areas in the wake of opening of Indo-China trade through Nathu La. The pre-investment feasibility study conducted by North Eastern Development Finance Corporation Ltd.[15] identified potential industries based on local resources availability in Sikkim. The study estimated the investment potential of Rs. 723.4

Table 4.9: Proposed Industrial Units, Location, Investment and Employment

Unit	*Location*	*Project cost (Rs. Million)*	*Total employment*
Agro based			
Potato chips (large scale)	Geyzing	27.8	244
Potato chips (small scale)	Gangtok, Geyzing (2)	4.2	192
Horticulture and plantation based			
Passion fruit vine		4.0	96
Orange plantation		3.0	96
Orange squash & jam/marmalade and mixed fruits jam and jelly	Rangpo, Singtam, Geyzing	3.6	320
Multi fruit juice	Gangtok, Singtam	110.7	744
Ginger oleoresin	East District (2), South District	45.5	624
Large cardamom oleoresin	Mangam (N), Rabangla	47.1	432
Animal husbandry based			
Pasteurized milk and cream	West District	10.0	92
Other industries			
Aluminum extruded household	Ranpo (1)	5.9	56
Nursing home cum diagnostic Centre	Gangtok (2), Namchi (1)	42.1	660
Garment unit	Gangtok, Rangpo	4.1	184
Cut flower	Namchi (2), Gangtok (1)	11.3	252

Source: NEDFi (2006)

million in the next ten years with a total employment generation of 3992 (Table 4.9).

Small and medium scale cottage industries, particularly, wool and silk-based units, have a rich potential to be developed. Raw wool and silk imported from China possess the finest qualities.[16] Spinning mills could be developed to make yarn and finished goods, which have a high export potential. Similarly, there is some potential for manufacturing of crockery by using clay imported from China. Handicrafts are one of the traditional industries of Sikkim and other northeastern states. The crafts like carpets, bamboo products and paintings made in this region possess special qualities and design. Besides Tibet, people in other parts of China have a passion for handicrafts made in northeastern India.

People of TAR and other Western parts of China still depend on traditional medicine. Given the serene and pollution free environment, Sikkim offers a great scope for development of pharmaceuticals industries. Food processing is another potential industry, which can be developed in a big way, given the demand for processed vegetables and fruits across the border.

(iii) Tourism

Tourism is one of the major activities in which about 42 per cent of main stream workers are employed.[17] Tourism related activities occupy the centre stage in the socio-economic development of a vast section of population. During the last ten years, the tourism industry of Sikkim has been growing at 8 per cent per annum. In 2005-06, about three lakh tourists visited various parts of Sikkim. Currently recorded direct revenue from tourism to the state government is about one crore of rupees only. Taking into account the total of tourism industry, including hotels and restaurants and transport, the total turnover will be around Rs. 135 crores in 2006.[18]

Nathu La opening is not only seen from the point of view of increasing bilateral trade between India and China, but also of boosting tourism related activities. Given its strategic location, the direct benefit from the increased tourism related activities would accrue to various stakeholders in Sikkim. If tourists are allowed to cross the border through Nathu La, the revenue from tourism related activities will almost double to Rs. 270-300 crores per annum.[19] The construction and transport industries will witness the spillover effects of increased tourism activities. The flow of private investment would increase to construct new hotels and restaurants and other amenities.

Religious tourism: Presently, thousands of Hindu pilgrims visit Mansarovar through trekking Pithorgarh-Nepal route, which takes a long time to reach. Mansarovar is located about 500 Km from Nathu La. The presence of motorable roads on both the sides will make the Hindu pilgrimage easy, thus diverting the pilgrim flow from the Nepal route to the Nathu La route. Further, Nathu La point will act as a gateway for Buddhists from India and Tibet to visit various Monasteries in the respective countries.

Business tourism: With increased trade flow through Nathu La, the visit of business people from various countries, including India and China, will increase. This will stimulate a host of secondary activities attracting business people to visit various places of tourist importance. Business tourism will promote the development of meeting and convention centres and exhibition halls in and around Sikkim.

Health tourism: Given a peaceful and pollution free environment, health tourism will get promoted in various parts of Sikkim. Various treatments like ayurvedic, herbal and other indigenous healthcare packages can be offered to the people visiting Sikkim.

(iv) Social Welfare

Being a land–locked state, most of the local demand in Sikkim is met through movement of goods from neighbouring states like West Bengal. The internal transportation cost is so high that when a particular commodity reaches Gangtok and other major towns in Sikkim, the price of that commodity increases by at least 25 per cent over the original price. Given the fact that most of non-durable consumer goods, which are mostly of Chinese origin, are transported through Nepal and Siliguri, the direct movement of the same or similar goods from China through Nathu La will reduce the transport cost considerably. This will make goods available at cheaper prices. The availability of goods at cheaper price will increase the implicit real wage rate, thereby increasing the overall economic welfare of people in Sikkim.

(v) Increased Revenue to Exchequer

The direct benefit to the state government from the increased trade flow through Nathu La will be enormous, if appropriate taxation policy is framed. Siliguri or New Jalpaiguri may act as a dry port, where goods can be assembled and transported to/from Kolkata port. However, transport and related facilities available in Sikkim will be crucial for a smooth freight movement. To get benefitted from a large volume of freight movement through Sikkim and to augment revenue to the state exchequer, the Government of Sikkim can levy new form of taxes like transit tax, environment conservation tax, parking tax and road development tax.

Summary and Conclusions

India and China have emerged as the important economic power centres with increasing influence in the world economy. During 1995-2003, India and China accounted for 11 per cent and 23 per cent of global output growth, respectively. With growing population and a vast skilled labour force, these two countries will have comparative advantage over other developed countries in propelling economic growth at a relatively high rate. A notable feature of warming political and economic relations between India and China is the rapid growth in bilateral trade. Bilateral trade between India and China was US$ 1.2 billion in 1995-96, which increased to US$ 25.7 billion during 2006-07. The whopping increase in trade volume is mainly due to the existence of trade complementarities and comparative advantage in export and import of goods. While India's export to China includes basic and intermediate goods, China's exports to India are relatively broad based, including electronic goods, organic chemicals, coal, medicinal products and textiles.

Building up on political relations initiated in the eighties, India and China agreed to open border trade between the State of Uttaranchal and Tibet Autonomous Region (TAR) of China in 1991. Both the sides agreed to use Lipulekh (Qiangla) as the border pass for the entry and exit of persons engaged in border trade and the exchange of commodities and means of transportation from both the sides. Trade takes place on the commodities approved by the Directorate General of Foreign Trade (DGFT), Government of India. About 29 commodities are allowed to be exported from India, and 15 commodities permitted to be imported from China. During 1993, India and China decided to extend border trade through another point between the State of Himachal Pradesh and TAR of China. Shipkila is the border pass for the entry and exit of persons engaged in border trade and the exchange of commodities across the two sides.

Meanwhile, India and China have agreed to expand border trade through an additional post on each side of the border. Both the countries decided to use Nathu La for entry and exit of persons, exchange of commodities and means of transport. Border trade through Nathu La was officially declared open on 6 July 2006. Nathu La offers a huge trade potential to be exploited by India and China in particular and the subcontinent in general. The advantage of Nathu La over other existing

Lipulekh and Shipkila passes is the presence of motorable roads on both sides of the border. It would be possible to have larger volume of trade because of ease of travel.

Both India and China have been sprucing up the required infrastructure facilities for a smooth conduct of trade. During the 2006 trading season, Travel passes were issued to Sikkim traders only. Trade took place on the restricted list of commodities approved by a DGFT. Non-Basmati rice was the major item accounting for about 78 per cent of total value of commodities exported from India. Wool was the only commodity that had an import demand from Sikkim. Sikkim traders provided a modest forecast of increase in the value of MFN trade in future. The total trade volume through Nathu La is expected to reach about US$ 22 million during 2007.

Nathu La provides strategic advantage for India and China as the point of entry and exit for movement of goods. The geographical proximity and presence of motorable roads between Kolkata and Lhasa provide greater scope for strengthening trade relations between India and China. The existing transport facilities can be used for freight movement through Kolkata port, which can act as a major hub for large volume trading. It could be possible to connect with other land-locked northeastern states, and to exploit trade potential to augment the benefit to the local people.

The opening of Nathu La provides a window of opportunities for generating various economic activities in Sikkim. It would be better from the economic and security point of view to make Nathu La a regular trading point between India and China. The increased demand from across the border will diversify the subsistent economic activities into commercially oriented ones. Producers of various potential by exportable commodities may reap the advantages of moving from subsistence to commercially oriented production. Indo-China trade through Nathu La will substantially improve the economic welfare of local people in Sikkim and other neighbouring areas by affecting the implicit real wage rate. The revenue to the Government of Sikkim is expected to increase through direct and indirect effects of Nathu La trade. It would also discourage informal imports of the Chinese goods entering into India via the Nepal route.

REFERENCES

1. World Bank, *World Development Indicators*, Washington: World Bank, 2007.
2. Rita Dulci Rahman and Jose Miguel Andreu, *China and India Towards Global Economic Supremacy*, New Delhi: Academic Foundation, 2006.

3. Dale Jorgenson and Khuong Vu, "Information technology and world economy", *Scandinavian Journal of Economics,* Vol. 107, No. 4 (December 2005): 631-50.
4. Dominic Wilson and Roopa Purushothaman, "Dreaming with BRICs: The path to 2050", Global Economics Paper No. 99, Goldman Sachs Global Economic Website, October 2003.
5. Memorandum between the Government of the Republic of India and the Government of the People's Republic of China on the Resumption of Border Trade, 1991
6. Protocol between the Government of the Republic of India and the Government of the People's Republic of China on Entry and Exit Procedures for Border Trade, 1992
7. India, China eye $40 billion bilateral trade. *Business Standard,* Tuesday, 21 November 2006.
8. Available at http://news.xinhuanet.com.
9. Available at www.travelchinaguide.com.
10. See www.china.org.cn.
11. *Traders Survey*, Sikkim
12. www.china.org.cn
13. Mahendra P Lama, "Sikkim-Tibet trade via Nathu La: A policy study on prospects, opportunities and requisite preparedness", Prepared by Nathu La Trade Study Group, Government of Sikkim, Gangtok, 2005.
14. Department of Agriculture, Government of Sikkim, Gangtok
15. *Pre-investment Feasibility Study on Industrial Potential Survey for Manipur and Sikkim*, North Eastern Development Finance Corporation Ltd. (NEDFi), Gangtok, 2006.
16. *Traders Survey*, Sikkim
17. *Sikkim: A statistical profile 2004-05,* Directorate of Economics, Statistics, Monitoring & Evaluation, Government of Sikkim, Gangtok, 2005.
18. Department of Tourism, Government of Sikkim, Gangtok
19. Department of Tourism, Government of Sikkim, Gangtok

Chapter 5

Looking at Nathu La through the Security Prism

Binoda Kumar Mishra

The 12,400 feet mountain pass between India and China has a long history. Being part of the "Silk Route", it served as a connector between India and China and accounted for a large volume of trade between the two countries for centuries. It accounted for 80 per cent of bilateral trade between India and China. The importance of Nathu La to both India and China is not only economic, but also the border pass is historic and holds implications for future Indo-China relationship. Its closure had Indo-China war as the cause. Thus, the opening of this pass is bound to create some apprehensions within Indian policy-making and strategic communities. The calculations of benefits from the opening of this pass is not just economic but strategic, too vis-à-vis a country with which India does not share a predictable action-reaction relationship. The question of opening this pass and using it for economic prosperity of the border areas of both the countries have to be considered from the overall political and strategic relationship the countries have shared in the past and expect to share in the future.

The end of the Cold War, among many things, generated the debate as to what kind of international system is emerging. Speculations varied from describing the emerging international system as a unipolar world with US at the head of the power hierarchy, to a multi-polar world with many states sharing the status of world power. In between these two extreme speculations was the speculation that the Cold War would continue between two great world powers, with China replacing the former Soviet Union as the competitor. For some, the possibility of a cooperative Sino-American world order can also not be overlooked. It is premature to give a verdict on the validity of any of these speculations. One thing is for certain that Asia has emerged as the centre of attention. Apart from the presence of China, the emergence of two rival nuclear powers, namely,

India and Pakistan, has drawn this attention to Asia. In many ways Asia now is a complete replica of the present international system – having four nuclear powers, diverse political and economic structures, regional and sub-regional associations, and the level of trust among nations, in the words of Fukuyama, is like 'a loose tray of sand'. Scholars of international relations are engaged in contemplating the role of these two most populous countries in the emerging international system and within the Asian continent. The projections vary from cooperatively leading Asia and the world to competing for space within Asia. These possible political speculations have long prevented cooperation between these two great Asian civilisations. History has a hand in building the distrust between these two nations, and of course there remain potential areas of conflict that might threaten their cordial relationship at any time.

The coincidence of the end of Cold War and the acceleration of the process of globalisation has created conditions wherein economic cooperation between nations is not merely a matter of expediency but a compulsion. A major component of the economic cooperation between nations is trade, and both India and China realise the potentials in this area. There has been substantial growth in trade between the two nations. There remains a great potential of border trade between the two countries, which not only would add to the economic growth of both the nations, but also, would automatically develop the frontier regions of both the countries. 'It is still early days in the courtship, though if it continues, 2050 may not look much different from 1750 when the two nations together controlled as much as 57 per cent of the world's manufacturing output.' But all depends on what kind of bilateral relationships these two countries share in the future.

The enthusiastic reopening of Nathu La in July 2006 after 44 years, threw up allusions of improved economic relations between the two nations, but the enthusiasm has not been reflected in the volume of trade. Restrictions of items by both the nations have made Nathu La a less than ideal trade route. This can be attributed to the difference of perceptions at the ground (border) and at the national (central) levels. A look at the items of trade between the two countries reveals an interesting fact. The top ten items in the export lists of both the countries differ substantially from the items traded through the border. The Sikkim government has urged the Indian government to increase the number of items for trade through the Nathu La pass. But both the central governments have their typical (security) prism look at both Northeast and Tibet. It is interesting to note that there are talks about the security threats from across the border if the trade through Nathu La is allowed but there is no clarification as to what constitute threat and to what kind of security. China experts who favour opening the Sikkim-Tibet trade route believe India had overplayed the security concerns.

Traditionally, security was interpreted as protection of territorial integrity of the nation-state. But in contemporary international politics, the definition of security is getting broader day by day. Along with protection of territory from military threats, security now includes: protection of economic interests both within and outside the country vis-à-vis competing countries; preserving the socio-cultural cohesion of the country; and retaining meaningful political sovereignty. If India is worried about the protection of her territory from possible Chinese aggression then we have an interesting argument. The only bone of contention between the two nations in their bilateral relations is the unsettled borders. We have even fought a war on the border question. But border trade has been identified as the beginning point for warming the relationship. This implies that both sides tacitly prefer the *status quo* to continue at the least or to settle the border issue amicably. It is quite clear that both do not favour any more conflicts over the issue. There are critics who are not fully convinced about the naivety of China in offering to open the Nathu La pass. According to them, China has solved its border issues with 12 of its 14 land neighbours. "Only India and Bhutan are having pending border issues with China."[1] They see a larger game plan behind China's demand to open up the border trade routes. It is difficult to arrive at the objective Chinese intentions but the caution on Indian side can be explained within the neo-realist framework of international relations and state behaviour under conditions of uncertainty towards potential competitors.

International cooperation is a complex issue and more so is bilateral cooperation between two countries not having the best of relationship in their recent history. The bilateral environment between India and China remains chaotic in the absence of identified common interests and defined norms / procedures to be followed in pursuance of national interests. India and China, in their 60 year history of mutual relationship, present a classic example of being "locked in an insecurity complex".[2] Laws of universal rationality do not always guide the mutual behaviour of states caught in this complex. The situation closely approximates the realist explanation of the international system in which both the states act as unitary actors trying to maximise their interests. Mutual behaviour is characterised more by caution rather than progressive cooperation. The neo-realist theory provides an apt explanation as to why nations remain ambivalent in their policies towards countries they consider potential adversaries or competitors. In the absence of transparency in mutual interaction, conjectures remain the main guide to foreign policy towards each other. The caution exercised by India in her China policy is a typical example. According to neo-realist theory, in their bilateral relationship, a nation remains more sensitive to the pay-off of the other (adversary) than her own. Each evaluates the expected pay-off of both the countries in relation to each other and cooperates only when the pay-off is favourable vis-à-vis the perceived adversary. If the adversary is expected to gain more from certain cooperative ventures between the two countries, the country gaining less prefers non-cooperation despite promises of absolute gains from that particular cooperative venture. This reasoning is well articulated by Kenneth N. Waltz:

When faced with the possibility of cooperating for mutual gains, states that feel insecure must ask how the gain will be divided. They are compelled to ask not "will both of us gain?" but "who will gain more?" If an expected gain is to be divided, say in the ratio of two to one, one state may use its disproportionate gain to implement a policy intended to damage or destroy the other. Even the prospects of large absolute gains for both parties does not elicit their cooperation as long as each fears how the other will use its increased capabilities. Notice that the impediments to collaboration may not lie in the character and immediate intention of either party. Instead, the condition of insecurity – at the least, the uncertainty of each about the other's future intentions and actions – works against their cooperation.[3]

The trade relationship between India and China is the classic example. In a situation where the level of trust between two nations is at the lowest, both seek to exploit the wealth of the other to enhance their own capabilities using trade as an instrument.[4] Despite gains for India from border trade with China, the Indian government is reluctant in increasing border trade with China. National Council for Applied Economic Research, in a recently concluded study, has projected that had both nations traded on Most Favoured Nation (MFN) basis across the border, the trade volume would have reached $22 million.[5] But the consideration is not what India can achieve from increasing trade engagement with China, rather what China can achieve from the same with India. The history of India-China relationship provides credence to the neo-realist explanation of bilateral behaviour of India and China vis-à-vis each other.

In a condition of anarchy, states tend to be cautious not only vis-à-vis known or potential adversaries, but also vis-à-vis countries with whom they share relatively cordial relationship. The rationale for such caution is the uncertainty over the future intention of the other state in question. Since there is a possibility of new dangers and opportunities arising out of change of leadership in the other country, [6] states tend to monitor the development of the relative capability of the other country with the fear that the other country might turn the relative advantage into greater bargaining power on certain military and non-military issues. Such relative advantage, states fear, may affect the autonomy of choice of the disadvantaged state on certain particular issues.[7]

The relationship of the two nations has not been uni-dimensional. The two civilisations have not enjoyed congenial relationship in the ancient past. The major religion of China, i.e. Buddhism, travelled from India through the silk route and facilitated religious and educational interactions between the two nations. During the period of colonialism in India, the relationship between the two countries got limited to trade and economic interactions only. But the geo-political developments of this time set the stage for the relationship the two countries shared after India got independence and China turned communist. However, the two shared a warmer relationship in the initial phases of India's independent existence. The then Indian prime minister described China as a sister civilisation and advocated closer ties between the two countries against the imperialist forces. He wrote, "We stand for the freedom of Asian countries and for the elimination of imperialistic control over them."[8] The intent in maintaining a friendly relation with China was evident from the fact that India extended recognition to Communist China, campaigned for her inclusion in the international community as an equal member. For positive bilateral engagement both agreed to the famous *Panchsheel.* But the warmth lasted for not more than a decade and a half. The question of Tibet was the beginning of the bitterness. This was followed or supplemented by the dispute over the boundary. The McMahon line drawn by the British in 1914 was rejected by the Chinese, while India claimed it as the official boundary as inherited from the British empire. The stand taken by China and the subsequent war made Indian leadership feel cheated. The Chinese victory in the war of 1962 did not resolve the border problem, rather, it perpetuated a sense of suspicion among Indians.[9]

The evolving Sino-Indian relationship from 1962 is characterised more by apprehension than eagerness for progressive engagement. This applies more to India than to the Chinese policy. Unlike China, India has a democratic system, which is more susceptible to public opinion and the opinion of the Indian strategic community in particular. The opinion of the Indian strategic community is based more on conjectures about the emerging world order and India's position in it. It is argued that a multi-polar world is in India's interest and India is destined to play a meaningful role in the international system by virtue of her size, economy and more importantly her firm belief in democratic values.

India's international position depends largely on her position in the Asia, and there it comes in for relative assessment with the other prominent world power of the region and the world that is China. By her sheer size, population and military might China is already an established power and her secretive authoritarianism keeps her as an enigma for all others to keep guessing about her global and regional ambitions. Since the emergence of the People's Republic of China in 1949, Indian policy makers and strategic community had been suspicious about the Chinese intentions regarding their territorial ambitions. India's first prime minister and foreign minister had expressed his apprehensions about the Chinese intentions. "He had experience of Communist Regimes and knew that they could be sweet reasonableness itself or pig-headed with conceit in turn."[10] The historic event of 1962 reinforced the apprehensions of the sceptical Indian strategic community and the policy makers about the sinister designs of China vis-à-vis India. Though there are various accounts of the 1962 India-China war, there is a consensus in India that it was a betrayal on the part of China. From 1962 till late 1980s, the China threat was dormant in Indian strategic and policy community. Three factors contributed to the resurgence of China as a potential threat to India in the late 1980s and 1990s. The phenomenal economic growth attained by China, massive military build up after the end of the Cold War, and the Chinese assertiveness in handling international affairs and its growing irredentism.[11]

With this historical background, the relationship between the two countries is approaching a new complex. This perception about China has forced the Indian strategic community to be overcautious in their prescriptions about India's China policy, and the policy makers are even more cautious in dealing with China. Given the fact that China has not showed her military aggression towards India for over four decades, there has been a slight shift in the dominant perception about China among the Indian strategic and policy making community. From a constant threat China is now viewed as non-threat for the present, but there is no guarantee that it will not be a threat in the long-term.[12] Such perceptions are grounded on the history of China's unilateral activities and current multi-lateral engagements with neighbours who are known or potential adversaries of India.

States, though sensitive to relative gains from cooperation with a particular country, are also calculative about absolute gains. In what circumstances a state would be sensitive to relative gains or loss varies. If the power base of a particular country is sinking, then that country is expected to be more sensitive to relative gains or losses than rising hegemons.[13] The level of trust is directly proportional to the likelihood of sensitivity towards relative gain or loss. In a condition of 'no trust' (like war), states are more likely to bother about the mutual pay-offs than their absolute gains.[14] Lastly, relative pay-off calculation is more likely to predominate on issue areas where the chances of the one party translating the relative advantage into capability to affect the other adversely are high.

The economic interaction seems to be moving in the positive direction. China has emerged as the second largest trading partner of India, though India is 10th in the list of trading partners of China. Bilateral trade between the two countries has crossed $40 billion. The visits of the Chairperson of the ruling Congress party Ms. Sonia Gandhi, followed by the visit of Indian Prime Minister Dr. Manmohan Singh, are evidences of India placing her China policy high on the agenda. One of the reasons that provides added urgency to Sino-Indian relations is India's so called "Look East" policy. India's renewed interest in Southeast Asia has brought her to deal with nations in China's neighbourhoods. There are, therefore, compulsions for both countries to engage each other in a positive manner. Among the positives, one should not lose sight of intermittent flare-ups over the long drawn out border question. The present Sino-Indian relation is far from trouble free and continues to oscillate between friendship and rivalry. Thus, the current (over) cautious approach of India needs to be looked through the perceived relative gains (security and strategic advantage) China is feared to get from increased engagement through interactions like border trade.

India's Threat Perceptions vis-à-vis China

Military/Strategic

Unlike the popular perception that clubs strategic and security concerns with similar connotations, I see security as a matter of immediate concern to the state's territorial integrity, its economic health, social cohesion and environmental balance. Strategic concerns, on the other hand, while not discounting the importance of territorial integrity and internal stability of a country, looks beyond to incorporate vital issues like the perception of neighbours, allies, potential competitors, not-so-friendly countries and the persistent importance of geopolitics in combination with international *real politick.*

There has been an identifiable perceptual position in India that influences the policy-making which characterises China as an adversary for both conspicuous and inconspicuous reasons. From the Indian point of view, there are chances of China posing a security threat. The strategic community in India cites Chinese actions that pose both direct and indirect threats to India. The most direct threat perceived by India is the presence of Chinese nuclear missiles in Tibet. It is alleged that since 1971, China has deployed medium range, intermediate range and long-range ballistic missiles.[15] The missile system deployed by China has the capability to carry nuclear payload. Though China has declined the presence of nuclear capable missiles in Tibet, various independent accounts point to the fact that most of the Chinese missiles in fact target India. Though China is committed to "No First Use," in the absence of and de-targeting agreement with India, which China has with other nuclear power states, there remains according to security experts in India, high possibility of China actually using these weapons against India. Along with the direct military threats emanating from Tibetan territory, there are other military concerns also. Chinese presence in Myanmar, particularly the building up of signal intelligence system in the Great Coco island and the setting up of a radar station on the Hiangyi Islands bother India, as from these facilities China can keep a close watch on India's defence activities in the Bay of Bengal.

The present inclination of China towards her neighbours including India is alleged to be an approach for a limited period of time. It is feared that China may change its approach and behave aggressively any time in the future. Thus it would be "imprudent for India not to institute adequate precautionary measures to cater for a possible reversal of China's policies..."[16] In this context, the building of rail road from Beijing to Lhasa, and the accompanied declarations by the Chinese authorities from time to time, are picked as allusions for possible reversals of the Chinese policies towards her neighbours, particularly India. It is no secret that China has been building road and train infrastructure in Tibet. In 2001, President Hu Jintao, describing the utility of the rail connectivity between Beijing and Lhasa, declared that, "Tibet of today presents a scene of vitality and prosperity with economic growth, social progress and stability, ethnic solidarity and solid border defence."[17] The reference to solid border by China is perceived in India as alarming and the present thaw or probable leaning of China is an *ad hoc* approach to buy time to prepare for strengthening the border and consolidate her peaceful rise.[18] The present fast paced infrastructure development by China in Tibet and its extension to Nepal are thus not viewed as economic measures only. India is worried that China will make use of these infrastructure to increase her military capability on the borders of India.

Another important Chinese action, that has a hand in generating antagonistic perception about China, is China's apparent resistance to India's position as a nuclear weapon state in the international sphere, despite the fact that China has violated the Non-Proliferation Treaty principles by assisting Pakistan and North Korea in developing their nuclear programmes. It is perceived in India that China intends to arrest India's nuclear capability through international pressure, and at the same time enhance the capability of India's adversaries, particularly Pakistan. The relationship of China with Pakistan and her covert support to Pakistani nuclear programme has kept India bothered. China's involvement in Myanmar and increasing proximity with Bangladesh is perceived by the Indian strategic community as strategic encirclement of India. Added to this, the Maoist dominated Nepal now seems eager to welcome Chinese involvement in Nepal. This is viewed as particularly dangerous for India.

Economic

At the bilateral level, there has been a realisation that the interests of India and China are not antagonistic to each other, and there remains a great potential for mutual gains from bilateral economic interaction. In objective terms, the economists are optimistic that bilateral trade between the two countries can complement each other's economy. A large number of studies conducted by Indian scholars present a very positive prognosis of the prospects of India-China border trade across Nathu La. The critics of the initiative also share the same optimism. Thus, one can conclude that trade across Nathu La is certainly a positive economic step for the interest of the people at both sides of the border. This is also evident from the enthusiasm shown by the political establishment of the state of Sikkim, which has worked over time to get the pass reopened. Then what is the concern? It is feared by China watchers in India, including some scholars from the Northeast itself, that by allowing border trade through Nathu La, Northeast India is being turned into a zone for extraction. As of now, owing to various factors Northeast India does not produce any major marketable commodity but houses a large amount of natural resources. It is feared that with the opening of the trade route the current "illegal but licit" trade practices would be stopped and this would hamper the lifeline of the small traders of the region who stand no chance to compete with the market forces.[19]

I do not dispute the primary assumption of the argument that small traders stand no chance in competition with the bigger players in the market. But this is not unique to the region and nor is it directly related to Nathu La. It is one of the evils of globalisation from which no country can escape. It certainly is a challenge for the developing countries to adapt to the principles of globalisation. Some call this process as "glocalisation". This remains a separate argument, and cannot and should not be counterpoised against the anticipated benefits of border trade through Nathu La.

The second argument is that border trade through Nathu La would open the floodgates for Chinese cheap goods to be dumped in the region and hollow out whatever potential the indigenous market has. This argument, to me, seems totally unfounded. This fear stems primarily from the typical conjecture Indians have towards China. I would just like to make a point that this fear of losing market is not one sided. As India is now trying to expand her connectivity with hitherto neglected regions traditionally considered to be Chinese strongholds, such as Southeast Asia, a section of Chinese academia considers that Indian goods will be preferred to Chinese goods in Southeast Asia once the market in Southeast Asia matures from the stage of mass consumption to search for quality. Therefore, it is up to the market to decide who is going to win in this genuine economic competition.

It is feared that China stands to gain a lot more than India from border trade. The argument is, if Chinese goods are allowed to flood the Indian market, it would be preferred by the Indian consumers and thus would ruin the Indian manufacturing sector. The second argument is that China is treating India as a competitor in matters of investment and employment. B. Raman argues that Indian companies having investments in China, mostly in the IT sector, employ Chinese youths and bring them to India to improve their IT skills and English language, whereas the Chinese companies having investments in India do not employ Indian youths. They prefer to employ Chinese youths. Raman attributes this to the Chinese attitude of competitiveness towards a potential rival.[20]

Political

The general population of Sikkim, it is argued, seems to be sceptical about the benefits of the resumption of border trade. They feel that it would simply legalise the smuggling of goods, which has hitherto been carried out via Nepal. They fear that instead of Bagdogra and Siliguri, now Gangtok would be flooded with Chinese goods. As far as employment generation is concerned, a few hoteliers and transporters seem enthusiastic about the reopening of Nathu La. The local population, on the other hand, sees more opportunities in the tourism sector than in border trade. Moreover, border trade would initially benefit only the residents of the East Sikkim district (especially Bhutias), since only they will be allowed to trade with their Tibetan counterparts. The people of Sikkim are also apprehensive that opening of the border pass would lead to a massive influx of Tibetan refugees. There is simmering resentment among the people of Sikkim towards the Tibetans. It is believed that during the late 1950s and early 1960s, a substantial number of Tibetans crossed over to India and settled in Sikkim. In course of time, they added "Bhutia" to their names and started availing of the reservation facilities extended to the Scheduled Tribes of the state.[21] Since the Tibetans were better educated compared to the local Bhutias, they were able to grab top positions in government as well as in other economic and social spheres.

In addition, a substantial influx of Tibetan refugees can also have adverse political implications. Sikkim is a small state with a population of approximately 5 lakhs. It has 32 constituencies with about 18,000 persons in each. Even a small addition of Tibetans to the voter's list can alter the political destiny of the state.[22] Even if the security arrangements and the terrain around the border pass do not facilitate large scale Tibetan infiltration, complacency in guarding the borders can cost us dearly. The case of Bangladeshi refugees and illegal migrants do serve a good example to assess the impact of illegal migrants in the socio-economic and political life of the border states of India. The opening of the border pass can usher in an era of prosperity, but India should be prepared to meet the challenges it might pose in maintaining the peace and tranquillity of the strategically sensitive border regions. Given the history of Chinese involvement in the form of supplying arms to various insurgent groups of India's Northeast, it is argued that all this may increase, once the borders are made permeable. Last but not the least, there is a fear that, China's eagerness in normalisation of economic, political and cultural relations without solving the border issues indicates that China wants to create stakes within India.[23]That will help the Chinese create an atmosphere in their favour before taking up sensitive border issues like Aksai Chin or Arunachal Pradesh.

Conclusion

The perceptual fears discussed above are certain to cross the minds of policy makers while thinking about engaging China. Similar perceptual fears can also be generated and in fact are being generated by the Chinese academia about India's moves and intentions.[24] But in the contemporary world of economic globalisation and regional integration, the compulsions of cooperation are well realised by both India and China. As mentioned earlier, there has been a quantum leap in trade and both countries are cooperatively pursuing common needs such as energy in the global market. On the strategic front, India and China have also established a framework for frequent high-level exchanges among the defence ministries and armed forces; an annual defence dialogue; joint military exercises and/or training programmes in the fields of search and rescue, anti-piracy, and counter terrorism.[25]

Although India's overall level of economic development lags behind that of China, it has made significant advances, especially in high-technology industries. Growing rapidly since New Delhi introduced economic reforms in the mid-1990s, India is aiming to become the fourth or fifth-largest economy in the world by 2020.[26] Currently ranked among the world's top 10 countries, India's economy is projected to claim the number three spot by 2050.[27] Therefore, the fear of losing out to China in an economic competition is too gross and simplistic. Legal trade, once it picks up, is bound to reduce, if not eliminate, illegal trade. Opening the Nathu La can enable both India and China to better monitor and curb illegal activities like smuggling. Last but not the least, Nathu La, by dint of better facilities in comparison to the other two passes, namely, Shipki La and Lipulekh, can serve the cultural purpose of Indian pilgrimage to mount Kailash and Mansarovar. There is no urgent need to return to the 'bhai-bhai' (brother-brother) cordiality of the 1950s, but it must be understood that there is a growing interdependence between the two countries and if this is complemented by some confidence-building measures, potential conflicts can certainly be deterred. Border trade, particularly through Nathu La, can be viewed as such a confidence building measure, and be pursued with a positive approach, keeping it outside the relative gain calculus.

REFERENCES

1. Srikanth Kondapalli quoted in Percy Fernandez, "Nathu La endangers Indian Security: Experts," 4 July 2006, available at http://intellibriefs.blogpost.com
2. See Waheguru Pal Singh Sidhu and Jing-dong Yuan, *China and India:*

Cooperation or Conflict?, New Delhi: India Research Press, 2003) pp. 45-78.

3. Kenneth N. Waltz, *Theory of International Politics*, New York: Random House, 1979, p. 105.
4. Joanne Gowa, "Rational Hegemons, Excludable Goods, and Small Groups: An Epitaph for Hegemonic Stability Throry?", *World Politics*, Vol. 41, p.307, cited in Andreas Hasenglever, Peter Mayer and Volker Rittberger, "Interest, Power, Knowledge: The Study of International Regimes," *Mershon International Studies Review*, Vol. 40 (1996), p. 202.
5. See K. Elumalai, "India-China Border Trade through Nathu La: Prospects for Growth and Investment in Sikkim," in this Volume.
6. Robert Jarvis, "Minds can be changed, New leaders come to power, values can shift, new dangers and opportunities can arise" in Robert Jarvis, "Cooperation under the Security Dilemma," *World Politics*, Vol. 30, No.2, 1978, p. 168.
7. Joseph M. Grieco, "The Relative-Gains Problem for International Cooperation: Letter to the Editor", *American Political Science Review*, vol.87, no.3, p.734 (pp. 729-35)
8. Jawaharlal Nehru, *India's Foreign Policy: Selected Speeches, September 1946-April 1961*, Bombay: The Publications Division, Ministry of Information and Broadcasting, Government of India, 1961, p. 24.
9. Rollie Lal, *Understanding China and India: Security Implications for United States and the World*, London: Praeger Security International, 2006, p.134.
10. Iqbal Singh, *Between two Fires: Towards an Understanding of Jawaharlal Nehru's Foreign Policy*, New Delhi: Nehru Memorial Museum and Library, 1998, p. 187.
11. The three factors are identified by Waheguru Pal Singh Sidhu and Jing-dong Yuan. See, Sidhu and Yuan, *China and India*, p. 49.
12. Steven A. Hoffmann, "Perception and China Policy in India," in Francine R. Frankel and Harry Harding (eds.), *The India China Relationship: Rivalry and Engagement*, New Delhi: Oxford University Press, 2004, pp. 39-40.
13. Andreas Hasenclever, Peter Mayer and Volker Rittberger, "Interests, Power, knowledge: The Study of International Regimes," *Mershon International Studies Review*, Vol. 40, No.2, 1996, p. 203.
14. "In general, [sensitivity towards relative loss] is likely to increase as a state transits from a relationships in …a 'pluralistic security community' to those approximating a state of war." Joseph M. Grieco, *Cooperatino among Nations: Europe, America and Non-Tariff Barriers to Trade*, Ithaca: Cornell University Press, 1990, p. 45. Cited in, ibid, pp. 202-03.
15. According to various reports, a launch site for Dong Feng Four (DF-4) missiles which are equivalent to Russia's CSS-2 was built in Tsaidam. These missiles, located at Large Tsaidam and Small Tsaidam are reported to have a range of over 4,000 km, placing the whole Indian sub-continent within striking distance

16. Jasjit Singh quoted in Hoffmann, "Perception and China Policy in India," p. 40.
17. Claude Arpi, "Chinese Consolidation in Tibet and its Impact on India's Security," in *South Asia Defence and Strategic Year Book 2007*, New Delhi: Panchsheel, 2007, p. 51.
18. Ibid.
19. Observation by Rajesh Dev in a Workshop on "Northeast India and Southwest China" in Kolkata on 15 November 2007.
20. B. Raman, "India and China: Reality Behind Statistics," Chennai Centre for China Studies Paper No. 101, 28 January 2008.
21. Pushpita Das, "Nathu La: Pass to Prosperity but also a Challenge", IDSA Strategic Comments, 4 July 2006, available at http://www.idsa.in.
22. Ibid.
23. Srikanth Kondapalli quoted in, Sheela Bhatt, "It is advantage China, says expert," June 25, Rediff.com.
24. In the Chinese perception, the warming U.S.-Indian relationship is an effort to contain China. India poses a risk to the territorial integrity of China's western provinces. India can play a big role in destabilizing Tibet. Finally, India poses a conventional threat with its stronger navy, sophisticated arms acquisitions, and growing nuclear arsenal declaredly built in response to the China threat. For a detailed discussion on the Chinese perception of India as a security threat, see Susan L. Craig, "Chinese Perceptions of Traditional and Nontraditional Security Threats," March 2007, available at http://www.StrategicStudiesInstitute.army.mil/
25. "Memorandum of Understanding Between the Ministry of Defence of the Republic of India and the Ministry of National Defence of the People's Republic of China for Exchanges and Cooperation in the Field of Defence," 29 May 2006.
26. Sun Peijun and Hua Biyun, "Yindu de jingji gaige: chengjiu, wenti yu zhanwang," *Nanya Yanjiu [South Asian Studies]*, No. 74 (2003): 3–11, 22; Sun Peijun and Hua Biyun, "Jiedu Yindu Jingji de Jueqi," *Nanya Yanjiu*, No. 76 (2004): 3–11; Wang Jiangang, "Yindu Jingji: Ganshang Zhongguo Shangxu Shiri," *Liaowang Zhoukan*, 17 May 2004, pp. 32–33. For a different assessment, see Yasheng Huang and Tarun Khanna, "Can India Overtake China?" *Foreign Policy*, No. 137 (July/August 2003): 74–81.
27. Goldman Sachs, "Dreaming With BRICs: The Path to 2050," Global Economics Paper, No. 99 (October 2003), available at http://www2.goldmansachs.com/insight/research/reports/99.pdf.

Chapter 6

Travel and Tourism: Economic and Cultural Ties and Buoyancy

Renzino Lepcha

General Overview of World Tourism

Rise in World Tourism

The mercury on barometer of the tourism industry is on a rise. With growing money power, falling dollar prices, better connectivity, people wish to travel. Their travel is not restricted to their countries or neighbours. People are travelling across the earth with jet lags of modern aircrafts for the sheer experience of different cultures, bounties of nature, contemporary towns, mega metropolis, or just family holidays.

Tourism is today one of the world's largest industries, creating 231.2 million jobs in 2007 worldwide, i.e. 0.3 per cent of total employment (*Source: World Travel and Tourism Council*). Clearly the tourism sector is an important economic activity for both developed and developing nations. The Madrid-based World Tourism Organization recorded the growth of world tourism from 766 million in 2004 to 808 million international arrivals in 2005. The figure was expected to increase by 5 per cent the following year. In less than a decade, international tourist arrivals are projected to reach one billion (*Source: World Tourism Organization*)

While in 1950 the top 15 tourist destinations, all in western Europe and North America, attracted 97 per cent of the world's total arrivals, by 1999 this figure had fallen to 62 per cent, with market shares increasing for developing countries, particularly in South-east Asia, Central and Eastern Europe, and Latin America. In 2005, in a report by WTO, Asian destinations were among the top 10 destinations worldwide, including the mighty Asian giants like China and Hong Kong, but the European

Table 6.1 : World's Top Tourism Destinations

Rank		*Series*					*Change (%)*		*Average 1995-2004*	*Market share*	*Population 2004*	*Arivals per 100*
			1995	*2000*	*2003*	*2004*	*2003/2002*	*2004/2003*	*(%)*	*2004*	*(million)*	*of population*
	World		**545**	**636**	**691**	**760**	**–1.7**	**10.9**	**3.8**	**100**	**6,376**	**11**
1	France	TF	60.0	77.2	75.0	75.1	–2.6	0.1	2.5	9.9	60	124
2	Spain	TF	34.9	47.9	51.8	53.6	–1.0	3.4	4.9	7.1	40	133
3	United States	TF	43.5	51.2	41.2	46.1	–5.4	11.8	0.6	6.1	293	16
4	China	TF	20.0	31.2	33.0	41.8	–10.4	26.7	8.5	5.5	1,299	3
5	Italy	TF	31.1	41.2	39.6	37.1	–0.5	–6.4	2.0	4.9	58	64
6	United Kingdom	VF	23.5	25.2	24.7	27.7	2.2	12.1	1.8	3.6	60	46
7	Hong Kong (China)	VF	10.2	13.1	15.5	21.8	–6.2	40.4	8.8	2.9	7	318
8	Mexico	TF	20.2	20.6	18.7	20.6	–5.1	10.5	0.2	2.7	105	20
9	Germany	TOE	14.8	19.0	18.4	20.1	2.4	9.5	3.5	2.7	82	24
10	Austria	TOE	17.2	18.0	19.1	19.4	2.5	1.5	1.3	2.6	8	237

Source: World Tourism Organization (WTO) © (Data as collect by WTO May 2005)

countries like France and Spain retained their first and second positions respectively.

The Asian Dark Horse

The notable change in the chart was Asia, stealing the show from other European counterparts. If not in the top 10 list, South Asian and North Asian countries have made their presence felt on the world tourism map. In 2006, Asian countries collectively earned $93.4 billion from international tourism, including air travel, according to the World Tourism Council. Almost 80 million people in Asia are engaged in the tourism industry for at least a part of their income.

Region	*Market share of the total world tourism*
Asia	**19 %**
Northeast Asia	11.5%
Southeast Asia	6.2%
South Asia	1.3%

Source: World Tourism Organization

Most Asian destinations grew by over 15 per cent in the year 2005, with growth rates reaching often over 100 per cent during April. Arrivals in Japan reported a positive 19 per cent increase. Arrivals in the Philippines and Singapore increased by almost 25 per cent, while Malaysia reported a growth of almost 60 per cent. Arrivals in India increased by 24 per cent after a very positive performance in 2003, while arrivals in Sri-Lanka and Nepal also did positively with an increase of 10 per cent and 43 per cent respectively.

Factors behind the Growth of Tourism in Asia

One of the major factors is the demand of tourism worldwide. Tourists are in search of unique products merged with quality standards and suitable pricing packages. The amalgamation of diverse elements like transportation, accommodation, dining, recreation, and entertainment that is across natural and cultural features, hospitality and ambience, are the highlight on Asian tourism platter. The countries are offering authentic experiences to tourists rather than a Mcdonaldized society – an experience that is unique and distinctive.

Some of the factors like the region's booming economy have steered the tourism growth. Economic growth has ranged between an average of 6 per cent to 9 per cent in the last decade, in contrast to 3 per cent to 4 per cent growth achieved by the rest of the world. The liberalisation of the economies like India's, has added to the growing influx of foreign investment in the tourism trade. Billions of dollars from the western markets are being poured into the region to upgrade tourism infrastructure, and to accommodate a burgeoning tourism industry in Asia. This has intensified trade, investment, and travel within the region and with the rest of the world.

In recent years, the South-east Asian region has become politically more stable. The opening of borders to both inbound and outbound travel, and the breakdown of political barriers, has provided tourists with opportunities to pursue their leisure interests. Easing of travel restrictions has contributed to a surge in the tourist inflow in regions like South Korea and Taiwan. Liberalisation of air transport, replacing the traditional policy of safeguarding national carriers, has only served to enhance trade and tourism growth in the region. Focussed marketing and themed campaigns like 'Incredible India,' 'Malaysia Truly Asia,' 'Uniquely Singapore' have put these countries on the world tourism map and provided a new impetus to tourism and transformed the clichéd attitudes towards these regions.

New Vogue of Tourism

Tourism has greatly expanded largely due to the revolution that is taking place on both the demand and the supply side. The changing population structure, improvement in living standard, more disposable income, fewer working hours and long leisure time, better-educated people, ageing population and more curious youth in developing countries, all add fuel to the tourism industry growth. But, on the other hand, the new world challenges such as terrorism, international political instability, economic turbulence and environmental consciousness have affected the tourism demand. The volatile situations always demand the creation of new products and diversification of existing tourism products or simply re-invention. The new and the emerging forms of tourism are catering to travellers around the world.

The innovations in tourism are: Ecotourism, Rural Tourism, Spiritual Tourism, Health Tourism, Adventure Tourism, Sustainable Tourism, Cultural Tourism, Memorial Tourism, Beach Tourism and many more. The South-east Asian region has all the galore. The region is home to the Himalayas, the oriental culture, traditional practices, ancient temples and monasteries, the ocean and its blue world, the people and amicable hospitality, the untainted places far from the crowd as well as the biggest cities, ancient arts and many such old wines waiting to be packed in new bottles.

New tourism trends are one of the key ingredients of rapid increase of tourist flow to South Asia. With countries like India, China, Malaysia, Maldives, Indonesia, Nepal, the tourism products are much more diverse than in any other region in the world. 'These new forms of Tourism are embracing a new dimension of Travel & Tourism. It is a mature response to a more complex world and the often unpredictable consumer behaviour. It is geared to deliver commercially successful products – but in a way that ensures benefits for everyone. New tourism trends look beyond short-term considerations. They focus on benefits not only for people who travel, but also for people in the communities they visit, and for their respective natural, social and cultural environments' (*Source: World Travel and Tourism Council*).

Incredible India!

In recent times, India has seen that scale of development, which has gone beyond the imagination of most economists. A badly battered economy of the late 1980s has moved to one of the top markets in the world. India, since liberalisation, has steadily gone up the graph with constantly increasing GDP and FOREX reserves. India's economic success has some unique features: India has one of the largest film industries in the world; the world's richest sporting body is Board of Control for Cricket in India; Indians head top places in some of the biggest corporations in the world. India sure is going places. But not too far from the glitter is the land itself: India is a tourist haven.

Recently, India topped the prestigious Conde Nast Traveller top travel destinations in the world. India Tourism office at Tokyo won two International Awards in Tour Expo held at Daegu in Korea for excellent tourism promotion. The Indian Pavilion won the Best Booth Design Award as well as the Best Folklore Performance Award competing with major players in tourism such as China, Japan, Thailand, Malaysia and Canada. Adding another feather to the cap was the successful and the high profile campaign 'Incredible India' by the Ministry of Tourism, which recently bagged the coveted PATA Grand Award for Marketing. India also bagged two PATA Gold Awards for Cultural Tourism (Aranmula) and Marketing Brochure (Kumarkom) awarded to Kerala Tourism. The World Social Forum, AdAsia, World Bamboo Congress, Commonwealth Games, Laureus World Sports Academy Global Summit, along with some of the biggest expos and conferences of the world, are choosing India as a destination to host their events.

India has the potential to become the number one tourist destination in the world with the demand growing at 10.1 per cent per annum, as predicted by the World Travel and Tourism Council (WTTC). A record 2.8 million tourists made their way from various parts of the world to India in 2003, registering a rise of 15.3 per cent over 2002. In 2004, the tourism industry registered a growth rate of 17.3 per cent in foreign tourist arrivals, which has been the highest in last 10 years.

India accounted for over half of the tourist arrivals in South Asia in 2006, in which arrivals were up 10 per cent over 2005, as per the data from the World Tourism Organization. Total international arrivals into India, as per the Ministry of Tourism, Government of India, were up to 4.43 million out of the 842 million globally, in 2006. South Asia, with India as the single largest destination, is forecast to receive 11 million visitors by 2010, and 19 million by 2020, taking its market share in global arrivals to 1.2 per cent by 2020 against 0.7 per cent in 1995 (*Source: World Tourism Organization*).

Factors of Growth

The buoyancy in the Indian tourism industry can be attributed to several factors. Since the liberalisation of the 1990s, the Indian economy has been growing at around 7 per cent per annum, and with rise in disposable incomes of Indians, an increasing number of people are going on holiday trips within the country and abroad, resulting in the growth of the tourism industry. Increasing number of companies are coming to India, which has improved the tourism infrastructure and facilities in the country. This has also prompted local players to raise the quality standards and give the best to their customers. India is a booming IT hub, and more and more people are coming to India on business trips. Aggressive advertising campaign "Incredible India" by the Tourism Ministry has played a major role in changing the image of India from that of the land of snake charmers, poverty, and pavement dwelling people to a culturally and naturally diverse country with modern as well as traditional lifestyles.

India's Magnetic Charms

India is a diverse country with numerous tourism opportunities. If the north has the mountains and snow peaks, the south has miles of beaches. The west has the bustling modern lifestyles, the east retains some unique features of ancient cultural traditions. Every corner of India is about 'variance in colours.' Major attractions in India are the world's highest mountains, miles of coastline with excellent beaches, tropical forests and

State-wise Domestic and Foreign Tourist Arrivals during 2000 & 2001

(Figures in lakh)

	2000		2001			
State/ U.T.	*Domestic*	*Foreign*	*Domestic*	*Foreign*	*% of Total Domestic 2001*	*% of Total Foreign 2001*
Andhra Pradesh	479.982	0.78713	525.3365	0.67147	22.5	1.2
Arunachal Pradesh	0.09932	0.02044	0.06349	0.00323	0.0	0.0
Assam	8.91433	0.05954	10.10651	0.06171	0.4	0.1
Bihar	55.20589	0.73321	60.61168	0.85673	2.6	1.6
Goa	9.76804	2.91709	10.47342	2.60071	0.4	4.8
Gujurat	114.0828	0.31748	82.72969	0.3093	3.5	0.6
Haryana	2.60442	0.01113	2.76287	0.00898	0.1	00
Himachal P.	45.71129	1.11191	52.11772	1.3576	2.2	2.5
J & K	53.93463	0.194	52.46948	0.21298	2.2	0.4
Karnataka	180	2.08	141.1746	1.40703	6.0	2.6
Kerala	50.13221	2.09933	52.40009	2.0883	2.2	3.9
Madhya Pradesh	47.96133	1.11036	50.48851	1.07824	2.2	2.0
Maharashtra	82.97158	10.75169	84.79695	9.15399	3.6	16.8
Manipur	1.05167	0.00429	0.76527	0.00183	00	0.0
Meghalaya	1.69929	0.02327	1.78697	0.0239	0.1	0.0
Mizoram	0.28221	0.00235	0.28771	0.00152	0.0	0.0
Nagaland	0.13272	0.00451	0.09948	0.0092	0.0	0.0
Orissa	28.88392	0.23732	31.09976	0.22854	1.3	0.4
Punjab	3.85682	0.03854	4.74305	0.03258	0.2	0.1
Rajasthan	73.74391	6.231	77.57217	6.08283	3.3	11.2
Sikkim	1.43105	0.10409	2.03306	0.31028	0.1	0.6
Tamil Nadu	229.8226	7.85876	238.1204	7.73073	10.2	14.3
Tripura	2.31902	0	2.54912	0	0.1	0.0
Uttaranchal	N.A.	N.A.	95.51669	0.44429	4.1	0.8
Uttar Pradesh	648.3	8.48	680.71	7.95	29.0	14.7
Chattisgarh	N.A.	N.A.	N.A.	N.A.	0.0	0.0
Jharkhand	N.A.	N.A.	3.53177	0.02979	0.2	0.1
West Bengal	47.37112	1.97061	49.43097	2.84092	2.1	5.2
Andaman & Nicobar	0.853	0.03156	0.84064	0.05539	0.0	0.1
Chandigarh	4.86355	0.14612	4.82133	0.15203	0.2	0.3
Daman Diu	0.74172	0.0833	N.A.	N.A.	0.0	0.0
Delhi	14.9789	11.2795	13.24636	8.30092	0.6	15.3
Dadar & Nagar Haveli	4.08639	0.00223	4.52	0.004	0.2	00
Lakshdweep	0.01087	0.00597	0.03501	0.0065	0.0	0.0
Pondicherry	5.27274	0.23878	4.76804	0.22115	0.2	0.4
Total	**2201.069**	**58.93542**	**2342.009**	**54.23667**	**100**	**100**

wildlife, desert safari, lagoon backwaters, ancient monuments, forts and palaces including the Taj Mahal. The tropical forests in Uttaranchal, Madhya Pradesh, Karnataka, Orissa, Kerala and Rajasthan are being developed into major tourist attractions. Every state of India offers a different experience than the other. India is probably the only country that offers various categories of tourism. These include history tourism, adventure tourism, medical tourism, spiritual tourism, beach tourism, cultural tourism, ecotourism, and many more such categories.

Impact of Tourism

There are numerous tourist destinations in the world; and more and more tourists are coming to these destinations. It is therefore essential to know the demand and supply, inflow and outflow, of the tourists for data analysis and overall information to assess the impact upon the economy, environment, people, industry and other related factors. The impact of tourism upon the country's economy, employment rate, etc. can be easily quantified. But when it comes to the cultural and environmental aspects, it is extremely difficult to quantify such elements. Such elements are researched only through observations over a period of years. In India, it may not be easy to build up systems for evaluation of cultural-environmental changes brought about by tourism.

Economic Impact

Tourism is among India's important industries. With an increasing number of international tourist traffic, tourism has already emerged as an important segment of the Indian economy. Tourism has helped in increasing foreign reserves and in uplifting the economy in economically backward states. Foreign exchange earnings from tourism during 2003-04 were US $ 3,533 million (Rs 16,429 crore). Tourism also contributes to the economy indirectly through its linkages with other sectors like horticulture, agriculture, poultry, handicrafts and construction. Besides such contributions to the economy, tourism also provides employment to millions of people in India both directly and indirectly. It is estimated that total direct employment in the tourism sector is around 20 million.

Alongside these economic benefits, there are some significant costs associated with tourism development. These costs include the costs of advertising and marketing the country as a destination and the establishment and operation of national tourism organisations as well as the costs associated with developing and maintaining relevant infrastructure. For example, the State Tourism Department of Ladakh has spent millions of rupees on publicity abroad to attract more tourists. And there has been very little planning and investment in sanitation, public health service, electricity, safe drinking water, and training of local people in servicing the tourism sector. The people of these areas are neither educated about the nature, needs and tastes of tourists nor about tourism related problems. There are no plans and programmes to make tourists realise that they have come to experience the things that make Ladakh special and different from other places.

Revenues from tourism vary with factors like seasonal patterns, international events, natural causes, etc. These can create inefficiencies in terms of the utilisation of tourism resources leading to excess or waste. High levels of tourist arrivals may cause problems like overload on local infrastructure, placing pressure on water, electricity, sewage provision, and on transport links. Finally, it is often argued that many of the economic benefits of tourism are lost because of high levels of leakages in the form of increased imports. The issue of leakages has long been recognised as problematic, and the extent of leakages can be difficult to estimate. In some isolated places as much as 40 per cent of tourist expenditure may be lost overseas, with food and beverages often found to have particularly high import content. In many other destinations, leakages are probably much lower and often less than 20 per cent.

Cultural Impact

In India, culture and heritage are the most important ingredients of the tourism industry. India has been traditionally, and even in recent times, promoted as a cultural destination. Cultural heritage creates a foundation for tourism's growth. Tourism has the power to generate funds that make conservation possible. But cultural heritage loses much of its true meaning to a society participating in tourism, and benefitting from it, as the monetary gains creep in.

With the growing interest in culture and community, tourism is finally being recognised as an industry that can boost rural economies, create entrepreneurs and jobs and help to preserve indigenous cultures. For example, tourism in the Himalayan regions have led to the transformation of the traditional subsistence farming of the local communities in the regions into income generating options, creating jobs and better standards of living.

There is also no denying that tourists do influence the host population's culture. The places in the mountains and many such interior parts of India have remained relatively isolated from the mainstream, and, therefore, the value system and traditions of the people are vulnerable. The interface with tourists sometimes results in insidious values creeping into a community's culture. Some of the remote places like India's Ladakh, Sikkim, Madhya Pradesh have suddenly become tourist destinations. Their tradition-bound society gets a severe culture shock from the permissive way of life of foreign tourists. But it need not always be so if proper care is taken in advance to prepare the host population to benefit from the interaction with tourists with diverse cultural backgrounds.

In recent times, the government has taken measures to ensure proper benefit sharing among the stockholders involved. The government is also promoting India as a cultural destination which prompts communities to display their distinctive identities and traditional lifestyles.

The Indian government has also adopted a multi-pronged approach towards promotion of tourism, which includes new mechanism for speedy implementation of tourism projects, development of integrated tourism circuits and rural destinations, and special capacity building in the unorganised hospitality sector.

The government is also running a nationwide campaign for creating awareness about the effects of tourism and preservation of our rich heritage and culture, cleanliness and warm hospitality, including a scheme of training and orientation, which was launched in 2004-05. The aim is to rebuild that sense of responsibility towards tourists among Indians, and reinforce the confidence of foreign tourists in India as a preferred holiday destination.

However, to ensure a sustainable form of tourism, India still needs to upgrade its tourism infrastructure and penetrate through the interiors to allow a proper flow of income through tourism, and promote awareness of cultural and environmental values in people engaged in tourism.

Sikkim Perspectives

The North-Eastern Sisters

The Northeastern Region of India comprises eight states, including Sikkim. This region is a relatively unexplored and unique area, in terms of both geography and cultural diversity, as it provides one with a glimpse of not just a 'mini India', but also of Southeast Asia, all within a space of 265,000 sq.km.

The indigenous people belong to mainly the Mongoloid and Tibeto-Burman stock, and have preserved their culture, language and way of life, even in the present century. Geographically, India's Northeast is a land of undulating hills and plains with luxuriant green cover and a wide variety of rare and exotic flora and fauna. The Bramhaputra valley with its near tropical climate is a fertile plain on the basin of one of the largest rivers of the world. The hilly terrain of the region ranges from Nagaland in the east to the Meghalaya in the west; the Mizoram lies in the south, while in the north lies Arunachal Pradesh, which extends to the snow-clad ridges of the great Himalayas.

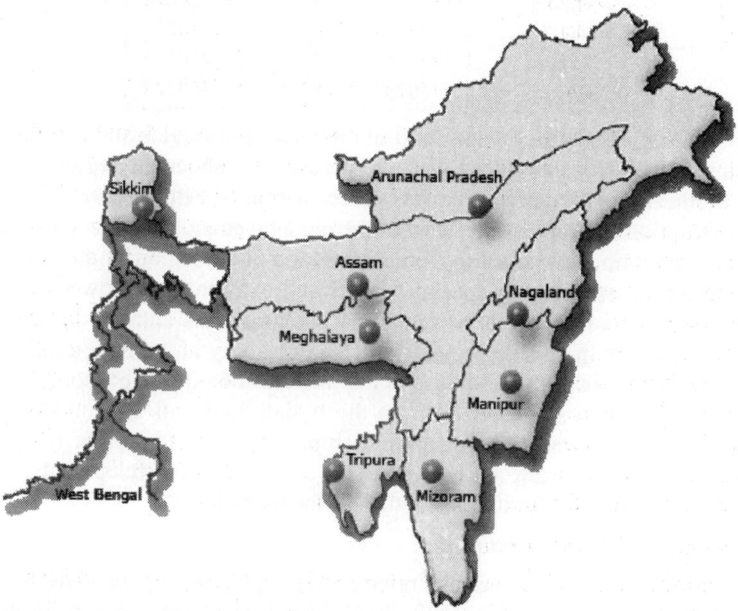

The entire region is the home of some of the most rare and endangered species of animals, including the renowned and world famous one-horned Indian rhinos. The virgin dense forest is the home of hollock tree, the tallest of its kind in India. Northeast is also the habitat of the maximum species of wild orchids, which number more than 500.

The region is endowed with diverse tourist attractions, and each state has its own distinct features. The attractions are scattered over the entire region and are largely located in remote areas within highly fragile environments. The tea estates, ruins of ancient kingdoms, temples, rivers, hills, the rich flora, fauna, and ethnic groups have recently started attracting domestic as well as foreign tourists into the region.

Tourist in Northeast Region during 2001-2002

States	*Tourist (2001-2002)*		
	Indian	*Foreigners*	*Total*
Meghalaya	268529	3191	271720
Assam	9973763	4265	9978028
Manipur	103854	409	104263
Mizoram	27417	197	27614
Nagaland	10395	438	10833
Tripura	257989	2564	260553
Sikkim	**160789**	**8539**	**169328**

Despite all the beauty and abundance, political instability and insurgency have produced negative perceptions about the region. The Northeast has become an area of violence, insecurity, extortion, trafficking, corruption and repression. Most of the ongoing ethnic insurgencies have turned criminals, and led to the militarisation of the region by the Indian armed forces enjoying special 'rights' and extraordinary powers. The Northeast is trapped in its economic backwardness and can be aptly described as India's neglected child. The volatility of the region has hit its growth prospects. And despite the liberalisation of the economy, the region still remains isolated from the Indian mainland. Sikkim stands apart in the Northeast region as an example of peace and prosperity. The serene and quiet state has been enjoying a high rate of development, and growing as a hub for tourists in the Northeast region.

Economy of Northeast India

The Northeast India is usually referred to in India as a region which is as interesting and varied as India itself. The pace of development in the hilly areas and plains differs considerably.

State-Wise Net State Domestic Product (at Current Prices)

State	*2000-2001*	*2001-2002*	*2002-2003*	*2003-2004*	*2004-2005*	*2005-2006*
Arunachal Pradesh	595	1729	1896	2160	2246	NA
Assam	28262	30674	33516	35700	38624	41842
Manipur	2517	2947	3054	3323	3680	NA
Meghalaya	3338	3699	3976	4349	4754	NA
Mizoram	1635	1777	2027	NA	NA	NA
Nagaland	3427	3864	4458	NA	NA	NA
Sikkim	878	974	1111	1242	1375	1541
Tripura	4869	5559	6044	6728	NA	NA
Total	46521	51223	56082	NA	NA	NA

The contribution of agriculture to the State domestic income is much higher in this region, except for Meghalaya and Nagaland. Mining in case of Meghalaya, and forestry and logging in the case of Arunachal Pradesh and Nagaland, are important contributors to NSDP. The contribution of construction is also high in this region. Growth in per capita income is almost stagnant in Assam since the 1990s. It is better than the national average in Meghalaya. An increasing trend is visible in cases of Arunachal Pradesh, Manipur, Nagaland, Sikkim and Tripura. The per capita income in the Northeastern region on an average is Rs. 12,918, as compared with the national average of Rs. 17,947 in 2001-02.

Tourism has emerged as one sector of prospective growth in the Northeast. Experts foresee an explosive growth in this sector in the coming decades. But despite being rich in natural resources, tourism development in the Northeastern region has lagged behind the rest of the country. The region faces the problems of inadequate infrastructure, geographical isolation, communication bottleneck, lack of proper transport, and lack of tourism awareness.

Government Efforts to promote tourism in the Northeast

The Government attaches great importance to the development of tourist infrastructure in the Northeastern region in view of immense tourist potentials of the region. Despite abundance of natural beauty, snow-peaked mountains and white water rivers, the flow of incoming tourists has been marginal due to lack of infrastructure and awareness. Accordingly, there has been a continued thrust on development and upgradation of various tourist facilities, namely, Tourist Accommodation, Wayside Amenities, Budget Accommodation, Beautification and Refurbishment of Historical Monuments/Monasteries, etc. Under Adventure Sports, River Rafting equipment, Water Sports equipment, Adventure Tourism equipment, have also been provided under the Central Government's Financial Assistance programme.

In order to develop and promote tourism in the region, the Ministry of Tourism has taken the following steps:

1. In pursuance of the PM's initiative for Northeast, a full-fledged Institute of Hotel Management and Catering Technology has been set up at Shillong.
2. A chapter of Indian Institute of Tourism and Travel Management has been opened at Guwahati.
3. The Food Craft Institute at Guwahati has been upgraded to the level of an Institute of Hotel Management, Catering Technology

and Applied Nutrition, and the existing infrastructure is being expanded.

4. The Department of Tourism has upgraded the head of the Government of India Tourist Office, Guwahati, from the level of Director to the Regional Director level. This will facilitate work of classification/re-classification of 1-3 star hotels located in the Northeastern States, which were earlier covered by the Regional Director, Government of India Tourist Office, Kolkata.
5. A video film on tourist attractions in the Northeast has been produced by the Ministry of Tourism in order to give wide publicity to the region. This is being screened by Air India in their flights.
6. Northeastern States are given a free booth in the world tourism fairs and festivals.
7. Financial Assistance for promotion of fairs and festivals is also being provided to Northeastern States every year on a continuing basis.
8. Northeastern States are given a special focus in the Marketing Conferences of Overseas Offices of the Ministry of Tourism. All these overseas offices are giving due publicity to the Northeastern States for the promotion of tourism in the region.

During the year 2000-2001, the Ministry of Tourism sanctioned an amount of Rs.24.52 crores for new projects relating to development and promotion of tourism, out of which Rs.7.79 crores were released to North-eastern states and Sikkim. In addition, an amount of Rs.4.96 crores was also released for ongoing projects. For the year 2001-2002, 121 projects relating to development and promotion of tourism amounting to Rs. 32.57 crores were prioritised for the Northeastern States including Sikkim.

Sikkim Overview

Small but beautiful, Sikkim is situated in the Eastern Himalayas. Spread below Mount Kanchenjunga (8598 mts.), the third highest mountain in the world, it is revered by the Sikkimese as their protective deity. This tiny state, bigger only than Goa and Delhi, is India's least populated. Sikkim was once an independent kingdom but now is one of the states in the Indian Union. Different people have given different names to this place. Nepalese call it "Sukhim" or "New Home", while Tibetans have named it as "Denzong" or "Valley of Rice". There are Lepchas as well, who are the original inhabitants of Sikkim, and they call their motherland as "Nye-Mal-Ale" or "Heaven".

The state of Sikkim is located in the inner regions of Himalayas and has no open valleys or plains but has varied elevations ranging from 300 to 8583 m above the sea level. Sikkim is picturesque and verdant with clean crisp air, deep blue mountain lakes, gorgeous Buddhist monasteries, and hillsides ablaze with rhododendrons against a backdrop of snow-clad mountains.

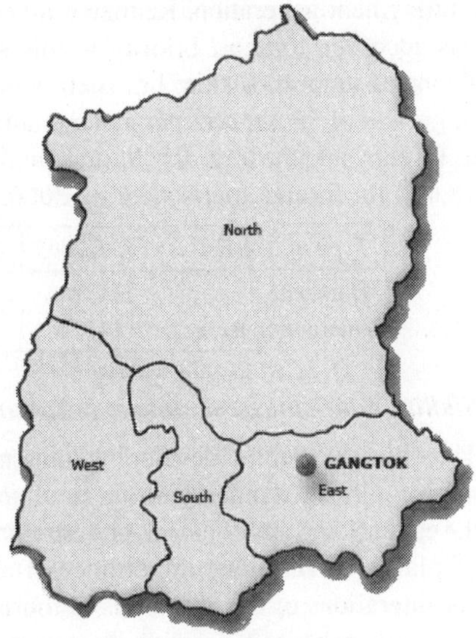

The capital of the state, Gangtok, is an attractive and interesting town in eastern Sikkim, well developed and with absolutely amazing views of the snow clad Himalayan peaks including the Kanchenjunga.

Sikkim: The Ecotourism Destination

Sikkim has been taking rapid strides in the ecotourism sector, and has now become a major ecotourism destination in the region. In 2005, more than 2.5 lakh domestic and 17,000 overseas tourists visited Sikkim.

Sikkim is often called the biodiversity 'Hotspot' of the lower Eastern Himalayas. And rightly, since the region is bestowed with abundant natural resources. Covering only just 0.2 per cent of the geographical area of India, it hosts 30 per cent of the flowering plants accounted for in the country. With its exhibition of the varied canvas of nature, Sikkim is now not only a natural hotspot but also a tourist hotspot. With the expansion and development of Sikkim, the state has determinedly adopted and implemented a policy for the management of natural resources based on the principle of conservation and sustainability. Inventing benefit mechanisms for the people has also been a part of the growing concept of ecotourism in Sikkim. Biodiversity management by the people has been blended in a conservation policy for the betterment of the communities in the environmentally sensitive areas.

Tourism is one of the fastest growing sectors in the state, and holds a tremendous potential for future economic growth with equity and employment generation. Realizing this potential, the State Government has accorded topmost priority to this sector with adequate policy and financial support. Sikkim has been witnessing a steady and healthy rate of growth of 15 per cent per annum tourist arrival, both domestic as well as foreign, and the total arrival stood at 3.2 lakhs for domestic and around 18,000 for foreign tourists during 2006.

Type of Tourist	*2004-2005*	*2005-2006*	*2006-2007*
Domestic	234574	261107	302693
International	14774	16472	18371

Sikkim Tourism: Economic and Cultural Buoyancy

The objective behind developing tourism is to generate employment and improve living standards of the rural areas, without adversely affecting the ecology and environment, or destroying the protected areas. Exhibition of places of religious importance is also one of the most important considerations of the promoters of tourism.

Low leakages are extremely important to the state of Sikkim, so that the state can take the road to progress with benefits reaching primary players involved in tourism. Another consideration for encouraging tourism is culture, which is at the heart of tourism in India and likewise in Sikkim. Creative adaptation to changes is equally important. And with growing environmental consciousness, an evaluation of the impact of tourism on the environment is also essential.

Economic Dimensions

Tourism, if utilised effectively, can be a force for positive growth and economic success for the state of Sikkim. Sikkim has the potential to become a top ecotourism destination in India. The tourism industry can enhance the state's income and generate income and benefits for the poor and isolated areas in Sikkim. It can act as one of the key employment generators.

Contribution of Tourism to the Economy

Tourism converts the natural and cultural resources of Sikkim into dynamic economic activities and marketable assets by bringing tourists to Sikkim. It is estimated that the 300,000 tourists who visit Sikkim at present pump almost 50-60 crores of revenue into the state every year. This is real money brought from outside by tourists, and spent in Sikkim on accommodation, food, transport, entertainment, purchase of souveniers and so on. Such expenditure of tourists has generated direct employment for the people in the hotels, transport and travel agency sector. But the indirect economic benefits in the form of multiplier effects are much more. For example, the commercial activities like supplies of vegetables, eggs, meat, etc. to hotels and restaurants during the tourist season add to the economic and employment benefits of tourism. Photographers' studios also thrive on tourist arrivals.

Job Growth: The implications and contribution of tourism to the mountain economy of Sikkim has been significant with the tourism industry providing the maximum employment opportunities after the Government. Now ecotourism has emerged as an important economic activity in the region, which includes trekking, mountaineering, river rafting and other nature oriented activities.

Tour Operators: The sudden upsurge of tour operators in Gangtok and in other parts of the country has given Sikkim the tourism destination status for the last decade or so. Tour operators have the potential to sell a destination to a wide audience. The increasing number of tour operators leads to better and broader networking, subsequently creating numerous jobs. The tour operators have expanded their activities to cover spheres like hotel, transport services, restaurants and infrastructure development, entertainment and media, education, training, etc.

Hospitality Industry: The hospitality industry contributes to the important process of job creation. As a labour intensive industry, it employs a large number of wage earners, whose taxes and disposable income add to the gross domestic output, and help to create further employment opportunities. Given that each hotel room typically requires one member of staff, every hotel room built has the potential to create an additional job.

Other than job creation, the hotel industry is a thoroughly tourist based source of income. Creation of hotels leads to more tourists, in turn leading to higher profits. The industry makes a major contribution to the gross domestic output of the state. Every penny spent by the tourist adds to revenue. Growing local community based tourism in Sikkim has helped the hospitality industry with various products like homestays and village guest houses. Increasing number of tourists are visiting such places, adding to the revenues of the local communities.

Cultural Dimensions

Tourism can be both a force for the preservation of, or, conversely, a threat to a community's natural and cultural heritage. Sikkim, like other parts of India, is rich in culture and heritage. The Sikkimese people, with their rare tradition and rich culture, add greater fragrance to India's diverse and composite culture. The three ethnic communities (Lepcha, Bhutia and Nepali) display a remarkable feature of Sikkimese society with its cultural harmony and peaceful coexistence.

In Sikkim, the demand of tourists to experience the culture of local people has helped revival of interest of local people in their culture. The people of Sikkim with their friendly and hospitable nature have welcomed tourists from all over the world. Sikkim Tourism has been organising tourism festival, where local traditional dance and music are displayed through the main thoroughfare of the Gangtok town. Various ethnic groups of Sikkim participate in these cultural carnivals with great enthusiasm and gusto. Different tourism destinations in the state have made tourism festivals an annual feature adding to the variety of activities for the visitors to sample. These festivals make an attempt to highlight the rich ethnic diversity in food, ornaments, songs, dances, traditional practices and folklore. Local people have begun to realise the importance of their own cultural heritage, and to promote the revival of interest and pride in their culture.

Case Study: Cultural Revival

Pastenga is a hub of three ethnic tribes, the Lepchas, Bhutias and Rais. The village is very rich in tradition and culture. With the introduction of homestay hospitality, the villagers took an initiative to entertain the guests with traditional dance and playing indigenous musical instrument. At the advent of the cultural programme, the dance troupe used to play songs in a tape recorder and dance to the music. Through the initiative of Mr. Pancha Bahadur Rai, a professional Maruni Dancer and Madal (Traditional Drum) player, the ladies and young men of the village started to play different musical instruments and sing folk songs together, which were once forgotten by the villagers, and especially the youth. Mr. Pancha Bahadur Rai takes pride in his tradition and culture; he teaches the youth and others to dance and play different musical instruments which otherwise were replaced by modern items. Whenever he has guests staying at his homestay unit, he entertains the guests playing "madal" and singing folk songs – sometimes his whole family joins together to entertain the guests. Ms. Shakuntala Rai, a relative of Mr. Pancha Bahadur Rai, who plays "madal" regularly to entertain the visitors said: "We have started to beat the drums again even at this old age, and I am happy to be a part of the cultural troupe."

With the introduction of traditional musical instruments like "Binayu and Machunga," there has been a cultural revival amongst the youth and women who now take pride in exhibiting these age old instruments. They have even started playing choruses for the visitors at the cultural programme. The introduction of cultural programme has not only led to cultural revival but has empowered the women to take active part in the cultural programme, performing dances, singing folk songs and playing age old traditional musical instruments like "madal, machunga and binayu".

Similarly, in Kewzing village, the local tourism committee of the village frequently hired a cultural troupe for their visitors in the tourist season. This practice was not appreciated as it did not reflect the true spirit of the village community. This posed a challenge to the local inhabitants. They made efforts to start practising their traditional Sikkimese Bhutia songs and dances. Initially the local committee members took the initiative and gradually during the village festivities, the villagers congregated and took part in it.

Nathu La Pass –The Ultimate Bolster

General Overview

Nathu La is a mountain pass in the Himalayas. It is located on the Indo–China border, connecting Sikkim with the Tibet Autonomous Region of the People's Republic of China. The pass, at 4,310 m (14,140 ft) above mean sea level, forms a part of the ancient Silk Route. *Nathu* means "listening ears" and *La* means "pass" in Tibetan. It is also spelled *Ntula, Natu La, Nathu La,* or *Natula.*

Nathu La is one of the three trading border posts between China and India. Sealed by India after the 1962 Sino-Indian War, it was re-opened in 2006 following numerous bilateral trade agreements. Its opening is expected to bolster the economy of the region and play a key role in the growth of Sino-Indian trade. The current agreements limit trade across the pass to exports of 29 types of goods from India and imports of 15 from the Chinese side. The opening up also shortens the distance that must be travelled to access the important Hindu and Buddhist pilgrimage sites in the region.

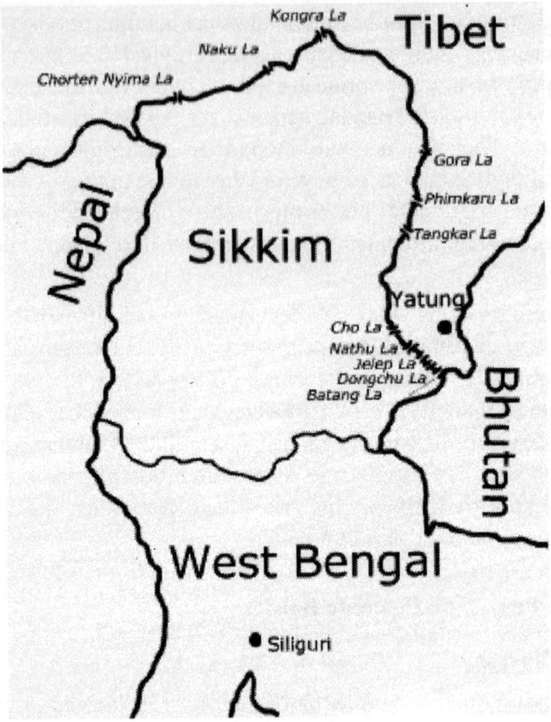

Economic Benefits for Sikkim and other States

Before the pass was opened, almost all the Indo-China trade went through the port of Tianjin more than 4,000 km (2,500 miles) away. With the opening, this distance has been reduced to 1,200 km (745 miles). This re-opening is expected to stimulate the economy of the region and bolster Indo-Chinese trade, which amounted to US$7 billion in 2004. Figures released by the Tibet Autonomous Regional Bureau of Commerce show that in the 51 days of trading in 2006, US$ 186,250 worth of trade passed through Nathu La.

It is estimated that Sino-Indian trade would increase by nearly 15–20 per cent within two years of Nathu La's opening. Trade volumes through the pass are projected to grow to Rs. 206 crore (US$ 44.6 million) by 2007, and Rs. 12,203 crore (US$ 2.6 billion) by 2015. The pass offers the Chinese companies access to the port of Kolkata (Calcutta), situated about 1,100 km (700 miles) from Lhasa, for trans-shipments to, and from Tibet.

To facilitate cross-border trade, the two countries have set up trading marts at Sherathang in Sikkim (6 km from Nathu La) and Rinqingang in Tibet (10 km [6 miles] from Nathu La) for the purposes of customs and checking. China has not placed any restrictions on cross-border trade, but India has, placing heavy restrictions on the commodities to be exported and imported.

The re-opening is also expected to boost up cross-border tourism. It will be open for tourists by 2011. On the Chinese side, 7,000 tourists visited Yadong County near the Nathu La border in 2006, and brought in 1.67 million yuan (US$ 216,000) as revenue. On the Indian side, only citizens of India can visit the pass on Wednesdays, Thursdays, Saturdays and Sundays, after obtaining permits, a day in advance, in Gangtok. Nathu La is one of the excursion highlights for domestic visitors and a must- see for most first timers.

Tourism through the Silk Road

The reopening of the Nathu La Pass is foreseen to bolster tourism sector too. Currently, only traders are allowed to cross the snowy Silk Road mountain pass between India and China. But tourism could thrive in this region with readily available land routes. That, in turn, can be developed into an integrated international tourist circuit.

The Sikkim Chamber of Commerce envisions making the high altitude area a trans-shipment hub like Singapore. By 2011, when Nathu La is scheduled to be open for tourism, more than 300,000 Chinese are expected to travel through mountain passes to India.

The flow of people, goods and services and enhanced communication facilities will create several new avenues for building mutual confidence and ensuring tranquility in remote border areas. Tourism will also bring prosperity to isolated communities on both sides of the Himalayan divide.

The Sikkim Government is working with the Centre for the introduction of bus services between Gangtok and Lhasa, the distance between which is about 500 km. The State Government is prepared to meet infrastructural requirements for the bus service on the Indian side. The new route would considerably boost tourism in the region on the lines of the Delhi-Lahore and the Kolkata-Dhaka services.

The Government is also taking steps to promote "religious tourism" in the state, and the proposed Gangtok-Lhasa bus service is expected to benefit pilgrims heading for Mansarovar in the south Tibetan region of China. Indian and Sri Lankan Hindu and Buddhist pilgrims would take the Nathu La pass to visit Lake Mansarovar or even Mt. Kailash. The journey to these holy places through Nathu La will be more comfortable and less time-consuming, compared to the route through Kathmandu. It would also attract a huge number of tourists, who would use Nathu La to travel to China to visit monasteries and other scenic spots. It will also permit Tibetan pilgrims to visit Buddhist monasteries on the Indian side. Another factor which will provide boost to the region is the start of the Qinghai-Tibet railway in July 2006. That ended Tibet's history of no railways and linked the region more closely with other parts of China.

The Sikkim Government has also planned to take up the airport project at Pakyong, about 20 km from Gangtok, to boost the inflow of tourists. State officials say that about Rs. 50 crores has already been allotted by the Planning Commission for the purpose. The demand by the travel and tour fraternity to convert Bagdogra airport near Siliguri into an international one would also boost tourism in the region. It is predicted that, out of the yearly tourist flow to Tibet from mainland China, a good number would like to visit Sikkim and the rest of India. It has also predicted that Sikkim will get an extra 300,000 tourists annually (*Source Sikkim Chamber of Commerce*).

Clearly the Nathu-La route will open a new chapter in tourism. The two countries are yet to work out the modalities on cross-border tourism, and State Government officials are not yet sure about the entire mechanism; but the private as well as public sectors are naturally euphoric about the prospects.

Nathu La and the Northeast

By reopening Nathu La, the two countries have given new hopes to the backward regions like China's southwest and India's northeast. Tourism can bring large economic benefits to the Tibet-Himalayan border region as well as the local economies in Tibet and Northeast India. The shorter route to reach the beautiful sights in Sikkim and the other Northeast Indian states plus Bhutan and Nepal, will greatly energise tourism.

West Bengal could register impressive growth in tourist inflows, leading to a growth in spending in travel and hospitality sector. Nathu La can lead to the north Bengal town of Siliguri turning into a transit point for travellers. The town, located at the foot of the Himalayas and well connected by road and rail, operates as the connecting link for the Northeast and northern Bihar. Siliguri could well emerge as the growth centre of Buddhist tourism in India. The city can position itself as the hub for Buddhist pilgrims from Japan, and for East Asian travellers to

Bodhgaya in Bihar, Rumtek in Sikkim and Tawang in Arunachal Pradesh and to the rest of the Northeast.

Challenges ahead

It has been more than a year since Nathu La was opened between India and China. The growth in bilateral trade has benefitted the region, and the future is getting brighter. The initial optimism has been reinstated with ground realities. The Nathu La will be opened for cross-border tourism only in 2011. Until then, the road to the Silk Road is not as smooth as its name. Some of the major challenges are:

Lack of infrastructure: Poor roads and communications, lack of banking facilities and lack of container depots constitute some major problems of infrastructure. These need to be addressed before tourism in the region takes off. Sikkim has no rail links or airports, it urgently needs more highways. Currently, only one national highway – NH 31A – is the lifeline of the state. The construction of an airport at Pakyong, East Sikkim, must be speeded up and taken more seriously.

Human capital: Despite China and India being the two most populous countries in the world, the region where Nathu La is located between both countries fall in scantily populated regions, i.e., the Southwest of China, Tibet, and Northeast of India. The regions are economically backward. Capacity building for tourism is therefore essential. It is upto the people in the region to stand up to the challenges ahead and against the wits of outsiders.

Monitoring: The threat of terrorism is one of the most daunting challenges in cross border tourism. Though the region is quite peaceful, it takes only an event to change the picture. The Central Government will have to be proactive in monitoring and checking the movement of people across the border. The State Government should be able to set up a counter-intelligence service in the State Police Department near the Nathu La Pass.

Military: The recent news about the Chinese invasion of 60 metres into India in Arunachal Pradesh will certainly affect the military's policies and the opposition in the region. The Indian Army is strongly opposed to the opening of the border, particularly on strategic grounds. The Army expressed its concern over the construction of road, rail and air-heads in the Tibet Autonomous Region. It fears that the 1,118-km railway project to link Gormo in China's Qinghai province with Lhasa in Tibet is an indication of the induction and sustenance capability of Chinese troops in Tibet.

Natural restrictions: With an elevation of 4,310 m above sea level, Nathu La receives heavy snowfall and remains impassable for normal traffic for several months of the year. Tourism through Nathu La can only be done for a limited period during the year when the weather conditions permit.

Last Words

The Nathu La Pass can easily become one of the most important tourism circuits in the world. This will act as a booster for the region's economy. The current cautious attitude of India makes Nathu La seem far from being a viable proposition for tourism between India and China. A lot needs to be done, particularly by the Indian Government, to unlock the real value of the route.

REFERENCES

"300,000 Chinese tourists through Nathu La by 2011". Retrieved from http://www.indiaenews.com/business/20060921/23155.htm

"Asian destinations on the rise in world tourism ranking". Retrieved from www.world-tourism.org/newsroom/Releases/2005/May/asian.htm.

"Indian Industries". Retrieved from http://www.indiacore.com

"Indian Travel Industry". Retrieved from http://www.indiandata.com/travel/

"Nathu La Pass on Sino-Indian border closes", *China Daily*, 15 October 2006.

"Nathu La reopens for trade after 44 years". *Times of India* (Kolkata), 6 July 2006.

"Nathu La reopens for trade after 44 years". *Zee News*, 6 July 2006.

"Report: Silk Road pass to increase tourists to India". Retrieved from http://www.chinadaily.com.cn/china/2006- 09/21/content_694208.htm.

"The Northeast of India". Retrieved from http://databank.nedfi.com/mod.php?mod=userpage&menu=10&page_id=3

Bijoy, Bagchi, *Heritage, Tourism & Development.* Retrieved from http://www.pcedindia.com/peoplescomm/heritage2a.htm.

D. Buhalis, *Information and telecommunications technologies as a strategic tool for small and medium tourism enterprises in the contemporary business environment.* In Tourism: The State of the Art, edited by V. Seaton et al. Chichester: John Wiley & Sons, 1994.

By 2020, Tourism in India could contribute Rs 8,50,000 crores to the GDP. (Source- WTTC). Retrieved from http://www.indiacore.com/tourism.html.

Somnath Chib, *Understanding the Economic Impact of Tourism.* Tourism and Travel Research Institute, 2003.

Renaud Egreteau, "India's troubled Northeast". CHS Occasional Papers, 2006.

M. Elliott, "Lie in the Sun - and Change the World", *Time Magazine*, 21 May 2001.

Government of Sikkim (2001). *Development of Eco-Tourism in Sikkim: A Case Study.* Sikkim Tourism.

Government of Sikkim (2001). *Sikkim, the people's vision*: Department of Forest, Environment and Wildlife.

Government of Sikkim (February 2006). *Sikkim Government Gazette the people's vision*: Indus publishing industry.

Government of Sikkim. *Ecotourism of India, Sikkim.* ENVIS Centre, Sikkim.

D.E. Hawkins, E. Finucane and M. Sharp (forthcoming). *Reducing Barriers to Tourism, Investment in Developing Countries.* International Institute of Tourism Studies. The George Washington. University. USA.

C. Holiday, and J. Pepper. *Sustainability Through the Markets - 7 Keys to Success,*

ILO, 2001: *Human Resource Development, Employment and Globalisation in the Hotel, Catering and Tourism Sector.* International Labour Organisation, Geneva.

'Incredible India' gets PATA award. Retrieved from http://www.ibef.org/artdisplay.aspx?tdy=1&cat_id=60&art_id=16809

India Travel. Retrieved from http://www.indiandata.com/travel/

Ashwini Kakkar, *Tourism*. Retrieved from http://www.bseindia.com/downloads/Tourism.pdf.

D. Killeen and A. Rahman. 2001: *Poverty and Environment.* London: International Institute for Environment & Development., 2001.

Northeast India Tour. Retrieved from http://www.northeastindiatour.com/index.html

Keshav Pradhan, "In the good ol' days of Nathu La", *Times of India* (Mumbai), 6 July 2006.

Amrik Singh, *Asia Pacific Tourism Industry: Current Trends and Future Outlook.* Department of Parks, Recreation and Tourism, University of Utah.

Tej Vir Singh, "Keep the Sharks Out of the Mountains", *Our Planet*, Vol. 10, No. 1.

Tourism India. Ministry of Tourism, Government of india. Retrieved from www.tourismofindia.com

Tourism Industry in India. Retrieved from http://www.economywatch.com/business-and-economy/tourism-industry.html.

Tourism Statistics of India. Retrieved from www.fhrai.com/mag-news/magTourismStatisticsIndia.htm.

T. Venugopalan, *Emerging Dimensions in tourism*

Sonam Wangchuk, *Tourism and its Impact in Ladakh.* Retrieved from http://www.pcedindia.com/peoplescomm/tourism_6a.htm

What border markets can bring? China Tibet Information Center, 5 July 2006. Shehla, Raza Hasan. "The India-China road to – somewhere" (2006). Retrieved from *Asia Times Online*.

World Business Council for Sustainable Development.

World Travel & Tourism Council (WTTC), International Federation of Tour Operators (IFTO), International Hotel & Restaurant Association (IH&RA), International Council of Cruise Lines (ICCL). *Industry as a partner for sustainable development.* United Nations Environmental Program.

WTTC, 2000 *Research: Overview and Definitions.* London & New York: World Travel & Tourism Council.

www.wbcsd.org/projects/pr_marketsust.htm.

Chapter 7

Linkages Across Borders: Implications for Northeast India

Shubhrajeet Konwer

The Northeastern states of India have a distinctive place due to their geographical, historical, social, cultural, and political features. Yet the eight states share a basic problem: they were never seen as individual states but only as "the northeast".[1] They are so treated owing to their peculiarities and location. They harbour 145 tribal communities, of which 78 have population strengths of more than 5,000. That adds up to about 12 per cent of India's tribals, and 25.81 per cent of the Northeast's population.

The area's inhabitants are Mongoloid tribes with close ethnic and cultural ties with tribes in China, Tibet and Myanmar. Their oral traditions, ethnic coalitions, and lifestyles are quite distinct from 'mainstream' India's. Moreover, almost all the hill tribes, except for the Khasis and Jaintias of Meghalaya, belong to the Tibeto-Chinese fold or the Tibeto-Burmese family[2], and they share racial, historical, anthropological and linguistic kinships. Indeed, the latter are more vital than their links with India's political centres – especially Delhi. This affinity, and the related (identity-based) issues, play a key role in the unrest, and insurgencies, plaguing the Northeast.

The region's sluggish industrial growth can be attributed to lack of infrastructure. It has lost out on the latter front despite possessing an abundance of natural resources and endless plans for modernisation.[3]

Nevertheless, the Northeast's terrain and location makes it unique. Administrative reorganisations have also been frequent, and there is a persistent demand for further subdivisions of administrative units.[4] Demands for change are continually put forth in the expectation that they would resolve the economic and social issues that dominate the region's politics.

Another vulnerability of the Northeast is its borders with Bhutan (8%), China (23%), Myanmar (55%), and Bangladesh (12%), and is compounded by the narrowness of 22 km wide 'chicken-neck' (Siliguri Corridor) that connects the Northeast to mainland India. Each one of the bordering countries is thus enabled to play a key role in India's domestic and international policies. The borders with Myanmar, Bangladesh and Bhutan are porous owing to the rugged terrain. That makes cross-border movements extremely hard to regulate. Meantime, cross-border affiliations across tribes are common – meaning that the international border is not a cultural border.

In short, the geography and politics of the Northeast provide just the right setting for the intervention of foreign power, which aims to aid and abet insurgency. And, not only do China, Pakistan, Bangladesh and Myanmar interfere, smaller nations like Bhutan and Nepal do the same.

But the silver lining is that even prickly borders can play a positive role in transforming the region's economies. But the authorities must address the problems associated with the borders and their management for that to happen. New Delhi's "Look East Policy" can generate goodwill and, in that way, contribute to development. More importantly, India's Northeast provides a gateway to Southeast Asia and to TransAsia road and rail links. Thus, any development of the region could transform it into an economically vibrant, conflict-free area. But there are major obstacles ahead.

These obstacles assume forms such as the proliferation of small arms, drug trafficking, illegal migration, shelter to terrorists in Myanmar, Bhutan and Bangladesh, border disputes with China and border skirmishes with Bangladesh's army. Such troubles have made the Northeast very vulnerable in the last few years.

This paper intends to identify the nature and problems of cross border terror linkages and the security challenges that the Indian state faces. It also analyses the implications of the Look East Policy – which is often viewed as being critical for the region's development.

II

The terror groups of the Northeast have numerous demands and are often overlapping or contradictory goals. What they have amongst themselves is a marriage of convenience. For example, the NDFB's quest for a "sovereign Bodoland" in areas north of the Brahmaputra is pitted against the ULFA's demand for a "sovereign Assam". Similarly, NSCN-IM, the outfit that aims to establish a "Greater Nagaland" ("Nagalim", or People's

Republic of Nagaland based on Mao Zedong's ideology), has made its presence felt in Wokha, Phek, Zunebhoto, Kohima, parts of Mokokchung and the Tuensang districts of Nagaland. Reportedly, the NSCN–IM also imposes a "House Tax" on every dwelling unit in Nagaland, and the quality of "voluntary compliance" is such that it would be the envy of even the most successful government department. It has also extended its influence to the Naga-inhabited areas of the North Cachar Hills and Karbi Anglong districts of Assam, and some parts of Arunachal Pradesh. Such territorial claims over "Nagalim" contradict the ULFA's goals.

Secondly, illicit trading – including the lucrative drug and arms trade – is all being conducted under the control of terrorist groups.[5] And despite counter-insurgency operations by the Police, Army and the Central Paramilitary Forces, new militant outfits crop up every passing year in Assam.

What is also novel is how both the ULFA and NSCN have been helping the smaller outfits. The ULFA provides a useful and complex agenda, combining underground and surface activities. The sympathisers, who paved the way for beneficiaries, existed in sufficient number for the ULFA to establish fronts.[6] But now even the ULFA stands divided, with one faction playing into the ISI's hands. According to the outgoing AOC-in-C of Eastern Air Command Air Marshal P.K. Barbora, "One faction, operating in lower Assam, is playing into the hands of Pakistan's ISI and other fundamentalist forces, while the other operating in Upper Assam has built up nexus with NSCN (K)".[7] It seems that the big outfits started to help smaller ones mostly for tactical reasons. That also explains why those that have recently cropped up have the backing of either the ULFA or NSCN.

The Black Widow group, which is active in the North Cachar Hills, is considered to be amongst the strongest recent groups. The outfit gets added leverage from the terrain of the hill district. Its declared objective is to create a separate state of "Dimaraji" for the Dimasa ("sons of the great river") tribe, comprising the Dimasa dominated areas of the North Cachar Hills, Karbi Anglong districts of Assam and parts of Dimapur district in Nagaland. The outfit operates mostly in Cachar, N C Hills, Karbi Anglong and the Nagaon districts of Assam. It has a strong presence also in the Dimasa dominated Dhansiri area of Karbi Anglong district. The DHD is also reported to have linkages with the National Socialist Council of Nagaland- Isak- Muivah (NSCN-IM) and the National Democratic Front of Bodoland (NDFB). DHD had also helped the Black Widow group to increase in strength when several of the former's members switched over to the breakaway faction. (The police has again pointed out that ULFA started helping the KLNLF to establish bases in the hill district – and that the recent killing of Hindi speaking people in Karbi Anglong was mostly a joint operation which had been undertaken by members of both outfits).

AANLA has stepped up its activities in Guwahati after the recent clashes between the Adivasis and locals of the Beltola area. In fact, the AANLA and the NSCN even signed an agreement to help each other, and NSCN's training greatly helped the Adivasi outfit. Security forces believe that the NSCN started to help the AANLA only in order to increase its domination in the areas which border Nagaland. As already noted, the Naga outfit has been demanding the creation of greater Nagalim, including areas of Assam.

According to Indian Intelligence, a strategy for the region was jointly fashioned in a meeting between ULFA, NDFB, and the KLO. Members of the Communist Party of Nepal (Marxist-Leninist-Maoist) too participated in the meeting. The focus of the meeting was believed to have been the prospect of creating a compact revolutionary zone – one that would allow a modicum of cross-border elbowroom to the groups concerned.[8]

Meanwhile, the demand of smaller outfits like the HPC-D is an independent Hmar State (Hmar ram) – comprising the Hmar-inhabited areas of Mizoram, Manipur and Assam. Ever since its formation, the HPC-D has aligned itself with the Northeast's insurgent groups. It maintained cordial relations with the NSCN in its formative years, and was rewarded with arms and training in return. The HPC-D also carried out attacks with the support of the Manipur-based People's Liberation Army (PLA).A close working nexus between militants and politicians was also recently revealed in Karbi Anglong. But it was different in the sense that the Congress leaders admitted that "some suggestions from them on development" were acceptable, though simultaneously discarding alleged links with the militant Dima Halam Daogah (DHD). A letter, drafted by Bhupen Hansu, EM of KAAC, had been addressed to Pronap Nunisia, the DHD's self styled commander-in-chief; the signatories of the letter included KS Ingti, CEM, KAAC. The letter mentions, "We shall give maximum employment opportunities in all the Government Departments for the educated youth of the concerned community and shall take prior approval of DHD in any appointment of jobs."[9]

Thus, the linkages between terror groups are part of a well laid out plan to tackle the Indian state. But the reports of overt linkages between civil society groups, politicians and terrorist organisations remain a major source of worry for the Centre. Indeed, the proliferation of militant groups is symptomatic of state failure.[10]

III

Normally, the major terrorist movements in India have enjoyed some foreign support, and been granted safe refuge in havens outside. But there are also times when the state's operational successes are high. The remnants of militant organisations can find shelter in the more accessible parts of India at such times; they do so by reverting temporarily to normal, civilian life. Military operations, consequently, can almost never entirely eliminate the forces of terrorism.[11] The terror network has become transnational.

The ULFA had decided to set up camps in Bhutan in the early 1990s, following Operation Bajrang and Operation Rhino in Assam. The militants' arrival from Assam, and the construction of camps and the associated infrastructure injected much money into an area that is economically backward going even by Bhutan's standards.[12] That was initially to Bhutan's benefit; but, by 2003, circumstances had changed. The Bhutanese Army had uprooted the ULFA's major bases in Bhutan. Despite that, terrorists continued to use the area for training. However, the ULFA is yet to establish permanent camps in Bhutan after its 2003 setback; but makeshift ones do get occasionally established in jungle areas to train cadres. Militants are helped by the fact that the terrain along the greater part of the Assam-Bhutan border eases the militants' task of sneaking into, and out of, Bhutan in small groups. That occurs despite the emplacement of SSB personnel along the Assam-Bhutan border. Reportedly, even smaller outfits – like KLO – assisted the Adivasi Cobra Force in setting up camps along the Bhutanese border. India is also concerned over reports of Naxalites setting up bases in the Himalayan kingdom. The Centre has already sanctioned the additional deployment for Sashastra Seema Bal (SSB) battalions along the Indo-Bhutan border in Assam and north Bengal. Apart from guarding the international border, SSB has also been instructed to escort Bhutanese passenger buses, trucks and other vehicles.

In totality the security of Bhutanese nationals and their merchandise increased following the December 2003 flush-out of rebels. Meanwhile, the arrest of Prabal Neog, the acting commander of ULFA's 28th Battalion, in Tezpur unearthed vital information about the outfit's bases in Myanmar. But the police reported that 28th Battalion's HQ (which is also the outfit's strongest arm) is still in Myanmar, while the same company's B Company is based in the neighbouring country.

As for ULFA's presence in Myanmar, the majority of fresh recruits from Upper Assam are sent to Myanmar to train. The ULFA currently has about 200 cadres in Myanmar, and is alleged to be launching the largest number of operations in the Upper Assam districts from bases in Myanmar. The militants infiltrate through either Nagaland or Arunachal Pradesh by taking advantage of the terrain.[13] The camps in that country are maintained along with the NSCN (K). The ULFA also has a council camp in Myanmar, which is headed by senior ULFA leader Jibon Moran, who is responsible for maintaining communication with the leaders of the NSCN (K).[14]

Over time, in fact, the NSCN-IM has developed extensive linkages both within, and outside, India. Neighbouring countries have also been giving it substantial assistance–ranging across logistical support, supply of arms and ammunition, the provision of safe havens and camping or training facilities. The US had been a major provider of arms, finance and intelligence until 1971. So also has been erstwhile East Pakistan; it used to provide money and arms. Even China provided support to the organisation until the late eighties. Today, it is Pakistan's Inter Services Intelligence (ISI), which provides a major part of the finance, arms and logistical support to the NSCN-IM (which has links with Myanmar-based Naga groups, with drug trafficking being a major source of income).

Security analysts, however, have admitted that it would be difficult to completely flush out the militants from Myanmar. That is because of the country's tough terrain, and because the militants are using the vast, unused, and under-administered jungle areas.

Naga bases, on the other hand, are located in a terrain that is more difficult than that of the Manipuri groups or ULFA's. It could well be that the Nagas are Burmese nationals and that their demand for being included as a part of the Greater Naga state is seen as a threat to Burmese sovereignty by the military junta. Myanmar's rebel bases serve three important purposes for insurgents from the Northeast: (a) They have been sheltering the rebel leadership after East Pakistan was lost as a safe base; (b) They are a crucial link via which rebels could access China for training and weapons; (c) They provide safe training and regrouping zones within which new recruits can be taught the art of guerrilla warfare. Active guerrilla units can also be shifted out when these come under pressure in India.[15]

The recent arrest in Guwahati of a Pakistani ISI agent has again proved beyond doubt that the agency is still active in the Northeast. The agent (S.M. Alam alias Mojibullah Alam) is a Bangladeshi national and a frequent visitor of Bangladesh–thanks to the very porous international border. Interrogated, he reportedly admitted to having links with more than 20 regional militant outfits. Clearly, the ISI can always engage the militant outfits linked with it and create disturbances in this part of the country. It need not even send in its own men to do the terroristic work.[16] Indeed, Assam Public Works says that there are 36 Jehadi groups in the state and that they possess arms which could easily penetrate into the Indian Armed Force's security zone.[17] Meanwhile, the Minister of State for Home Affairs, Sri Prakash Jaiswal, has confirmed that the Northeast's insurgent groups are operating out of Bangladesh, and have links with the ISI. He has also noted that New Delhi has taken up the issue with Pakistan.

According to the information available with Indian security agencies, the ULFA has about 250 to 300 militants in camps located in Myanmar and in the HQ of the outfit's 28th Battalion – the latter located in the neighbouring country's territory. Based on available inputs, some Indian insurgent groups with ISI links, active in the Northeast, have been using Bangladesh. According to Sri Prakash Jaiswal, there have been reports of inter-linkages between these outfits for tactical purposes like sheltering, concealment, arms procurement and training.[18] A large number of Islamic militants are fleeing Bangladesh and taking refuge in the districts of Assam bordering Bangladesh. Hence the ISI-DGFI nexus continues to haunt the Northeast's security forces.

Thousands of Bangladeshis daily cross the border into India. Most of them are driven by poverty, but some others take advantage of anonymity in numbers and infiltrate with the specific agenda of *jehad*. This is not just the result of a handful of fundamentalists working in Bangladesh. Political analysts affirm that such a movement would have been impossible without tacit support from the ruling Bangladesh Nationalist Party (BNP). The BNP is allied with two influential fundamentalist groups – the Jamaat-e-Islami and the Islami Oikyo Jote – that reportedly oversee the infiltration into India with the purpose of changing its demographic pattern, particularly in West Bengal, Assam, Tripura and Bihar.[19] Needless to say, the porosity of international borders has simplified matters for them in border districts like Karimganj, Dhubri etc. Assam too has become a safe haven for militants.

A similar influx is being witnessed in the neighbouring states of West Bengal and Tripura.[20] According to newspaper reports, apart from running several training camps, in Bangladesh, the ULFA has launched several income-generating projects, set up media consultancies and run units that manufacture soft drinks. It also, reportedly, owns three hotels, a medical clinic, and two motor driving schools in Dhaka. Paresh Baruah is believed to own, or have a controlling interest in, several business in Bangladesh. The latter include a tannery, department store chains, garment factories, travel agencies, shrimp trawlers, and transport and investment companies.[21] The Government of India had submitted the list of camps of Bangladesh's militant groups. But, instead of acting to evict the camps, the Bangladesh Government denied the very presence of any member of the Indian militant group.

In fact, the growth of jehadi forces inimical to India in Bangladesh also poses a grave security threat to the Northeast. Several jehadi attacks in different parts of India in recent days have been traced to Bangladesh. This highlights the gravity of the security threat, but Bangladesh's government refuses to act despite requests from India. That is further proof of the fact that the neighbouring country was indirectly involved in encouraging the forces behind the creation of disturbances in India.[22] Importantly, relations between the Indian government and Bangladesh's have been far from warm; the regularity of clashes between the BSF and BDR reflect the rockiness of this uneasy relationship.

Meanwhile, China is currently not involved in supporting any terror group, but there are immense problems along the Indo-China border. Zhou Gang, the former Ambassador of Beijing to New Delhi, said that India must make "substantial adjustment" in the eastern sector – including the return of the Buddhist enclave of Tawang to China – in order to reach an early settlement on the border issue. "As the Chinese people will never accept the 'McMohan line', India must make substantial adjustment in the East sector." "I cited the following example that during my tenure as Chinese ambassador to India, I made it clear on many occasions to the Indian public — Tawang belongs to China, it is the birthplace of the sixth Dalai Lama and the Dalai Lama is 'China's Dalai Lama', who cannot be 'India's Dalai Lama'."[23]

Reports of intrusion by China into India's territories have led the Army to tighten its vigil along the international border in Arunachal Pradesh. But, the Indian Army has been maintaining a stoic silence on the issue of regularly reported intrusions by the Chinese Army. Even the Centre has denied such reports on the floor of Parliament, and clarified that Arunachal Pradesh is an integral part of the country. New Delhi has even gone to the extent of denying that China had intruded into the North eastern sector and destroyed forward posts and bunkers in Sikkim; but it has admitted that perceptions on the Line of Actual Control between India and China differed. A.K. Antony said, "there was no incursion by the Chinese troops in Indian territory, be it in Sikkim or Arunachal Pradesh". "We have a long border with China, and dispute regarding most of them are settled. But it doesn't mean that there is no problem. There are differences in perception — we have our own perception and they have their own (over boundary)."[24] Thus, there are divergent perceptions of India and China on the Line of Actual Control. The Defence Minister admitted that the isolated incidents on the borders may arise out of this difference of perceptions on territorial jurisdiction between the two countries.

IV

Perhaps the answer lies in the fact that India's relation with neighbouring countries has seldom been positive. Accordingly, the latter find the terror groups of the Northeast India, and New Delhi's cross-border affinity, to be ideal tools to maintain pressure on the government. For instance, Bangladesh's long-term goal might be to keep the region unstable and encourage its nationals to infiltrate into the region. Land shortage is a major problem, and Bangladesh is considering this part of India for expansion.

With the smooth flow of development in Indian economy, investments too are increasing in the Northeast. This encourages labour immigration, particularly, since construction activities require a huge labour force.

Sources, in fact reveal that the government at Dhaka has had reasons to assist the Northeast's militants. They have beer doing so for years, while senior Army officials of the neighbouring country have floated theories that say India might invade Bangladesh to take over Chittagong port. This explains why Bangladesh implements a dual strategy to force India on the back-foot: it is, firstly, to assist militants in sustaining the disturbances in the Northeast – and, secondly, to maintain close ties with Pakistan and China.

Meanwhile, Bangladesh has not been looked upon favourably by the international community for increasingly becoming more fundamentalist in character. Bangladesh is becoming a "cocoon of terror" (*Far Eastern Economic Review*, 2003), "next Islamic Revolution" (*New York Times*, 2005).[25] In fact, the 'eastward surge of the jehadi elements has gained ground in the wake of operation enduring freedom'.[26] Bangladesh is a major source of tension in the region. More importantly, many analysts in Bangladesh feel that the "'opportunity cost' of an antagonistic Indo-Bangladesh relationship is rising".[27] Further more, the involvement of

ISI in this region may be a policy of Pakistan to open up a second front in Northeast India. Pakistan is very keen to see India preoccupied with internal security issues, as well as, threat from neighbouring countries. It is here that the ISI-DGFI nexus becomes clear. India needs stable democracies in the neighbour to prosper, but unfortunately, India's neighbours are losing their democratic character.

Myanmar needs India to help revive its economy. But it also realises that terror groups of India operating from Myanmar can be a vital bargaining chip in the long run. Myanmar of late has shown concern about the presence of Indian militant groups in the territory of the neighbouring country. India is keen to start several development projects including road construction schemes and construction of a mega power project. Moreover, India wants to counter the growing Chinese presence in Myanmar. In order to enhance the volume of regional cooperation, road-rail access is critical. India needs Myanmar, and needs good relations with it.[28] India's ultra-conservative Myanmar position arises from four considerations: eagerness to enlist Myanmar's help in fighting insurgencies in the Northeast; interest in Myanmar's natural gas; anxiety to counter China's regional influence; and concern for "stability" in the neighbourhood.[29] Lately, there has been a considerable improvement in the relations between the two governments, and the two countries are on their way to becoming strategic partners. Strategically, Myanmar is New Delhi's only land bridge to the rest of ASEAN. Therefore, India has little option left.

India's borders with China will continue to be debated on both sides of the fence. In May 2007, China denied visa to Ganesh Kayu, an IAS officer who was to visit China as part of a 102-member delegation of IAS officers drawn from all over India, just because Kayu is an Arunachali. China claims the whole of Arunachal as its territory.[30] In contrast, a few months later, it granted visa to a native of Arunachal Pradesh, raising hopes for an early resolution of the border dispute. It is, however, unlikely to materialise into any concrete step for a dispute resolution. This relationship seems to be of limited adversarial nature and is likely to continue. Therefore the rhetoric regarding Tawang and Tibet is also likely to continue on both sides.

Of course, border trade with China has started across the Nathu La Pass, and that does signal a certain degree of positivism. But India cannot afford to lower its guard. It appears unlikely that either side can agree on historical facts as to the ownership of various portions of the land through which runs their border.

V

Ironically, India's policy in fighting cross-border terrorism and its network has not yielded the desired results. Myanmar has been ineffectual in preventing the Northeast's insurgents from establishing camps on its soil. It has only restrained the National Socialist Council of Nagaland (Khaplang), with which it has a cease-fire agreement. It has taken token, or desultory action against other groups. Myanmar has very conveniently played China off against India, while milking both for assistance.[31] However, India has received no gas or gas supply contracts from Myanmar. Thus Myanmar has played its cards carefully, and India has only fallen prey to economic greed.

It must be mentioned here that the India-Myanmar border terrain is not easy to completely seal. So, although the Government of India has entrusted Assam Rifles with the task of guarding that border, and a few posts of theirs have been established, there is still a crying need to raise and deploy more Assam Rifles battalions.[32] Adequate planning and coordination can, of course, yield the desired results – but only in a limited number of cases.

Ratachera, on the 'Naga Trail' that once used to serve as a cross-over point for Naga militants from Bangladesh, is now a quiet place, owing to the experimental mobile patrol posts established by the BSF. About the influx of militants across Ratachera that started after the Mizoram uprising of the 1970s, has fallen to just a "trickle" after mobile posts were set up between Ratachera and the Donna Border Observation Posts. Ratachera was in the news in the 1990s, after the Naga militants used it extensively as a cross-over point, while accessing Nagaland and Manipur.[33] Even today, says Tripura Frontier's BSF IG, J.A. Khan, there are still a total of 58 hideouts of the Northeast's outlawed groups in Bangladesh. Of that total, eighteen Tripura-based groups are operative within 5 km of the Indo-Bangla border. The BSF IG even asserts that the insurgents now use the eastern international border for infiltration. That shift of operations owes greatly to the fencing, which has been coming up along the western border. And it has happened despite the border fencing having helped in containing the movements of insurgents along the border.[34]

The peace process or ceasefire agreements signed with different groups have had limited effects. The PCG has had three rounds of talks with the central government but a solution to 'sovereign Assam' is still not near. The extension of the ceasefire with NSCN has yet to address the issue of 'greater Nagalim'.

The region's state governments have nevertheless achieved some success in their quest for peace. In Assam, more than 13,000 militants have laid down arms following the start of the formal surrender of militants since 1991. That figure included about 2,600 militants belonging to the Bodo Liberation Tiger (BLT), who surrendered following the signing of the ceasefire pact with the Government of India. Some outfits, including the Bengali Tiger Force and Rabha Security Force no longer exist after the arrests and surrender of senior members of the outfits. The surrendering militants get a monthly stipend of Rs 2,000. But that was only true of those who stayed in the rehabilitation training camps; many others who returned home were deprived of the same.[35] Today, the surrendering militants get vocational training from the Indian Institute of Entrepreneurship, SIRD and different government departments like Veterinary, Fisheries, etc.

Meanwhile, the ULFA has changed tactics and, instead of engaging the security forces in gun battle, the militants have started planting explosives. The outsourcing of urban terror is the new *modus operandi*, and children, drug addicts, etc. have been used to do this work. According to police records, 276 civilians were killed and 750 others received injuries in Assam in 2007.[36] The attack on Hindi speaking people in the districts of upper Assam in early 2007 by militants belonging to the ULFA resulted in the increase of death toll. Sources pointed out that the Hindi speaking people were attacked in the remote parts, and it was not possible to provide security to each and every citizen. Perhaps the ULFA is sending a message to New Delhi that hurting the interests of Hindi speaking people would make the central government stand up and listen to the demands of the group.

The demands for a dialogue have led to a series of talks between the ULFA-appointed Peoples' Consultative Group and the Government of India. However, these have not made much headway towards a peaceful solution of the problem. Government officials believe that ULFA's offer for dialogue stems from two immediate problems. One is the fact that the Bhutan government's action has deprived it of safe bases and entailed a heavy loss of cadres in encounters with the security forces. Many trusted leaders and activists seem to have given up the struggle and surrender to the Army. Secondly, ULFA is fast losing mass support, because of the violence that Assam has been experiencing for quite some time. The state's economy is shattered since no meaningful development work could be undertaken in the last 15 years. Plus, many of ULFA's cadres have lost all hopes of an "independent Assam".[37]

This situation has been exacerbated by high unemployment, corruption and nepotism – all of them leading to growing frustration amongst the region's youth. Even the best efforts of the police and security forces have been unable to plug the routes which militants use to smuggle in arms and explosives from Bangladesh.[38] No wonder Tarun Gogoi, the Chief Minister of Assam, raised an alarm at a CMs' meeting about the ISI activities in the state. There he also referred to the recent arrest of a Dhaka-based ISI activist in Guwahati.

VI

The benefits of a well-managed border are immense. Enunciated in the 1990s by the then Prime Minister P.V. Narasimha Rao, India's 'Look East' Policy owed its origin to the end of the Cold War. It coincided with a shift in India's foreign policy, when it embarked on free market restructuring at home and sought new markets and economic partners abroad. The focus, then, was on Southeast Asia considering the geographical contiguity of Northeast Indian states with the economies of the Association of South East Asian Nations (ASEAN). Things, however, are yet to go India's way.

Regional co-operation got a boost ever since the first BIMSTEC (Bay of Bengal Initiative of Multi Sectoral Technical and Economic Co-operation) summit of July, 2004. The countries concerned were Bangladesh, India, Sri Lanka, Thailand and Myanmar. Meanwhile, the Thailand-Mekong-Ganga Co-operation Project aims at developing overland trade, tourism, communication and transport between India, Myanmar, Thailand, Laos, Cambodia and Vietnam. These developments will facilitate the 'Look East' Policy and brighten the development prospects of Northeast India.

Despite such positive predictions, the Northeast has not reaped any benefit from the policy. Even the road and rail links and riverways between Bangladesh and the Northeast have not been fully operationalised. Meghalaya shares 443 km of international borders with Bangladesh, and it proposed a Shillong-Dhaka bus service. State Chief Secretary Ranjan Chatterjee even says that the state government is trying to suppress restrictive practices for foreign tourists like stiff immigration laws and the practice to report on arrival. On the ground, meanwhile, the state government is concentrating on developing the infrastructure at Dawki – the only viable road-link between Meghalaya and Bangladesh. A Dhaka tourist office is also on the cards.[39]

The states of Northeast India want to maximize its benefits from cross-border relations. The Stilwell road, built during the World War II, connecting Ledo with Kunming in China, which would have provided road connectivity between the Northeast and China, remained unused, as a major portion of it lying within Myanmar needs extensive repairs. The Asian car rally organised earlier raised hopes that such steps would be taken by the governments concerned, and that the road would become motorable throughout the year. But India faces a diplomatic dilemma vis-à-vis Myanmar. India's natural instinct, as the largest democracy, would be to fully support the restoration of democracy in Myanmar. Its geopolitical interests, on the other hand, make it reluctant to offend Myanmar's present governing apparatus. Myanmar, by all accounts, is the key to the Stilwell route, and the Northeast can initiate business with the ASEAN countries if Yangon consents to its reopening. Failure on that front will negate the spirit of 'Look East'. Till date, nothing concrete has emerged on the ground in that direction. Hence, the oft-talked of policy remains an elitists' policy perspective.

There is, therefore, a huge infrastructural backlog. To cover this up, networks of roads, trans-shipment facilities, customs stations, and cold storages must be put in place by India to promote India's border trade with Myanmar, Bangladesh and China. This would help to develop the Northeast, too. Border trade, goods trans-shipment, and tourism can effectively promote the economies of the area, and impart a boost to the local economy. The sectors with potential are agriculture, horticulture, food processing, minerals, oil and gas, paper and wood. These should be tapped and harnessed by promoting economic linkages – with the ASEAN, and through Myanmar. But the hard reality is that none of that potential has yet been translated into concrete achievements.

In October 2007, Mani Shankar Aiyar, Central Minister for Development of Northeastern Region (DoNER), at a conference on "India's Look East Policy - Challenges for Sub-Regional Cooperation" in Guwahati, remarked: "The Look East policy is not even a written document yet and the harvest of the initiatives is so far nil." The minister's candid remarks prove that India's 'Look East' policy is, in fact, a non-starter, and lacks focus. The minister went on to say that "Economic ties with neighbouring countries like Bangladesh were not good, there was an ongoing dispute with China, while Myanmar's own internal problems were hindering trade prospects with the Northeast. ...the Northeast cannot really establish relations with China unless the disputes are resolved." So the key to the success of the Look East policy lies in a stable foreign policy and achievement of peace in the region. Problems of cross-border terror networks, drug trafficking, human trafficking, illegal migration, extortion – and the emergence of new, smaller terrorist groups along with the unabated growth in unemployment – will undermine the successes, if any, of the Look East policy.

Unemployment is high in the Northeast. Assam has a huge backlog of the unemployed (3 lakhs). Other states including Manipur and Mizoram, too, share a similar fate. Thus, 25 per cent of the region's active workforce is unemployed.[40]

Moreover, the patronage of politicians, touts and government functionaries makes the detection and deportation of infiltrators an insuperable problem in Assam. The game of 'settlement for vote' continues to be played openly in the region.[41] It should be understood that the Look East Policy would be hurt by more alienation within the Northeast, stagnation of growth opportunities and the growth of ethnic assertion.

Yet, leakage of funds, corruption and red-tapism continue to be the region's dominant features. So much so that, on 14 June 2001, after a meeting of Rural development Ministers of NR states at Shillong, the Union Rural Development Minister Sri Venkiah Naidu felt impelled to say that "the Centre would stop disbursing rural development funds to those states, where a bulk of the funds go to the coffers of the extremist outfits." Yet the high costs borne by the central government in pursuit of peace cannot be compromised in the name of corruption and duplication, misuse, and non-use of funds. Many of the problems of Northeast India are deeply related to New Delhi's neglect of the region – especially during the 1960s. It has been, thus, more because the Centre has always treated the Northeast as one single unit. The states, which are hardly homogeneous, can never be treated as identical. They possess unique problems, which need to be addressed individually.

Finally, the central government's dilemma is that the success of 'Look East' depends greatly on India's relations with the neighbouring countries. But that, unfortunately, is an area where little has been achieved in terms of positive gains. Nor will the resolution of this particular dilemma be easy. For, if the central government ignores security concerns while pushing ahead with its 'Look East' agenda, that will result in profits being concentrated among the creamy layer. Economic benefits will therefore never reach the majority, thereby leaving them out of the development loop.

Issues of terrorism and cross border networks must be looked into from a larger perspective, especially in context of economic inequality in the region, coupled with state neglect. Simply pushing Look East Policy without taking adequate precautions will result in 'look east' by-passing Northeast. While foreign investment and trade with ASEAN countries will multiply positively, it is unlikely to benefit the Northeastern region of India. Therefore, the Northeastern states must not be seen merely from the prism of Look East. The states of Northeast must get adequate attention from the centre irrespective of the potential benefits of looking eastwards.

REFERENCES

1. Bhaskar Ghose, "Always only a corner of India", *Frontline*, Vol. 22, No. 21 (8-21 October 2005).
2. V.I.K. Sarin, *India's North-East in Flames* (New Delhi: Vikas Publishing House 1980), p. 10.
3. B.G. Verghese, *India's Northeast Resurgent: Governance, Development*, second edition (New Delhi: Konark Publishers, 1996), p. 336.
4. B.C. Bhuyan, *Political Development of the Northeast* (New Delhi: Omsons Publication, 1989), p. 90.
5. Ajai Sahni, "The terrorist economy in India's Northeast", *Faultlines*, Vol.8 (2001), p. 140.
6. Jaideep Saikia, "Allies in the closet: over ground linkages and terrorism in the North East", *Faultlines*, Vol. 8 (2001), p. 107.
7. ULFA a divided lot, claims Barbora , *The Assam Tribune,* 17 December 2007.
8. "Armed struggle for a separate Kamatapur", *Frontline*, Vol. 21, No. 1 (3-16 January 2004).
9. "KAAC-DHD nexus, comes to the fore", *The Assam Tribune*, 19 Decdember 2005.
10. Sanjib Baruah, "Gulliver's troubles: state and militants in North East India", *Economic and Political Weekly*, Vol. XXXVIII (12-18 October 2002), p. 4178.
11. Sahni, "The terrorist economy in India's Northeast", p. 128.
12. M.S. Prabhakara, "Crackdown in Bhutan", *Frontline* ,Vol. 21, No. 1 (3-16 January 2004).
13. "Myanmar, India to launch joint action", *The Assam Tribune*, 21 February 2007.
14. "ULFA using Bhutan, Myanmar soil", *The Assam Tribune*, 5 October 2007.
15. Subir Bhaumik, in a seminar on 'Gate way to the East' in June 2005, argued on this line in his paper "Guns, Drugs and Rebels, Seminar".
16. "ISI activities", *The Assam Tribune*, 19 December 2007.
17. "Govt not taking steps to thwart Jehadis: APW", *The Assam Tribune*, 25 December 2007.
18. "Parliament concern over Bangla influx", *The Assam Tribune*, 6 December 2007.

19. Surhid Shankar Chattopadhyay, "Challenges in the East", *Frontline*, Vol. 23, No. 1 (14-27 January 2006).
20. "Islamic ultras may take shelter in state", *The Assam Tribune*, 12 December 2007.
21. "For sovereign socialist Assam", *Frontline*, 16 January 2004.
22. "Bangla's DGFI fomenting trouble in NE", *The Assam Tribune*, 3 February 2007.
23. "Former Chinese envoy calls for Tawang's return", *The Assam Tribune*, 1 November 2007.
24. "Centre denies reports of Chinese incursion", *The Assam Tribune*, 2 December 2007.
25. "Fatwa Against freedom", *The Telegraph*, 8 December 2005.
26. Jaideep Saikia , "Islamic resurgence in Bangladesh", *Aakrosh*, Vol. 6, No. 21 (October 2003).
27. Pinaki Bhattacharya, "Bangladesh at crossroads", *Aakroash*, Vol. 8, No. 28 (July 2005), p. 38.
28. "Why India needs Myanmar— MD Nalapat", *The Assam Tribune*, 30 October 2007.
29. "India's policy flounders on Myanmar— Praful Bidwai", *The Assam Tribune*, 23 October 2007.
30. "Hopes in Arunachal for better ties with China", *The Assam Tribune*, 24 December 2007.
31. "BSF checks influx through 'Naga Trail' RATACHERA", *The Assam Tribune*, 26 November 2007.
32. "Ultra camps in Myanmar", *The Assam Tribune*, 15 February 2007.
33. "BSF checks influx through 'Naga Trail'" *The Assam Tribune*.
34. "NE ultra hideouts still exist in Bangla: BSF", *The Assam Tribune*, 4 December 2007.
35. "Cadres disillusioned with top leaders' activities", *The Assam Tribune*, 5 November 2007.
36. "286 civilians, 129 ultras killed in State last year", *The Assam Tribune*, 3 January 2008.
37. Kalyan Choudhury, "A peace initiative", *Frontline*, Vol. 18, No. 26 (22 December 2001-4 January 2002).
38. "Cadres disillusioned with top leaders' activities", *The Assam Tribune*, 5 November 2007.
39. "Meghalaya reviving B'desh connection", *The Assam Tribune*, 20 December 2007.
40. "The Look East Policy— Walter Fernandes", *The Assam Tribune*, 6 July 2007.
41. Archana Upadhyay, "The Infiltrator Issue", *Economic and Political Weekly*, Vol. XL, No.28 (9-15 July 2005), p. 3003.

Chapter 8

Teesta Eco-Region and Bio-Resources: An Awaited Future

Jyoti Prakash Tamang

The Teesta Eco-region includes the biosphere regions of the Darjeeling hills and Sikkim. It is rich in bio-resources – which includes plants, animals and micro-organisms. Also, it is one of the world's 12 mega-biodiversity rich zones, and an active centre of evolution of many new gene pools. These gene pools contain valuable components that have many applications for the region's sustainable development. Indigenous food crops, ethnic fermented food, edible wild plants and their fruits, wild honey, etc. provide the source of food security of the region. Medicinal herbs, orchids, ornamental and wild flowering plants, ginger, oranges, large cardamom are Northeast India's 'cash-cows'. The eco-region's economy has remained self-contained as most needs get met from within, and with limited amounts of externally sourced inputs.

But this self-sufficiency has recently been breaking down owing to demographic pressure – and the effect of population pressure on traditional agricultural systems is that they progressively become inadequate for meeting basic needs. Meanwhile, the region's people nowadays tend to aspire to higher, different living standards. That has been the fall-out of societal improvements, access to other areas, plus increases in information flow. But, now that the latter has raised aspirations, there has also arisen the need to impart instruction! Everything is driven by the development of the region's bio-resources, while its products would have special advantages in terms of resource endowments. That too can improve the livelihoods of the people. So, clearly the development paradigm of the Teesta Region should focus mainly on bio-resources and biotechnology.

Trade in bio-resource products would be a sunrise industry for the region, with emphasis on tradition, socio-culture, cost-effectiveness and health. There is tremendous scope for trading these bio-resource products across the Indo-China border – at Nathu La as well as through the Northeast's other proposed borders.

As for re-opening the Nathu La border, that has been a key demand of Sikkim's local authorities, it has found echoes in Darjeeling Gorkha Autonomous Hill Council and the Tibet Autonomous Region in China since the 1980s. The denouement came when the closed gate was opened on 6th July 2006. It initiated a new chapter of trade between India and China; indeed, the report by the Nathu La Trade Study Group predicts that the volume of trade via Nathu La will be of the order of Rs. 206 crore by 2007, and Rs. 12,203 crore by 2015. But that prediction has remained hypothetical. There are 15 imports from China such as silk and yak pelts and horses, while India can export 29 items from textiles to tea, rice, vegetables and herbs.

India and China, however, have agreed to make joint efforts to increase the volume of bilateral trade to $ 30 billion by 2010. That would be propitious for India, being the world's second largest producer of foods after China. India is also the second largest producer of vegetables in the world – ranking next only to China and accounting for 15 per cent of world vegetable output.

Taking this into consideration there is a great opportunity to invest big in the agro-processing sectors in the Teesta Eco-region. The output would involve value-adding on the region's food and vegetables, fruit juices, jams, pickles, meat and poultry, milk and milk products, alcoholic beverages, wild edible plants, mushrooms, soybean-based products, mineral water, exotic foods, etc. The intervention of science and technology will work wonders. Indeed, biotechnology-related business of this sort has the potential to generate revenue to the tune of US$ 5 billion and create 1 million jobs by 2010 (*National Biotechnology Strategy Policy, 2006*). That, in turn, can lift India into a significant position in the global bio-tech market. Bio-pharmaceuticals alone have the potential to be a US$ 2 billion market, and are driven largely by vaccines and bio-generics. Also, the Northeast and the Teesta Eco-region can meet the demand for herbal drugs – as purified bio-active compounds – for global bio-pharmaceutical companies.

Cymbidium orchids, and the other wild orchids of Darjeeling and Sikkim produce quality cut flowers, which already have a ready market in Delhi and Kolkata and might also triumph in the Chinese market. Asiatic lilies are cultivated at around 2000m for the production of flower-bulbs in selected areas. Gladiolus corms are grown in areas between 1000m and 1350m, both for cut flowers as well as to supply markets. Finally,

Anthuriums andreanum are suitable for cut flowers and are grown in the warmer areas around 400m. All these have market potential as cut flowers. The market potential for flower bulb produce is good as well. The bulbs could be of *Eucaris, Haemanthus, Curcuma, Zephyranthus, Dutch Amaryllis, Gloriosa, Caladiums*, etc. In sum, the Northeast's exotic flowers could very well access global markets through the Indo-Chinese border. The progressive farmers and agencies should be helped to do so by the national R&D institutes. It is up to the latter to provide cultivators with modern technology.

Other agro produces that hold market potential include guava, oranges, avocados, kiwis, certain chilli varieties, and high-protein legumes such as soybeans and black lentils. Of these, there is high demand for guava fruit and jellies, and amongst chillies 'dalley khorsani', 'uamorok' (Manipur), 'raja' (Nagaland) – and the main need is to value-add, analyse bio-active compounds, packaging, etc. Legume crops need better grading, too. All these are possible tradable commodities.

The Teesta Eco-region is also a rich repository of 500-odd species of medicinal herbs. Phyto-medicines are produced from them, depending upon the requirements of traditional and modern medical systems and the degree of sophistication of preparation. Health benefits and economic considerations are of global importance. Major categories of plant-derived products include phyto-pharmaceuticals, herbal medicines, natural health products, and phyto-cosmetics. The traditional Indian system of medicine was developed and practised by ethnic groups. It has variants like Ayurveda, Unani, Sidha Jamu, and a Tibetan one. Based mainly on medicinal plants, they are an important source of health-care for millions of Asians.

Better regulations are needed if India is to profit from this rich resource. It will also introduce the sector to monitoring. However, until that happens, we will have to live with insufficient information on demand sources, about the dynamics of medicinal-plant trade – and channels of supply. But things could change if the information on major user-groups and international supply-demand trends are made available. Meanwhile, the major cause for concern is the rise in global interest rate, which in fact has created an underground market in medicinal plants, herbal drugs and plant materials. India urgently needs to regulate export and allow only sustainable harvesting of Northeast India's medicinal plants.

More than 350 varieties of traditional and ethnic foods and beverages, and 300 species of edible wild plants are consumed in the Teesta Eco-regions – i.e., all of the Northeast – as staple food, vegetables, pickles, condiments and herbal materials. Wild edible plants form an important constituent of ethnic food in these regions and they help supplement the micro-nutrients and bioactive compounds the body needs. The food security of the region rests on edible mushrooms, honey, meat (yak-products), river fish, milk and milk products (cow and yak), and wild edible plants.

Given the above, the Northeast can become a veritable centre of processed foods, with emphases on tradition, socio-culture, cost-effectiveness and nutrition. But the following would also be needed for successful industrialisation of traditional food: availability and consistent raw material supply, infrastructure, R&D, a well-defined administrative policy, suitably priced capital, legislation and trade issues.

Ethnic fermented food have a special place in this pantheon and relate to it in terms of culture, tradition, cost-effectiveness and nutrition. And three possible avenues for product development from ethnic food include the re-creation of authentic food products, extolling their functional properties and the utilisation of technology. (Already, many commercial products have been developed using food fermentations as the basis.) But technical parameters contribute only partly to the successful commercialisation of ethnic food products/processes. Where and how these might fit into a given market will largely define business success.

Some ethnic fermented food and beverages have medicinal values. Though clinical study of these food has not been done yet, people strongly believe they have certain therapeutic values. Studied properly, such food may be projected in global markets with value adding via biotechnology. We need a much larger perspective, and a global approach for a successful commercialisation of the ethnic food of the Teesta Eco-regions and the Northeast.

Some of the areas where the intervention of science and technology is urgently needed in the regions are: the setting up of the supercritical fluid extraction technology for agricultural crops such as ginger, cardamom; extraction and purification of bio-active compounds from some important medicinal herbs and aromatic plants; development of bio-fertilisers and VAM cultures for organic farming; development of probiotics or starter cultures for the production of functional food; and the setting up of a biotechnology park for entrepreneur development in biotechnology-related business, and also to frame policy guidelines for such biotechnology-related business in Northeast India.

Once we trap the track for trading of bio-resource products of Teesta Eco-regions across the Indo-China border, the market will flourish due to the high demand for such organic and natural products with no, or minimum, side-effects and high biological values. The following may be recommended to strengthen the initiatives on the bio-resource products of the Teesta Eco-region for trade across Indo-China border:

- Institutional mechanisms may be developed to commercialise the products of bio-resources.
- Strengthen the existing R&D institutes in the Northeast with modern scientific requirements to focus on biotechnology.
- Redesign the courses in universities of the Northeast regions and make them relevant to the development of the region.
- NEC/DONER should constitute a Task Force to prepare a perspective plan with reference to S&T in the Northeast.
- Every Northeast state should constitute a Scientific Advisory Committee to formulate a Northeast-friendly policy on R&D.

The potential is ample and it can easily be exploited – provided there is due attention given (both by the Central and State governments). The establishment of good bio-resource management is, therefore, a must for Teesta's Eco-regions and the entire Northeast.

REFERENCES

S. Dewan and J.P. Tamang. "Dominant lactic acid bacteria and their technological properties isolated from the Himalayan ethnic fermented milk products." *Antonie van Leeuwenhoek International Journal of General and Molecular Microbiology*, Vol. 92, No. 3 (2007): 343-352.

A.K. Rai, R.M. Sharma and J.P. Tamang. "Food value of common edible plants of Sikkim." *Journal of Hill Research*, Vol. 18, No. 2 (2005): 99-103.

B.Tamang, J.P. Tamang, U. Schillinger, C.M.A.P. Franz, M. Gores and W.H. Holzapfel. "Phenotypic and genotypic identification of lactic acid bacteria isolated from ethnic fermented tender bamboo shoots of North East India." *International Journal of Food Microbiology*, Vol. 121 (2008): 35-40.

J.P. Tamang, N. Thapa, Rai, B., Thapa, S., H. Yonzan, S. Dewan, B. Tamang, R.M. Sharma, A.K. Rai, R. Chettri, B. Mukhopadhyay and B. Pal. "Food Consumption in Sikkim with special reference to Traditional Fermented Foods and Beverages: A Micro-level Survey." *Journal of Hill Research*, Supplementary issue, Vol. 20, No. 1 (2007): 1-37.

J.P. Tamang, "Indigenous fermented foods of the Sikkim Himalaya: socio-economical prospective." In *Sikkim- Perspectives for Planning and Development*, edited by S.C. Rai, R.C. Sundriyal and E. Sharma. Dehradun: Sikkim Science Society - M/S Bishen Singh Mahendra Pal Singh, 1998: 513-523.

———, "Traditional fermented foods and beverages of the Sikkim Himalayas in India: Indigenous process and product characterization." In *Proceedings of the 1997 International Conference on Traditional Foods* (6-8 March 1997), edited by the Director, CFTRI. Mysore: CFTRI, 2000: 99-116.

———, "Food culture in the Eastern Himalayas." *Journal of Himalayan Research and Cultural Foundation*, Vol. 5, Nos. 3-4 (2001): 107-118.

———, "Food Culture of Sikkim." *Sikkim Study Series*, Vol. IV. Gangtok: Information and Public Relations Department, Government of Sikkim, 2005: 120.

———, "Fermented Foods for Human Life." In *Microbes for Human Life*, edited by A.K. Chauhan, A. Verma and H. Kharakwal. I.K. New Delhi: International Publishing House Pvt. Limited, 2007: 73-87.

S. Thapa, and J.P. Tamang. "Product characterization of kodo ko jaanr: fermented finger millet beverage of the Himalayas." *Food Microbiology*, Vol. 21 (2004): 617-622.

Chapter 9

Linkages between East India's Tea Industry and the Development of Sikkim: Dimensions, Challenges and Prospects

Sohel Firdos

The opening up of the Nathu La pass is a landmark in raising bilateral trade between India and China to newer heights. Their mutual trading potential has considerably enthused the Sikkim government since it sees this as opening up fresh development opportunities. The Sikkim government even constituted a Study Group headed by Dr Mahendra P. Lama to study the prospects of border trade. The Study Group's Report, titled "Nathu La Trade: Prospects, Potentials and Opportunities", was submitted in September 2005 and was optimistic in tenor. The report not only said that opening up Nathu La would benefit landlocked Sikkim, it also concluded that it would benefit the adjoining regions in the Northeast and West Bengal. The report also envisioned that border trade would transform Sikkim into a dry port and transform Siliguri, in West Bengal, into a major trading centre.

Siliguri is well connected by road, rail and airways with capital cities like Kolkata, New Delhi and Guwahati, and it acts, at present, as the transit point for goods and services for the Northeast and northern Bihar. In future, it can be the trans-shipment point of all trade through Nathu La. The initial daily transit may be of 100-150 trucks over the 154 km Siliguri-to-Nathu La route, and that by itself could generate annual employment for nearly 10,000 people (drivers, cleaners, mechanics, loaders, warehouse keepers etc). The choice of Siliguri, and its twin city, Jalpaiguri, as the point for customs, warehousing, storage and freight-handling infrastructure, seems obvious. Also, both cities are on the East-West Corridor of the National Highway Development Project, which makes them ideally placed as cargo-transfer points, into more powerful carriers capable of crossing Nathu La at 14,500 feet. Their being in the plains also implies that they would need less expensive infrastructure. Indeed, the eternal optimist would aver that economic activity across the entire eastern hinterland would be unprecedented if the old silk route gets re-opened and a Kolkata-Lhasa trade link established. Moreover, the port facilities of Kolkata and Haldia are nearer to China's southern and western regions. The ability to use these ports would, accordingly, help it to cut transportation costs – and would also immensely benefit Kolkata and Haldia. The situation will be a welcome contrast to current reality, where all of southern and western China is bottled up and must trade via Myanmar's ports. The latter are about 5,000 km away, while Kolkata port is just 1,200 km removed.

According to Prof. Mahendra P. Lama, leader of the Nathu La Trade Study Group, it has been estimated that, on the higher side, the value of bilateral trade through Nathu La would be Rs 206 crore in 2007, and go up to Rs 12,203 crore by 2015. On the lower side, the value of bilateral trade through Nathu La has been pegged at Rs 353 crore in 2010 and Rs 450 crore in 2015. The value of Indo-China bilateral trade in 2004 was $9.8 billion, which is seven per cent of India's bilateral trade globally (*The Hindu*, 19 December 2005).

Although the eight states of the Northeast will gain the most, none bar Sikkim has taken any initiative. Yet, the region provides a 650 million strong market, and China would very much like to form an Indo-China study group for market research. Lama said the ADB is "eager" to spend $1 billion for developing the NE market.

Prospects for trade have increased significantly due to the opening up of Nathu La – while Sikkim is located close to West Bengal's tea-growing regions. We shall therefore examine if the tea trade between India and China will contribute to Sikkim's development.

Tea Industry in India

Tea is an important commodity item in international trade. The world's supply of tea as well as its demand is steadily on the rise – and yet there was a global surplus of 113.48 million kg in 2006 (Tea Board of India). The estimated total of world production was 3,523.48 million kg, while the demand was 3,410.00 million kg.

India and China apart, the other tea producers are Sri Lanka, Kenya, Vietnam and Indonesia. India contributes 27.12 per cent to world tea production, next to China's 28. 94 per cent. Also, India ranks fourth in global tea exports. Sri Lanka, Kenya and China are the main exporters, while India – the largest consumer – contributes only 12.91 per cent to global tea exports. Earlier on, there were legislative measures to control the production and export of tea under India's 'Tea Control Act' of 1933. The regulation of tea prices, and the fixing of export quotas, lowered India's aggregate tea output by 12 per cent, and raised by 80 per cent the average price of tea in the Calcutta auction. That changed however after 'liberalisation' and the opening up of markets; the tea trade became less regulated after the advent of the WTO Regime and agreements on free trade.

The industry comprises both organised and unorganised sectors. The plantation sector is organised, and employs 12,58,800 lakh workers in a permanent capacity. The small tea grower, in the unorganised sector, is a more recent phenomenon. The contribution of the latter to India's tea production is currently about 21 per cent of the total.

Table 9.1: Estimated number of Labour employed in Tea Plantation

Category	*2001*	*2002*	*2003*	*2004*	*2005*
Women Workers	606009	618134	618630	620750	623727
Male Workers	579471	589607	589854	597835	600035
Adolescent	46,670	47,359	47726	39,025	35,038
Total	**1232150**	**1255100**	**1256210**	**1257610**	**1258800**

Source: Tea Board of India

As per the Tea Board of India, there are 126,256 STGs in India with a tea acreage of 106,748 hectares. This segment extends in 15 Indian states – namely, Assam, West Bengal, Bihar, Uttaranchal, Himachal Pradesh, Arunachal Pradesh, Nagaland, Manipur, Mizoram, Meghalaya, Tripura, Sikkim in North India and Tamil Nadu, Kerala and Karnataka in South India. Estimates suggest that approximately 5 lakh people (including STGs families) derive their livelihood from this unorganized sector.

Table 9.2: Distribution OF STGs in India (2005)

States	*Number of STGs**	*Area (in Ha)*	*Registered with Tea Board*	*% of Registered STGs*
Assam	42492	41249	1852	4.35
West Bengal	8398	9500	479	5.70
Tamil Nadu	61985	43157	59111**	95.36
Kerala	5999	4810	2648	44.14
Other States	7382	8032	7586	102.76+
Total	**126,256**	**106,748**	**71,676**	**56.77**

The shift from production to processing, and thence to marketing by companies or corporates has been accompanied by the closing down, and abandoning of tea estates. A coterminous development has been the mushrooming and growth of small tea growers.

The Eighth Five Year Plan saw the Tea Board of India introducing the expansion of new tea cultivating areas, in the form of small growers in the vicinity of tea estates. They formed the nucleus of tea estates and, through the institutional demonstration effect, this segment gradually expanded into other areas. In a parallel development, farmers – after failing to receive remunerative prices from fruit and vegetable crops – started switching to the cultivation of tea

Tea Industry in China

China still has millions of tea lovers, but many of the young Chinese are losing interest in it. The FAO says that tea consumption there is growing only by an annual 2 per cent. This explains why third-generation cultivators are exporting increasing amounts – causing alarm in India, Sri Lanka, Indonesia, Bangladesh, Kenya, Malawi and Zimbabwe. So, although the focus is more on its resurgent competitiveness following the end of global textile quotas, it is China's tea industry that poses the greater challenge to some of the world's poorest economies. Meanwhile, it is poised to become the world's largest exporter of tea by tonnage, overtaking both Sri Lanka and Kenya.

Indeed, figures show that China's tea production rose 8.7 per cent last year, and accelerated rapidly as (recently planted) tea bushes reached maturity. Another factor behind output growth is that the older, inefficiently managed, state-owned farms are being turned over to output-conscious entrepreneurs. The tea industry has even benefitted from Beijing's goals of rural poverty alleviation and the flattening of income inequalities between the (rich) coastal cities and (poor) rural areas. Municipal and provincial governments now vie to offer subsidies to an industry that is seen as the answer to persistent poverty and rural unemployment. They are paying upto half the cost of planting new tea farms and building tea-processing factories. Beijing has also eliminated an 8 per cent tax on tea production as a way to increase rural income. Tea promotion policies, which include heavy spending on research institutes to develop better strains of tea as well as subsidies, do seem to bring greater prosperity to tea-growing areas.

Government-support helped produce an 18.9 per cent jump in China's tea exports last year, to $437 million, in a nearly stagnant global market.

This version is in accord with official Chinese figures released at a conference in Hangzhou on 28 September 2007. But, according to the Food and Agriculture Organisation, Chinese officials have become a bit reticent about future levels of tea production.

China's surge in tea caught many off-guard. Tea growers in India, Sri Lanka and Indonesia invested in new processing equipment to produce green tea instead of black, only to discover that China has recently become their competitor. Only now are they beginning to see the steps – giant ones, such as investments in infrastructure – that China has been taking to improve its tea-making ability. Meanwhile, advanced infrastructure such as that far outpaces anything that is available to tea growers in India, Sri Lanka, Vietnam, Indonesia and other countries. The latter must settle for dirt roads and power failures – while China's wide roads lower the cost to ship-in the diesel that is needed to power the processing factories and subsequently ship-out the tea. Power failures were a problem in China last year, but they have disappeared as more generating plants got built.

Tea Growing Regions of China

First of all, tea is grown in the southern half of China. The birthplace of tea (Yunnan to be specific) has an ideal climate, while northern China is simply too cold. Tea has spread all across the world mainly due to European explorers. But it still has the greatest integrity when grown and processed in China or Taiwan. The growing regions of China are: South West, North of the Yangtze (Gansu, Shanxi, Henan and Shandong), South of the Yangtze (Hubei, Anhui, Jiangsu, Hunan, Jiangxi and Zhejiang) and South China (Guangxi, Guangdong, Fujian, and Hainan). The total area that is covered by these regions is 38 degrees east to west and 19 degrees north to south.

The South West district comprises Yunnan, Sichuan, Guizhou and southernmost Tibet. This region has a sub-tropical monsoon climate – perfect weather for tea to thrive in. Yunnan, the birthplace of tea, is the most famous province and is made up chiefly of red clay. The oldest living tea tree is an incredible 1700 years old and the oldest cultivated tree is 800 years old. Yunnan produces mainly black tea and also some which are white, green and oolong. Nearly all *pu-erh* is also made in Yunnan.

Guizhou is famous for growing Yunwu, a rare style of green tea that is rare in the US. Sichuan produces mostly green, as well as black and yellow tea. Tibet grows very little tea, but what it does is mostly made into low-grade *pu-erh* (or black) tea. The soil in these provinces is mainly yellow or brown. The north of the Yangtze district refers to the territory north of the lower reaches of the Yangtze River and includes Henan,

Shanxi, Gansu and Shangdong. The region also includes the northern sections of Anhui, Jiangsu and Hubei although many of the famous gardens in these provinces are not part of this region. The region produces mainly green tea and is not famous for quality. Tea in this region may suffer drought due to uneven rainfall. This means there are microclimates, some of which are great for tea growing, while some others are not. The soil is chiefly yellow and yellow-brown. Liu An Guapian, Xinyang and Maojian are grown in the more favorable microclimates here.

The district South of the Yangtze refers to the territory south of the lower reaches of the Yangtze River and includes Zhejiang, Hunan, Jiangxi, Anhui, Jiangsu, and Hubei. This region is the bread and butter so to speak of tea production in China. It has some incredibly famous gardens and micro regions and their annual production totals about 66 per cent of China's total output.

There are four clearly defined seasons and the region produces mainly green, black and scented tea. The region is also home to 5 of the 10 famous tea of China. The soil-type is mainly red, with some that is yellow and yellow-brown. Rainfall-wise, 60 to 80 per cent of the region's precipitation occurs during summer and spring.

The South China district includes Guangdong, Guangxi, Fujian and Hainan, an island off the south coast of China. The soil type is classified as old clay, and red clay in other parts. It is very nutritious, and the region gets much annual rainfall. The growth period for tea trees is 10 months of the year. Black/red, green and oolong tea are grown here. The most noteworthy of these is oolong. Anxi and Wuyi Shan, two of the most famous growing areas for oolongs are located here. The Phoenix Mountain is just to the north, in Guangdong.

Challenges before China's Tea Business

Erosion has become a problem with the clearing of so many hillside forests to accommodate more tea bushes. Also, prosperity is raising wages and drawing in migrants from other provinces. Sometimes, even prison labour has been used.

Winters, although milder than in northern China, mean that central China's tea bushes stop producing new leaves for harvest during mid-October to mid-March. Contrast that with the tea bushes of warmer climates like those of southern India and western Java; those can be harvested all the year long.

Finally, even a small appreciation in China's currency "will really affect our business", said Xu Hairong, deputy director of the Zhejiang

University's Tea Research Institute. But the bigger worry for the global industry is about the amount of Chinese tea, which will be arriving in world markets. That will amount to a flood if the people of China keep switching to other beverages.

India: Export of Tea

There was a declining trend since 1997, but there has been a significant increase in export over the longer term: India's tea exports increased by 16 per cent over the period from 1950 to 2000. That represented a reverse in the decline of tea exports. The decline started in July 2004 and continued until November 2004, but exports again rose marginally in December. Thus, 2004 was the year in which the export total rose 2.23 per cent and attained 177.55 million kg (up from 2003's export figure of 173.68 million kg).

The chief determinant of the decline had been the sharp fall-off in exports to Russia and the CIS countries. But, even today, a major share of India's tea goes to the Russian market; that accounts for around 34 per cent of India's total tea exports. The EU countries import another major proportion, and latest export trends show that there are potential markets in Pakistan and Iraq.

India: Import of Tea

Free trade policies and the availability of tea that is cheaper are the major factors that have been influencing the increase in tea imports into India.

But the penetration of cheap teas from Indonesia, Kenya and China into India will affect the growth of the domestic market for Indian tea. Yet, the duty free entry of tea had only been allowed for re-exports from India; imported tea cannot be sold in the local market. But imports, which came to 9.86 million kg in 2003, registered a phenomenal increase, to reach 23.95 million kg in 2006. The processed re-export includes imported cheap and low-grade tea from other countries. And they are re-exported to India's traditional markets where such tea commands a premium.

India's Tea Trade with China and Opportunities for Sikkim

As per the estimates for 2006 provided by the Tea board, India imported 2.0 million kg of tea from China with a market value of Rs 7.94 crore. Table 3 suggests that tea imports from China declined slightly over 2004 to 2005 but increased again in 2006. It is possible that imports from China may increase in future and that the import may be channeled via Sikkim if the Nathu La trade route is properly developed.

Also, since imported tea is meant for re-export after value addition, Gangtok may be developed as a destination centre for the imported tea to act as a blending centre. The tea may be re-exported from there after blending! It may help generate revenue for the Sikkim government and provide employment to people in the blending centres.

Table 9.3: Import of Tea from China

Year	*Qty (million kilograms)*	*Value (Rs Crore)*
2004	1.66	6.22
2005	1.08	5.46
2006	2.00	7.94

Source: Tea Board of India

The export of tea from India to China has also increased by more than five times. It has gone from 62,000 kg in 2003 to 3,47,000 kg in 2005. This phenomenal increase in exports could spell a boom for Sikkim were they to be canalised through Nathu La. That would generate much revenue for the state in the form of customs duty and local levies; it would also create employment.

Table 9.4: Export of Tea to China from India

Year	*Qty (in '000 Kgs.)*	*Value (in '000 Rupees)*
2003	62	12135
2004	126	23482
2005	347	70071

Source: Tea Board of India

Problems of Trade

It should be apparent from the above that Sikkim may benefit a lot from tea trade between India and China, but only after over coming certain impediments. Firstly, in terms of shipment facilities, the ports of Kolkata and Haldia have been plagued by shallow draft – the fallout of silt deposition. Saugor and the Sandheads offer deeper drafts that can handle very large ships and crude oil carriers.

Meanwhile, major steps have been taken within Kolkata to improve rail connectivity with other regions. The port trust is repairing the infrastructure at Kolkata and Haldia docks to handle additional cargo. It has also embarked upon a project to develop cargo handling in areas that possess deeper draft, such as Saugor Island and the Sandheads. The port has ended its long tiff with railways to work on a new container handling facility at Kolkata docks, which Container Corporation (Concor) will manage. Concor will set up a modern container handling facility within Kolkata Dock System. The port has also entrusted the Eastern Railway to spruce up 78 km of rail tracks within the dock area to move other break bulk cargo. Now, goods can move by rail direct from Kolkata to Siliguri – and they can also switch between rail and ship modes.

Secondly, the road between Gangtok and Nathu La needs to be widened to allow for more movement of trucks. The present single lane road will be broadened by the National Highway Authority of India within three years on a high priority basis. Besides, the chief minister of Sikkim also has plans for an alternative highway via Kupup. Moreover, the National Highway 34 and 31 needs to be widened and reconstructed to provide faster and more efficient road connectivity between Kolkata and Siliguri, and Siliguri and Gangtok respectively. Thirdly, tea is not in the import list of commodities. The government needs to include it in the import basket so that Gangtok may emerge as a major blending centre, from where tea may be re-exported after value addition.

REFERENCES

Pushpita Das, "Nathu La: Pass To Prosperity But Also A Challenge" (2006). Downloaded from www.idsa.in.

Manas Das Gupta, *Sikkim, Problems and Prospects of Development.* South Asia books, 1992.

Draft Report on the International Commodity Agreement of Tea. New Delhi: Centre for Education and Communication.

Mahendra P. Lama, *Sikkim: Society, Polity, Economy and Environment.* New Delhi: Indus Publications, 1994.

S.C. Rai, R.C. Sundriyal and E. Sharma. Eds. *Sikkim: Perspectives for Planning and Development.* South Asia Books, 1998.

Epilogue

Rakhee Bhattacharya

While contemplating about this beautiful hill State of Sikkim, the foremost thing that strikes one is its remarkable economic advancement within the last decade, which has been achieved only due to an honest and determined visionary approach of the State's political leadership and because of relatively good governance. This may serve as an example in the Indian scenario. As the noted economist Shankar Acharya said once, "the cause of inequality is not growth as it has driven down the poverty ratio. The cause is lack of governance and asymmetry of opportunity." So Sikkim's growth in this paradigm of progress is indeed path breaking, where we all agree to the fact that the other Northeastern States have manifested as problem-arenas in the political and economic milieu of contemporary India. Their issues are intimately connected with the intra and inter-regional inequalities, degree of alienation and isolation, rampant corruption, dismal failure of governance and above all, the issue of insurgency and the issue of security, which is again debatable at various levels. And despite Binoda Mishra's circumspection about Indian Government's security dilemma on Nathu La, Sikkim has a different story to say, as P.D. Rai strongly argues, since it does not suffer from such endemic insurgency issues as other Northeastern states do.

Amongst the eight Northeastern states, Sikkim tops the list in terms of its per capita income with Rs 13,353 while Assam is positioned at the bottom of the list with Rs 7020 during 2005-06. Though Sikkim is much behind the top scorer small State, namely Delhi, whose average income is Rs 31,345 for the same year, it is well ahead amongst the Northeastern peripheral states. The state has made this tremendous jump just within a decade. Its per capita income was Rs 8402 in 1993-94. Assam could just marginally improve from Rs 5715 in this decade (all in 1993-94 prices). And the growth rate of net state domestic product in Sikkim during the period from 1993-94 to 2003-04 was 8.31 per cent (Delhi 8.33 per cent), while in Assam the figure for the same period was 2.53 per cent. As an *India Today* yearly report (2007) on the status of Indian states rightly says, "The smallest state in the Northeast region, Sikkim is the leader." This is because, in the region, Sikkim ranks top in terms of overall prosperity, law and order, primary health, investment scenario and also in terms of budget and prosperity. It ranks second in primary education and infrastructure. So one can unmistakably make a vision of Sikkim as the most happening state in the region due to its exceedingly good economic performance compared to other Northeastern states. And this small state can possibly be compared with the other most successful small state, i.e. Goa of West India. Sikkim has proved that, though remote, it could progress very well with its economic initiatives, right political dynamism and social safety.

And now with the opening of Nathu La, the cross-country trade and other aspects of economic ties can hopefully be widened, and thus this 'model state' awaits a great future. As K. Elumalai has rightly pointed out in his essay, Nathu La provides strategic advantage for India and China as a point of entry and exit for movement of goods. As an important corollary to this argument, the immediate reflection of this volume has been on the development dynamics within the State along with its border pass, the historical Nathu La. The primary focus through this pass is trade - both border as well as full-fledged trade, which can give a fillip to the frontier regions of both India and China. M. G. Kiran, reflecting the State government's perspective, has made some very vital observations in this regard. To him, the reopening of Nathu La is indeed an emotional episode for the people of Sikkim, after a gap of 44 years. The Indo-China war in 1962 had ended this historical connection, and ever since this was exposed as a hostile zone. While the Sikkim Democratic Front Government deserves credit for its bold initiative for a successful opening of this door, the other doors of Northeast India also need to be opened now, so that the region can truly become a development hub along with its neighbours. It now lies in the hands of both the countries to make economic resurgence a success. Kiran has also enlightened us about the initial teething problems of trade through this route. This is probably also expected. After so many decades of truncation and distrust, this lost link needs to be reestablished first with trust, goodwill and understanding. The distrust should be erased by more people-to-people contact, friendship network, goodwill visits and restoration of cultural links, which can create an ambience for future strength of economic cooperation. In this regard, tourism along the

Buddhist circuit can be one of the best ways to begin. This landlocked State also needs resurgence in road infrastructure to stress the benefits of trade and travel up to West Bengal. Also, some purposeful special economic zones in the border areas may help this initiative.

All the States in this region, with a long harsh history of exploitation, along with failure of governance and rising corruption, could never focus on capacity building and self-sustenance of their economies. Due to shortage of revenue and meaningful productive activity generating resources, they are heavily dependent on central assistance to avoid a possible economic collapse. The result was that, when India actually transformed itself from the Licence-Permit Raj to the era of reforms and globalization, the rest of the country could enjoy the high economic growth trajectories brought by it, but the Northeastern States were oblivious to the reforms and their fruits. This failure to develop a skill-based competitive attitude is partly due to the obsession of the perceived 'ethno-cultural identity', which has eventually failed to develop a mindset to accept the 'modern identity', which evolves through economic development, diversity and professionalism. All this while, central assistance was pumped in generously for various developmental programmes, but their misutilization, and untimely dispatch, had hindered and prevented achievement of the scheme deliverables. It is time to revisit and question the earlier policies in the light of present requirements, in order to explain through a multi-stage analysis – the problem and the paradox, the gap between economic potential and performance in Northeast India. Unless this is hammered, development resurgence will most likely be unsuccessful in the region.

Sikkim in particular should ideally make this resurgence in the perspective of eastern India and West Bengal in particular due to their geo-economic proximities. What we need again is a vision to erase the political differences, and tie the states fruitfully and gainfully. For example, J.P. Tamang has talked about what he calls "the self-contained economy" of Teesta eco-region, which can have a spillover effect upon its neighbours from both sides. Sohel Firdos has also rightly observed that the opening of Nathu La can possibly change the fate of Sikkim and West Bengal. It is being realized today that the geographical boundaries, to demarcate one nation state from another, are gradually on a thinning trend in this flat world of technology and globalization. The emphasis today is more on integration than on fragmentation, and in this paradigm, the Northeastern states of India, with their eastern neighbours like West Bengal and other adjoining eastern states, can actually make a "geographical heart land" for the Asian economies, which are still marked by lack of governance, political volatility, proliferation of poverty, increasing urban slums, stagnating rural economy and choking urban imbalances. In the economic growth trajectories of modern India with 9 per cent, east and northeast India are yet to catch-up, and they are certainly not in this gravy train. This economic reality is the political challenge of the day for the people of eastern India. The depressing political games like Nandigram add more to the list of failures in east India today.

But all is not dark; the region can also rightly be claimed as "embedded" between the two fastest growing economies of the world – India and China. Thus northeast India, southwest China and Southeast Asia can be a "triangular economic zone" and can bring prosperity to this region through appropriate vision and initiatives. That is what calls for a "Look East" policy as the urgent need of the hour. It is in this light that the national perspective for development of eastern India shall have to be charted out. Keeping this in mind, the present volume therefore has aimed to search for a strategy to foster the growth of cooperation of eastern and northeastern regions of India along with its immediate neighbours like China, as a hub of regional growth, outlining the planning parameters of economic, social and cultural cooperation. This approach of cooperation should be the need of the hour for development of east and northeast India.

This volume has tried to touch upon these urgent issues through various thematic essays. It is expected to provide the readers with an opportunity to attend to diverse views from scholars belonging to diverse disciplines of social science, attempting to trace the roots of, and connections between, many problems, and ultimately forging a common strategy to address the issue of lack of development in the region. The volume has also attempted to see that the pressing impulses and agonies that confront us today are appropriately articulated so that the meaning of *development as freedom* is enunciated. As "Resurgent India", an ambitious project of Divya Jeevan Society, an NGO founded in 1996, campaigns appropriately for east and northeast India, that development does not mean mere physical development in the form of roads, bricks, building, plants and machineries. Rather, it embraces the fullest realization of the rated capacity of human resources, balancing environment and habitat. We find evidence from our age-old spirit, philosophy and ethics dating back from its ancient past, which is now being reiterated over and again by Prof. Amartya Sen, emphasizing the idea of human development as the centre of all developmental visions and plans. But the modern occidental frame unfortunately witnesses how human greed can bypass all such ancient oriental values, and can invite all sorts of shameful and disgraceful activities to challenge this world with multi dimensional threats of inequities and other non-traditional threats. India's northeast is one such vulnerable zone, which needs no elaboration in this regard. In its broadest and most ambitious scope, this volume has sincerely attempted to provide a thought-provoking platform where India's traditional spirit once again reflects itself in shaping modern India with human face. It is hoped that more of such attempts will help us to find out the future road map for *inclusive development* of east and northeast India.

Documents and Photographs

Agreements signed on June 23, 2003

Documents signed between India and China during the then Prime Minister Vajpayee's visit to China June 23,2003

Memorandum between the Government of the Republic of India and the Government of the People's Republic of China on Expanding Border Trade, 23 June 2003

The Government of the Republic of India and the Government of the People's Republic of China (hereinafter referred to as the two sides), with a view to promoting the development of friendly relations between the two countries and two people's,

Pursuant to the Memorandum between the Government of the Republic of India and the Government of the People's Republic of China on the Resumption of Border Trade signed on 13 December 1991, and Protocol on Entry and Exit Procedures for Border Trade signed on 1 July 1992,

Desirous of opening another pass on the India-China border and setting up an additional point on each side for border trade, Have agreed as follows:

Article I

The Indian side agrees to designate Changgu of Sikkim state as the venue for border trade market; the Chinese side agrees to designate Renqinggang of the Tibet Autonomous Region as the venue for border trade market.

Article II

The two sides agree to use Nathula as the pass for entry and exit of persons, means of transport and commodities engaged in border trade. Each side shall establish checkpoints at appropriate locations to monitor and manage their entry and exit through the Nathula Pass.

Article III

All the provisions of the Memorandum on the Resumption of Border Trade signed between the two Governments on 13 December 1991 and the Protocol on Entry and Exit Procedures for Border Trade signed between the two Governments on 1 July 1992 under the Memorandum shall also be applicable to the border trade through the Nathula Pass.

Article IV

This Memorandum may be amended or supplemented by agreement in writing between the two sides.

Article V

This Memorandum shall come into force as from the date of its signature and shall be valid during the validity of the Memorandum on Resumption of Border Trade signed between the two Governments in New Delhi on 13 December 1991.

Done in Beijing on 23 June 2003 in two originals each in the Hindi, Chinese and English languages, the three texts being equally authentic.

For the Government of the Republic of India	For the Government of the People's Republic of China

Source: 1. Pawan Chamling, *Nathula Trade Route: Harbinger of Greater Peace and Development,* Department of Commerce and Industries, Government of Sikkim, 2006: pp. 27-28.

Agreed Minutes of the meeting to Operationalize border trade through Nathula

To implement the Memorandum on Expanding Border Trade signed between the Government of Republic of India and the Government of People's Republic of China signed in June 2003, an Indian delegation led by Dr. Christy Fernandez, Additional Secretary, Department of Commerce, Ministry of Commerce and Industry, visited Tibet Autonomous Region on 17-20 June 2006. The Chinese side was led by Mr. Hao Peng, Vice Chairman of the People's Government of the Tibet Autonomous Region.

The two delegations agreed as follows:

1. The border trade between India and China will promote the development of friendly relations between the two countries and their peoples.
2. The border trade through Nathula Pass will resume on 6 July 2006 at the Changgu border trade market in the Sikkim State of Republic of India and Renqinggang border trade market of the Tibet Autonomous Region of People's Republic of China.
3. The two border trade markets shall be open from 1st June to 30th September every year. It will be open to the designated authorities of the two sides through mutual agreement to extend or reduce the period of the trade where such extension or reduction may be considered necessary and desirable on account of exigencies like weather conditions. Where such extension or reduction is mutually agreed it would be notified to traders by public notice on the two sides by their designated authorities.
4. The border trade markets will be open from Monday to Thursday every week. The daily opening time of the markets for border trade shall be from 1000 to 1800 hrs Beijing Time and from 0730 to 1530 hrs Indian Standard Time.
5. The opening ceremony for resumption of border trade through Nathula shall be held at Nathula at 1130 hrs, Beijing Time (0900 hrs. the Indian Standard Time) on 6 July 2006. Officials of the Ministry of Commerce of People's Republic of China, Ministry

of Commerce and Industry of Republic of India, other relevant Ministries of both sides and respective provincial officials of Sikkim State of Republic of India and Tibet Autonomous Region of People's Republic of China will be present on this occasion. The list of names of officials to be present at the opening ceremony will be exchanged through diplomatic channels by 25 June, 2006.

6. Both sides shall provide a certain number of fixed stalls in their respective border trade markets for the border traders.
7. Issues pertaining to exit and entry of border traders, import and export of goods, supervision over means of transport, entry and exit of drivers and cleaners, lists of items to be traded and requirements for inspection and quarantine, are at attachments I, II and III.
8. Both sides will establish a periodic consultation mechanism to address routine trade related operational issues, including customs, inspection quarantine, and border control. In this regard, both sides will designate a nodal officer, whose details will be exchanged through diplomatic channels by 25 June, 2006.
9. The two sides will implement the Agreed Minutes.

Signed in duplicate at Lhasa, Tibet Autonomous Region of China on 18 June 2006 in the English and Chinese languages, both texts having equal validity, but in case of any divergence of interpretation, the English text shall prevail.

For the Ministry of	For the Peoples'
Commerce and Industry	Government of the Tibet
Of the Republic of India.	Autonomous Region of the PRC

ATTACHMENT (ENTRY AND EXIT PROCEDURES)

The Provincial Border Control Bureau of Tibet Autonomous Region has consulted with the Indian delegation on entry and exit of persons, vehicles and other movements. The two delegations agreed as follows:

1. All the provisions of the Memorandum of the Resumption of Border Trade Signed between the two Governments on 13 December 1991 and the Protocol on Entry and Exit Procedures for Border Trade signed between the two Governments on 1st July, 1992 under the Memorandum shall also be applicable to the border trade through the Nathula Pass.
2. Persons and vehicles of each side engaged in border trade

through Nathula pass must enter the other country through Nathula pass with valid border pass. The traders from the Chinese side shall enter or leave the border region with the CHINA-INDIA BORDER REGION ENTRY AND EXIT PASS. Government of Peoples Republic of China will issue the BORDER REGION VECHILES' BORDER PASS to vehicles. The traders and vehicles from the Indian side will be issued the TRADE PASS. Movement of vehicles as mentioned above will be an interim measure. Both countries will subsequently enter into a motor vehicles agreement for trans border movement of vehicles through Nathula Pass for border trade.

3. To start with, each side will issue the pass to 60 four wheeled vehicles including passengers buses, if any. Both sides can increase or decrease the number of vehicle passes only after mutual agreement after assessing the requirement of border trade.
4. Indian side agrees that Yandong Border Control Inspection Station can collect RMB per trip in accordance with related Chinese regulations. Similarly, Chinese side agrees that all Chinese vehicles entering Indian Territory will be charged Rupees 30/-pertrip by the Indian Border Control.
5. Chinese side will stamp on the CHINA-INDIA BORDER REGION ENTRY AND EXIT PASS from the first page, and Indian side will stamp on the CHINA-INDIA BORDER REGION ENTRY AND EXIT PASS from the last page. Similarly Indian side will stamp the TRADE PASS from the first page and the Chinese side will stamp the TRADE PASS from the last page.
6. The traders engaged in border trade through Nathula Pass have to stay in the sphere of activities in Renqinggang Border Trade Market and the Changgu Border Trade Market in accordance with the Memorandum on Expanding Border Trade of June 23rd, 2003 signed by the Governments of China and India, and can not go out of the sphere of activities.
7. Yadong Border Control Inspection Station and Immigration offices of Government of India should establish a periodic meeting system through their designated officer.
8. The border trade mart will be open at BEIJING TIME 1000 hrs (Indian Standard time 0730 hrs.), and close at BEIJING TIME

1800 hrs (Indian Standard Time 1530 hrs). Raising and lowering of the respective national flags will mark the opening and closing of Nathu La Pass for Border Trade respectively. Raising and lowering of the National flags will be done in a coordinated manner between both the sides on the days of the trade.

ATTACHMENT II—CUSTOMS MATTERS

The representatives of both Indian and China Customs held discussions on the customs matters related to the opening of border trade between India and China. The following issues were discussed:

1. Supervision and control over means of transport and the destination:

The inward and outward vehicles movement between the two countries trade markets will be recorded by the customs. At the time of transport entering into or leaving from customs territory of People's Republic of China, both countries' transport shall submit transport declaration form to China customs. This procedure is required to be followed only for the first time a vehicle crosses the Nathula Pass. The vehicles, after being checked can leave the customs supervision spot and move along the designated route. Indian customs will have similar control over vehicle movement and agree to exchange the details of inward and outward transport on reciprocal basis.

The border trade market of the respective sides will be the terminal point.

2. Declaration of merchandise carried by inward and outward Traders:

The traders entering into customs territory of People's Republic of China, shall submit (Lhasa Customs Border Trade Declaration Form) and China customs will take the Export declaration filled by the trader with Indian Customs as annexure. Similar procedure will be followed for exports from China by the Indian Customs.

3. Issues Related to Prohibitions and Restrictions:

The traders from both the countries cannot carry or transport prohibited articles. For carrying restricted articles or articles which require permit, the trader shall produce required license. Customs of both sides agree to exchange prohibited and restricted articles list.

4. Meeting between both Countries customs:

It was agreed that officers from China customs and Indian customs may cooperate operational level through exchange information and assistance in investigation, to counter smuggling through Nathula, on approval from the respective customs administrations.

5. Tax Exemptions:

Two sides would provide duty free access to items on the agreed list for border trade. China side requested that India considers reciprocating the duty regime that China has extended to items subject to value limits. It was agreed that duty regime on the items that are not included in the agreed list should be negotiated separately.

Both sides also agreed to provide the documents in respect of Customs policy, procedures and standard forms.

ATTACHMENT III
(Inspection and Quarantine Issues)

The two delegations agreed as follows:

1. All the provisions of the Memorandum on the Resumption of Border Trade signed between the two Governments on 13 December 1991 and the Protocol on Entry and Exit Procedure for Border Trade signed between the two governments on 1st July 1992 under the Memorandum shall also be applicable to the Border Trade through Nathula Pass.
2. Establish a consultation mechanism between the Chinese Inspection and Quarantine authorities through the designated equitable officers once in a month on the two sides to address inspection and quarantine related matters.
3. The Indian side suggested that 29 items of exports from India to china be categorized into Quarantine and non quarantine lists. Tibet Entry-Exit inspection and Quarantine Bureau will study each conscientiously and give an early response.

Source: 2. Pawan Chamling, *Nathula Trade Route: Harbinger of Greater Peace and Development,* Department of Commerce and Industries, Government of Sikkim, 2006: pp. 29-34.

Summing up Remarks on the Nathu La Trade Route Report

Presentation by Nathu La Trade Study Group led by Prof. Mahendra P. Lama

Hon'ble Cabinet colleagues, MPs, Vice Chairman of the Sikkim State Planning Commission, MLAs, respected trade experts, professionals from different institutions, Chief Secretary, officials, ladies and gentlemen.

The power-point presentation on Nathu La trade today has been highly relishing. All of us have been made all the more wiser on the various aspects of the ensuing trade with the Tibet Autonomous Region of China. This presentation is an eye-opener in many respects. This brings a vivid recollection of long forgotten history with a punch of nostalgia. This presentation tells us how the changing global dynamics have facilitated the process of bringing the two greatest civilizations to a common platform once again. Both India and China are willing to forget the bitterness and coldness that submerged them in the precious forty past years.

This presentation by an eminent set of professionals and experts make us greatly proud by reminding how Sikkim and Sikkimese always strived and aspired to reopen this trade route. I have been personally a hardcore advocate of this reopening. Therefore, I have in me a deep sense of satisfaction today.

This presentation of Prof. Mahendra P. Lama made a very lively and realistic projections of how Sikkim and Sikkimese will benefit from the operationalization of this trade route. It is interesting to note that the neighbouring states and the countries will be an equal stakeholders in this entire paradigm shift triggered by Sikkim.

I remain deeply impressed by the way the presenter has depicted the various announces of other trading routes in Shipkila, Lipulekh and Khasa. Their field visits-based narrations are of very high value to us. I am particularly delighted to see the way the Chinese side is preparing for this trade operationalization. It tells us many things which we are yet to even think of.

Each and every policy options and implications recommended by this Expert Group are worth implementing. I am sure we will soon be

---

Speech delivered on 17th June 2005 al Chintan Bhawan in Gangtok, Sikkim.

able to put in place all the projects and operational details for making Sikkim as the trade mart like Hongkong and Singapore and not a small location Sherathang alone.

I congratulate the entire team of experts and the author of this report for carrying out such a challenging task with professional finesse and serious commitment.

You are aware that resumption of trade through Nathu La has been made possible due to government's policy and programme. Having realized that the globalization process will have far and wide impact on the life of every citizen, we decided to open up to the outside world. We held a series of meetings with the financial institutions, NGOs and other private companies in all parts of the country including New Delhi and Kolkata. And historically speaking, this is a unique achievement of the State Government and the Sikkimese people at large. It will benefit the Sikkimese people materially and will also greatly enhance the significance of this land-locked state doing a quiet business across the border. We look forward to seeing the Sikkim people and especially the youths playing a crucial role in all these exercises. They must be able to take advantage of the route as an economic instrument for development of the state.

When I say this here, I do not only refer to trade in isolation but the fruitful engagement of the Sikkimese people in all trade-oriented business opportunities generated by the trade. The trade and tourism integration is so vital to us. The issue of capacity-building of our people is again a key concern, which will empower ordinary people to tap all prospective opportunities. In all fronts, we are in a win-win situation.

The opening of Nathu La trade may have given rise to some apprehension in the minds of the Sikkimese people, both with regard to influx and migration. This only betrays a case of utter lack of understanding and lack of correct information. Initially, it is going to be a dawn-to-dusk business transaction along the defined post and trade mart in both sides of the country. And it all depends on the wishes and the preparedness of the Sikkimese people to further enlarge the trade activities both in terms of volume and tourism scope across the border.

Nathu La trade as part of globalization process is all set to grow as we begin. Our basic policy has been to Sikkimize the globalization process through creation of our own environment by maximizing the benefit and minimizing the fallout.

Our government in Sikkim has a two-pronged development strategies—both short-term and long-term. We want to see the opening of the cross-border trade as an inexhaustible trade engagement that would cater to the interest of people many generations down the line. Our endeavour has been to encourage change in people's vacation and a shift from traditional occupation to service sectors on the basis of our natural resources. This is where the recommendation of this report to firmly integrate trade and tourism stands out as the panacea of our development laggardness. The government, may I record, has already formalized plans and programmes to this effect.

Lastly, I would like to thank all experts, trade professionals, who took all the pains to come over to Sikkim and share their expertise. The very distinguished members of the National Advisory Board of Nathu La Trade Study Group deserve our warm applause and heartfelt gratitude. I also thank the Government of India for acceding to our genuine demand to open the border for trade. Equally thankful I am to the Principal Secretary and all officials from Industries Department for their steady commitment, all hoteliers, entrepreneurs, bureaucrats, and technocrats for their crucial contributions.

Wishing you all great success in the future.

Thank you.

Source: 3. Sikkim: *Exploring the New Frontiers*, Vol 3, Information and Public Relations Department, Government of Sikkim, 2007: pp. 133-135.

Address to the Media on the Reopening of Nathu La Trade Route

I am delighted to announce that the Nathu La trade route to Tibet Autonomous Region of China is now scheduled to be reopened on 06 July 2006. It is a historic occasion for the people of India in general and of Sikkim in particular as:

(*i*) It re-establishes the historical-cultural-commercial linkages between the two great civilizations—India and China.

(*ii*) It not only acts as a handsome confidence-building measure but also broadens the scope of cooperation and friendship between these two emerging economic powers of Asia.

(*iii*) It reopens a major point of cultural, social and economic contacts between the state of Sikkim in India and Tibetan Autonomous Region of China,

(*iv*) It is the shortest and most viable land route that gives India access to Chinese economy and vice versa,

(*v*) It brings pride, joy and credit to Sikkim for providing India and China a space for reiterating and promoting *Punchsheel,* the five principles of coexistence that govern the relationship between these two powers.

Nostalgic Recollection

The history of the initiation of formal trade linkages between British India and Tibet through the passes of Sikkim dates back to the late 18th century. It was the report written by John Edgar, the Deputy Commissioner in Darjeeling in 1873 that really captured the attention of the British India Government with regard to the great strategic and commercial potentials of this route in Sikkim. The trade through Nathu La (the path of listening ear—4310 m) had been the outcome of the repeated deliberations and discourses at the highest administrative levels between the British India/ Sikkim and the Tibeto-Chinese Governments.

The later half of the 1890s, witnessed a fairly good trade of British India with Tibet through Sikkim passes as highlighted by the extract of the diary of the Political Officer for Sikkim. The diary extract of the 16th

---

Speech delivered on 25th June 2006 at Samman Bhawan in Gangtok, Sikkim

January 1898 states, "the trade for December are very good, amounting to Rs. 3,41,290. This includes a consignment of gold worth Rs. 16,800—the finest that has been sent in for some years".

The adventurous Younghusband Mission launched from Sikkim with a military escort (1903-04) accomplished its task of reaching Lhasa thereby leading to 1904 Convention that firmed up the Anglo-Tibet trade.

Mention may be made here that regular trade between Tibet and British India was carried out on the basis of various conventions drawn between China and Great Britain from time to time in the distant past. There used to be altogether thirteen routes operational from the Indian side for the trade: (i) From Ladakh, via Rudok, Mansarowar Lake, Mariamzla and Shigatse to Lhasa; (ii) From Srinagar, via Leh, Ladakh, Tashigong and Indus valley to Gartok; (iii) From Kulu and Lahul, via Shangrang la, and Chumurti to Gartok; (iv) From Simla via Shipki to Gartok; (v) From Tehri Garhwal, via Nilang to Gartok; (vi) From Badrinath (British Garhwal), via Mana la, and Toling (Totlingmath) to Gartok; (vii) From Almora, via Jashinath (British Garhwal) Niti la and Daba to Gartok; (viii) From Almora, via Milam and Uttadhaura to Gartok; (ix) From Almora, via Darma or Noe Pass and Gyanema to Gartok; (x) From Almora, via Lankpya, Lekh and Gyanema to Gartok; (xi) From Almora, via Lipu Lekh and Purang (Taklakot) to Gartok; (xii) From Siliguri, via Kalimpong, Jalep la and Chumbi to Gyantse; (xiii) From Siliguri, via Gangtok, Nathu La and Chumbi to Gyantse. Hence, the reopening of this route is like re-establishing the traditional bonds between the two countries.

Let us recall that Nathu La used to be one of the most vital trade routes that connected India with China. There are very interesting oral accounts on this trading route. One of them gathered by the Nathu La Trade Study Group in its report Sikkim-Tibet Trade via Nathu La: A Policy Study on Prospects, Opportunities and Requisite Preparedness mentions that:

"Deorali village was mostly used as a starting point for the mule train caravan. All the mule trails were "kuccha" and un-metalled and most were susceptible to the wrath of nature. Starting early in the morning, in the break of day, the caravan used to trudge along the mule trail to the Naya Bazaar; 10th mile was the next stop and then came the uphill climb to 15th mile. Thegu, was the next stop before coming to the hamlet of Tshango. The next climb involved crossing the cold pass and the last outpost of India, Nathu La. Once the pass was climbed, it was down-hill all the way into the Tibetan hinterlands of the Chumbi valley. The very first village was that of Lathung after which places like that of Phari La, then Gyantse, etc. came before coming to the very end of it, i.e. Lhasa.

There used to be custom checks at 15th mile. Yaks were used only from Phari onwards. Upto that point, mules and occasionally, coolies were used to ferry the goods. An average mule train consisted of between 15-50 mules. Each mule used to carry 40-60 kg of goods. 5-10 mule riders would accompany the caravan in the company of a group of Tibetan mastiffs. It was the Chinese who were the inventors of the 2-wheel carriage pulled by mules. It was more in use from Phari onwards because of the level terrain of the Tibetan plateau. It is estimated that the mules could now ferry upto 4 *'moan'* or *'mound'* (1 *moan* = 40 kg) of goods in this new invention. There were post offices en-route the trade trail. They were also couriered on mules.

All trade were regulated via the India Trade Agent (Central Government) who issued trade permits to the traders, especially so in the case of high value commodities like that of petrol, diesel, auto parts, liquors etc. The trade was that of an open market. Most of the trade, especially from Nathu La was done on the basis of cash transactions whereas the trade from Jelep la was mostly done on the basis of barter, even to the later days. The preferred currency for trade was the Indian currency but later on in the post-1950s the Chinese dollar called "dyang" (1 dyang = INRs 3-4) gained prominence. It was a pure silver coin.

The trade exports of India then were that of ghee, sugar, tinned goods, hardware, motor parts, mechanical items, construction materials, edible oils, leather goods (especially shoes), western watches (Rolex black dials) etc. The Indian imports were that of raw wool, Chinese silk and Chinese dollar.

Among the Indian goods having the most demands in Tibet were petrol, rice, sugar etc. Also in the demand list were high priced products like that of the West End watches and the Rolex and the Laungis brand of watches. There were talks of 40 kg of these watches being transported every now and then.

Profitability of the trade was almost 3 times the cost of production. The trade brought with it a lot of employment linkages directly and indirectly. Indirectly, the trade agents, the mule agents, the mule suppliers, the mule riders, the fodder suppliers, the wooden crate makers, the inn-keepers (called "nhe'zang" inTibetan), the blacksmiths etc. were employed. Among the big names in the Indo-Tibet trade were that of Bhaju Ratna Sau (Jyoti Brothers, now in Kathmandu), the Sarraf Brothers, Nandu Ram, Mintri Bros., the Diplas (Gangtok traders), Musk house's Guwahatiwalla, etc.

It was easier to transport goods via Nathu La, as there was better road connectivity, at least upto Deorali the goods would have more chances of reaching its final destination safely. Not that there was any reports of robbery or dacoity enroute, rather time played an important factor and this route was an easier route. But we were always on the mercy of nature. Dangers of mudslides, landslides, avalanches, blizzards and generally, the slipping of some of the mules while on their walk did have a toll on the overall breakage. There wasn't any system of insurance then.

It took almost 15 days to reach the said destination from the date of order from the Indian side. The trade was done using only the two main routes; it was an open market with no knowledge of there being any black marketing. There was enough safety and security as well as strict custom rules especially regarding "prohibited items" and import of silver and gold for the trade to carry on.

The immediate impact of the abrupt closure of the Indo-Tibet trade in 1962 was the downfall of both Sikkimese and Kalimpong's economy."

From this flourishing trade route for traders from Calcutta, Madras, Amritsar and Delhi both in the pre- and post-independence period, the situations have transformed and paradigms have greatly shifted. The reopening of the Nathu La trade route has been a long drawn process.

The Vision

We have consistently worked hard towards the reopening of this trade route. We have consciously built our case brick by brick. It was impossible to think about the reopening of Nathu La trade route even a decade back. Both our party Sikkim Democratic Front and our government when we were for the first time voted to power in 1994 have been very clear and conscious from the very beginning that Nathu La trade route reopening would be a major boost to our development efforts. Anywhere in the world, trade and development are so integrated. Look at any developed countries and contribution of foreign trade in their national income. Therefore, we included this Nathu La trade route in our party's manifestos and economic objectives. We took following steps to reach this goal.

i) We mentioned reopening of Nathu La trade route as a very vital aspect of our election manifesto. In our manifesto for the 1994 general elections, we have categorically mentioned, "to expand scope of trade transaction after facilitating opening up of Nathu La trade with Tibet and to deliver local produces at the national and international markets". Further, we have again made a forceful mention of the Nathu La trade also in our

1999 manifesto which read, 'To fulfill this demand is the established policy of the Sikkim Democratic Front party".

The election manifesto of 2004 further mentions, "...We shall endeavour to reorient some of our economic activities in the state to match the needs arising out of Nathu La trade. This will bring maximum benefits to the state."

ii) This plea of ours on the reopening of this trade route has been mainly on account of:

- traditional trade linkages;
- possibility of finding a major market in Tibet and mainland China;
- improving the competitiveness;
- integrating trade with tourism and other services-related activities; and
- finding other options for sustainable livelihood and development.

iii) Since we came to power in 1994, we very consistently put this demand before the Union Government.

iv) We sensitized the civil society, media and various other crucial segments of our country including political parties both about our interest in reopening this trade route and also about the variety of benefits it would bring to our country.

v) We discussed this issue in various intellectual, social and political fora and mobilized the opinions of all sections of the Sikkimese society including the NGOs, media, private sector, businessmen, industrialists, service providers and professionals.

vi) We brought eminent media persons and other experts from various national media and institutions to Sikkim and briefed them as to why reopening of Nathu La trade route is vital for both the state and the nation.

vii) When the then Prime Minister Mr. Atal Behari Vajpayee visited Sikkim in April 2003, I again put forward this demand to him. He assured us of positive action on this. He was visiting China in June 2003. While doing all these, we had our national interest and the issues of national security uppermost in our mind.

Fortunately for us, there had been a steady improvement in Sino-India relations after the breakthrough visit to China of the then Prime Minister late Mr. Rajiv Gandhi in 1988. Both these two emerging economic powers wanted to look forward and leave the past discomfort behind. The opening of Changu lake and the Nathu La pass to the tourists in the late 1990s—though in a very regulated manner—by the army indicated a major shift in the Union Government's policy. Since then a series of high level visits were exchanged and relationship steadily warmed up. A number of far-reaching agreements were signed during these visits. These visits included: (i) the then Prime Minister Mr. Narasimha Rao's visit to China in 1993; (ii) the then President Mr. Jiang Zemin's visit to India in 1996; (iii) the then Prime Minister Mr. Atal Behari Vajpayee's visit to China in 2003; and (iv) Premier Mr. Wen Jiabao's visit to India in 2005.

The Historic Agreement

The process of rapprochement between India and China started with a memorandum signed in 1991 for the resumption of border trade with the Tibet Autonomous Region (TAR) of China through two passes of Shipkila in Himachal Pradesh and Lipulekh in Uttar Pradesh (now Uttaranchal) in India. The consolidation towards a more dynamic relationship is aptly indicated by the remarkable jump in bilateral trade between India and China from a mere US $ 49 million 1990 to US $ 11332.7 million in 2005.

India-China bilateral trade (million US $)

Year	-	Volume of trade
1970	-	3.4
1980	-	88
1990	-	49
1995	-	1094
2000	-	2508
2004	-	7008
2005	-	11332.7

It was during the visit of the then Prime Minister Mr. Vajpayee to China, this historic Memorandum between the Government of the Republic of India and the Government of the People's Republic of China on Expanding Border Trade, was signed at Beijing on 23rd June 2003.

"The Indian side agrees to designate Changu of Sikkim state as the venue for border trade market; the Chinese side agrees to designate Renqinggang of the Tibet Autonomous Region as the venue for border trade market."' (Article I)

This brought significant politico-strategic gain to India as China formally recognized Sikkim as a constituent state of India. During the visit of Premier Mr. Wen Jiabao to India in April 2005, he formally presented a map showing Sikkim as a constituent state of India. Prime Minister Dr. Manmohan Singh and Premier Mr. Jiabao decided to establish a strategic and cooperative partnership for peace and prosperity.

Nathu La Trade Study Group Report

The moment this Memorandum was signed we started preparing for the reopening of this trade route. Besides a much broader consultation with the Union Government, at this juncture we needed a comprehensive report that dealt with all aspects of reopening of this trade route. This was essential because we did not have a proper knowledge base and documents that would provide even preliminary guidance to the state and the Union officials for the smooth conduct of trade.

Therefore, we commissioned this Report to a high level Nathu La Trade Study Group led by Prof. Mahendra P. Lama, a well known development economist and the Chairman of the Centre for South, Central, South East and South West Pacific Studies, School of International Studies, Jawaharlal Nehru University, New Delhi. This Group was advised by a very eminent set of public figures and experts drawn from various related fields. This National Advisory Board consisted of the following:

Chairman: Prof. Muchkund Dubey, former Foreign Secretary, Government of India and President, Council for Social Development, New Delhi and Vice Chairman, Sikkim State Planning Commission.

Members: Mr. O.K. Balraj, Vice President, Finance, New Business Development Group, Mumbai and formerly IIcad, Andhra Pradesh & Eastern Region, Infrastructure Development Finance Company Limited (IDFC).

Dr. Veena Jha, Project Coordinator, UNCTAD, New Delhi.

Mr. C.V. Ranganathan, former Ambassador to China and former Convener, National Security Advisory Board.

Mr. Prabir Sengupta, Director, Indian Institute of Foreign Trade, New Delhi.

Mr. S. Sen, Deputy Director General, Confederation of Indian Industry, New Delhi.

Prof. Patricia Uberoi, Director, Institute of Chinese Studies, Centre for the Study of Developing Societies, Delhi.

The Group while conducting the study examined a major portion of the historical documents and manuscripts. It conducted interviews with a large spectrum of people and stakeholders in various parts of India, Nepal and Tibet Autonomous Region in China. It made field visits and extensive studies of trading places in Nepal-Tibet border, Shipkila pass in Himachal Pradesh, Lipulekh in Uttarakhand, Moreh-Tamu border between Manipur and Myanmar and Petrapol-Benapol border between West Bengal and Bangladesh. The Group had extensive discussions with the high level officials of Tibetan Autonomous Region Government (TARG) on trade, customs, transport, communications and other infrastructure and tourism. This Group submitted its report in 2005.

This Report gives a road map, provides new vistas of knowledge and information, takes us back to history and gives us a comparative picture of various similar trade routes that exist in various other locations both in the mountain areas and in the plain lands of India. This brings a vivid recollection of long forgotten history with a punch of nostalgia. This report tells us about how the changing global dynamics have facilitated the process of bringing the two greatest civilizations to a common platform once again. It is a very detailed and comprehensive report that places the entire perspective of trade and tourism through Nathu La route for the next 20 years. The Union Government is highly appreciative of the findings, analysis and policy recommendations of the Report.

The Study Group has presented two scenarios for trade volume projections. Scenario

I. of higher projection shows that trade flow through Nathu La will be Rs. 206 crores by 2007, Rs. 2266 crores by 2010 and Rs. 12,203 crores by 2015. Under the Scenario

II. of lower side projection, trade volume passing through Nathu La route will be Rs. 353 crores in 2010, Rs. 450 crores in 2015 and Rs. 574 crores in 2020.

The Study Group has mentioned that on a very simple assumption also the charges on tourists visiting Sherathang and Nathu La could generate a revenue of Rs 1.81 crores in 2006 and Rs 3.47 crores in 2010. The income and employment effects on roadside hotels and restaurants, handicrafts and transport and communication and many other backward and forward linkages are likely to be immense.

The Report provides an interesting dimension. It mentions that the Nathu La reopening very much coincides with "develop-the-west" campaign launched by the Chinese Government since 2000. China's western region covers two-thirds of the nation's territory, with a population making up nearly 23 percent of the national total. It comprises of nine provinces and autonomous regions with plenty of land and natural resource including Gansu, Guizhou, Ningxia, Qinghai, Shaanxi, Sichuan, Tibet, Xinjiang and Yunnan. After eastern China's 14,000 km long coastlines brought fortunes to China in the last two decades, it is now western China with 3500 km land frontier lines that will become second golden area of reopening. The completion of 1142 km long railway line—an engineering feat—connecting Lhasa with mainland China through Golmud city in Qinghai brings a much larger dimension to this reopening.

The successful conduct of the business through this route could generate scope for a range of such openings between the neighbour-locked North Bengal and whole of North-East region and the neighbouring countries. This includes Stilwell Road built during the Second World War that connects Assam with Kunming (Yunnan, China) via Myanmar. The ports of Kolkata and Haldia could be used more elaborately. This more scientific openings of borders for economic and commercial purposes could in fact steadily replace the dominant security debate by the development discourse and gains in this conflict-torn North-East region. This is the way to realize the larger goals of India's 'Look East' policy and consolidate sub-regional groupings like South Asia Growth Quadrangle (SAGQ) and Bay of Bengal Initiative for Multi-Sectoral Techno-Economic Cooperation (BIMSTEC).

Besides many other prospects, this trade route is likely to bring revenue to the state, the Study Group also mentions that annual revenue generation by Sikkim Nationalized Transport (SNT) or by private truckers through movement of 100-500 trucks daily between Siliguri and Nathu La at the existing rate varies between Rs. 13.97 crores and Rs. 69.90 crores. If this rate is doubled by 2010 the total annual revenue generation is likely to be between Rs. 27.94 crores and Rs. 139.80 crores.

The Study gives great details about how China is preparing for the same and what should be the preparation mode of India. The large scale investment opportunities including making the entire Sikkim a trade mart has been identified and recommended.

Besides generating a huge revenue for the state in terms of license fees, toll taxes etc., the daily movement of 100-500 trucks could alone lead to direct employment of 4000 to 10,000 persons per annum (including drivers, cleaners, mechanics, loaders, warehouse keepers etc.) and other major cascading impacts like income and employment through opening of restaurants, shops, petrol pumps, telephone booths, banking, hotels and other civic and administrative amenities on the roadside.

There are several other gains in terms of price effect, multiple options for passengers and freights, boost to tourism, expansion in industrial and tertiary sector activities, infrastructure development and revenue generation from taxes etc.

While warmly congratulating Prof. Lama and his team of the Nathu La Trade Study Group for preparing this report in such a short time, let me mention that there are very interesting and far-reaching policy suggestions made in the report. This includes the following:

2005-2010: Initiation of trading on both sides backed by existing and some additional infrastructures. Meanwhile start building wider and deeper infrastructural facilities.

2010: Trading on a larger scale start taking place based on upgraded and more developed infrastructures.

2012: Integration of trade with tourism for which a fresh bilateral legal framework needs to be concluded to facilitate the movement of tourists across the border.

Package tours: During 2012-2015, only Indian and Chinese tourists are permitted to cross the border through Nathu La on a package tour basis.

Open tourism: 2015 onwards movement among Indian and Chinese tourists both on package and individual basis.

2015: Inclusion of movement of freights to and from the neighbouring countries including Bangladesh, Bhutan and Nepal through this route.

2018 onwards: *SAARC tourism,* integrate with tourism activities of third countries of the region including Bangladesh, Bhutan and Nepal. Open for all the tourists to cross the border.

It has very vital policy recommendations on safeguarding Sikkim's interests, setting up of Centre-State Border Trade Coordination Committee, lifting Ban on Foreign Tourists, Tourism Infrastructure Package, facilities at Sherathang and Nathu La alternative roads to Nathu La and linking Sikkim with the Golden Quadrilateral project. It has proposed Gangtok-Lhasa bus service and an Infrastructure Development Package of Rs. 1650-1700 crores.

There are policy recommendations related to airport, transport and containerization, banking, customs facilities, quality control and standardization facility, market intelligence, role of private sector, insulations from *bandhs,* security dynamics, trade corridor and trade pass, trade mart and tourism corridor, environmental concerns, and public information and knowledge base. It recommends setting up of a chain of institutional linkages including Indian Consulate in Lhasa, India-China Joint Action Team (ICJAT) and Sikkim-Bengal Coordination Group (SBCG) and Nathu La Museum.

We shall have to make best use of the findings and policy suggestions made in this Report. I have presented this Report before the State Legislative Assembly for both discussion and adoption.

Preparations on War Footing

As follow up to this, there have been several visits by the Union Government officials to the state to assess the state of preparations on our side and also to provide resources and technical support. The Chinese officials also visited the state and exchanged their views with us on the final reopening of this trade route.

From our side, we worked on a war footing and have completed the basic infrastructure required for the initial level of trading. With limited resources at hand and minimum time, we have been able to provide over 30 structures in the trading mart complex at Sherathang to house all important offices and residence including Warehouses, Custom office, Post Office, Banks, Immigration posts, BSNL and ITBT posts. We have also allotted offices to the IT, our health officials, cafeteria, waiting sheds. The shopping units are particularly dedicated to showcase our exportable items for the prospective traders/buyers from across the border.

Potable drinking water is being provided to the entire complex which is being fed by a nearby stream through source tapping. Power supply is being made through two numbers of gensets with an installed capacity of 320 KVA. The Border Roads Organization has undertaken the work of further improvement, strengthening and expansion of the existing road connectivity.

However, we require a much bigger infrastructure to really make full use of this trade route. As the volume of trade may also increase in the near future, we will upgrade or add new infrastructure on modem lines to cater to the burgeoning activities in terms of movement of goods and people. In fact, we have submitted a detailed plan for the same to the Union Government.

The Final Move

Only a couple of days back, an Indian team led by Dr. Christie Femandes, Additional Secretary in the Ministry of Commerce and Industry visited Lhasa and reached an agreement with the Chinese Government to finally reopen this trade route on Thursday 6 July 2006. In another historic move the team for the first time in last 44 years crossed over to Nathu La in Sikkim from the Chinese side. The Indian delegation after returning from Lhasa called on the Chief Minister here in Gangtok. He informed about the date of actual opening of trade and all the important decisions agreed upon by both the delegations with regard to the modalities and procedures for operationalizing the border trade. Talking about our level of preparedness to handle trade transaction, he said, "Sir, I must say that you, your colleagues and your officers have done a wonderful job with a minimum possible time with limited resources at your disposal, which was commendable. You have done a good job especially after seeing what was in the other side. I have no hesitation in reporting it to the whole world that Sikkim Government has put the best foot forward."

Some of the highlights of this agreement reached between the two delegates are given below:

i) Border trade through Nathu La pass will formally resume on 6th July, 2006.

ii) Border trade markets shall be open from 1st June to 30th September every year.

iii) Border trade markets will be open from Monday to Thursday every week— four days in a week and from morning 7.30 a.m. to afternoon 3.30 p.m. Indian time and 10 a.m. to 6 p.m., the Chinese time would be the timings for the border trade.

iv) A permit fee of Rs. 50 each will be levied for every vehicle entering Sikkim side from China. Similarly, a fee of 5 Yuans (Rs. 5 equal to one Yuan) will be levied for every vehicle crossing over to the Chinese side upto the trade mart point at Renqinggang.

v) The list of 29 items from India exportable to China are as follows:

(1) Agriculture implements
(2) Blankets
(3) Copper products
(4) Clothes
(5) Cycles
(6) Coffee
(7) Tea
(8) Barley
(9) Rice
(10) Flour
(11) Dry fruit
(12) Dry and Fresh vegetables
(13) Vegetable oil
(14) Gur and Misri
(15) Tobacco
(16) Snuff
(17) Spices
(18) Shoes
(19) Kerosene oil
(20) Stationery
(21) Utensils
(22) Wheat
(23) Liquor
(24) Milk processed product
(25) Canned food
(26) Cigarettes
(27) Local herb
(28) Palm oil
(29) Hardware.

vi) The list of 15 items that are importable from China are as follows:

(1) Goat skin
(2) Sheep skin
(3) Wool
(4) Raw silk
(5) Yak tail
(6) Yak hair
(7) China clay
(8) Borax
(9) Seaibelyipe
(10) Butter
(11) Goat Kashmiri
(12) Common salt
(13) Horse
(14) Goat
(15) Sheep.

(Import of items from 13 to 15 could take place only from four designated seaports of Kolkata, Mumbai, Cochin and Chennai).

Realization of Our Dream

Historically speaking, this is a unique achievement of the State Government and the Sikkimese people at large. It will benefit the Sikkimese people materially and will also greatly enhance the significance of this land-locked state doing a quiet business across the border. We look forward to seeing the Sikkimese people and especially the youths playing a crucial role in all these exercises. When I say this here, I do not only refer to trade in isolation but the fruitful engagement of the Sikkimese people in all trade-oriented business opportunities generated by the trade. The trade and tourism integration is so vital to us. The issue of capacity-building of our people is again a key concern, which will empower ordinary people to tap all prospective opportunities. In all fronts, we are in a win-win situation.

The opening of Nathu La trade may have given rise to some apprehensions in the minds of the Sikkimese people mainly with regard to environment, influx of goods and migration. Let me assure that with the full support from the Central Government, we have strong mechanisms and institutional basis to regulate all these negative impacts. People have to be vigilant against any forces that try to misuse and misappropriate the opportunities generated by this trade route.

Our government in Sikkim has a two-pronged development strategies—both short-term and long-term. We want to see the opening of the cross-border trade as an inexhaustible trade engagement that would cater to the interest of the people many generations down the line. Our endeavour has been to encourage change in people's vocation and a shift from traditional occupation to service sectors on the basis of our natural resources. This is where we think trade and tourism integration stands out as the panacea of our development laggardness.

We are Grateful

The people of Sikkim wish to express their heartfelt thanks and gratitude to our Prime Minister Dr. Manmohan Singh for extending all support and cooperation to make this happen. We express our deepest thanks and gratefulness to our former Prime Ministers late Mr. Rajiv Gandhi, late Mr. Narasimha Rao and Mr. Atal Behari Vajpayee for their epoch-making role in reopening this traditional trade route.

We also salute the efforts and commitment made by various constituents of the Union Government including Ministry of External

Affairs, Ministry of Commerce, Ministry of Home Affairs, Ministry of Defence and Ministry of Finance. We are very thankful to the army and other defence officials posted in Sikkim for so smoothly facilitating the process. I also thank the recent delegation led by Dr. Christie Fernandes, Additional Secretary of the Ministry of Commerce, for leading the whole process to a concrete conclusion and which facilitated the actual resumption of trade with China.

I am very thankful to our Governor Mr. V. Rama Rao for his constant support for this great cause. Let me also express my gratitude to all my colleagues in the Sikkim Legislative Assembly for their unstinted support and advice. Our very high appreciations and thanks are due to the members of the Nathu La Trade Study Group and its National Advisory Board. Equally thankful we are to the Principal Secretary and all officials from Commerce and Industries and other related departments including Forests, Roads, Power and Communications for accomplishing this task of operationalizing the trade. I also thank all hoteliers, entrepreneurs, technocrats and other professionals for their crucial contributions.

Let me thank the people of Sikkim and India for their good wishes. The media has played a very vital and positive role. My hearty thanks to all constituents of both local and national media.

Win-Win Matrix

Besides its immense economic, social, historical and political significance, the reopening of Nathu La trade will convert the present hard border between India and China into a soft border. We will continue to play the most vital role of peace-builder and sustained peace-promoter. The peace dividends will be incessant and priceless for India, China and the global community.

I have personally been an advocate of this reopening. Therefore, I have in me a deep sense of satisfaction today. The countdown has begun. Let us celebrate. Let us share these joys. Let us hope that this historic action will benefit everyone in India and China.

Thank you.

Source: 4. *Sikkim: Exploring the New Frontiers*, Vol 3, Information and Public Relations Department, Government of Sikkim, 2007: pp. 136-149.

Historic Occasion of the Reopening of Nathu La Trade Route between Sikkim (India) and Tibet Autonomous Region (China)

Your Excellency, Mr. Champa Phunstok, Chairman, Tibet Autonomous Region of China, Vice Chairman, Mr. Hao Peng, Your Excellency Mr. Sun Yuxi, Ambassador of the People's Republic of China to India, hon'ble Ministers, very distinguished officials of the Government of India and China, Chief Secretary, State Government and all other officials, Major General K.T. Parnaik, GOC, 17 Mountain Division, media both from India and abroad, members of the defence personnel, business and industry fraternity, ladies and gentlemen.

It is a great honour for me to express our warm greetings to the distinguished delegates from China and from our country who have gathered at this unique point to participate in the historic event of the reopening of the Nathu La route for trade purposes.

I, on behalf of the Government of India and State Government of Sikkim, welcome all of you to one of the most beautiful, peaceful and fastest developing states of India. Today is a historic day for us. A route that linked the two great civilizations from time immemorial is being reopened. A contact that started centuries back is being reestablished.

Our first Prime Minister Pandit Jawaharlal Nehru had eloquently cherished the civilizational links between these two nations. In his speech in Paris on 23rd July 1938 he said "to the people of China, knit to us by a thousand bonds since the dawn of history, we stretch out our hands in comradeship. Their perils are ours, their suffering hurts us, and we shall hold together whatever good or ill-fortune may befall on us."

And today, the reopening of this trade route through Nathu La deeply justifies the historical statement to mutually share this great moment with you all and multiply our joy and happiness in great measures. The formal re-opening of this great Himalayan pass after forty-four years of closing down augurs well for the collective well-being of both the countries.

This was the route that linked vast masses of South Asian subcontinent with China and Central Asia. This cultural highway once triggered a chain

---

Speech delivered on 6th July 2006 at Nathu La in Sikkim.

of religious contacts, commercial exchanges and sharing of mountain commons. The representatives of King Ashoka in India and travellers-scholars like Fa Hien and Hiuen Tsang from China were the harbinger of such contacts.

This route has the rarest distinction of bringing together nomads and city-dwellers, pastoral people and farmers, merchants and monks, soldiers and pilgrims and scientists and literary figures. It was through this trade route we together shared our artistic traditions. And we together managed and conserved the ecological sanctity and pristine glory of nature and further boosting of world peace and harmony.

The travellers like Doughlas Freshfield, David Robertson, DJF Newall and John Clarke provide us with beautiful and nostalgic accounts of situations surrounding this trade route. We have a rich heritage of folk songs and folk literature based on the movement of people, their cultural exchanges and exhibitions of social habits and expressions on this trade route.

In 1890s, the exports from India were of products like superfine cloths, watches, snuffboxes, indigo, pocket knives and scissors, chant shells, cloves, and imports from Tibet were gold dust, talents of silver, musk, tincal, yak tails and goat's wool. By 1950s, there was a significant change in the traded lists. The exports from India included petrol, Rolex watches, Parker pens, food, vegetables, candles, pashminas, vaseline, tweed cloth, shoes, cigarette and religious items like butter lamps. And the imports from Tibet were Chinese silver dollar also known as *'Dyangs'*, gold, salt and bundles of the raw wool.

We have travelled a long way. The means of transport also saw a major change. The mule caravans of the 19th century were gradually replaced by the early 20th century *"tharkas"* 2-wheel axle strapped on the back of the mules that ran through the flat terrain of the Tibetan plateau. Banks, post offices and trade marts also came into being on both sides. And now in the 21st century, we will have the most sophisticated vehicles to transport the goods on both sides of the border. In other words, this route symbolizes the fading creaking sounds of burdensome mules' caravan and virtual extinction of "postal runner". It heralds the beginning of a modern means of transport and communication culture ticked with strong sense of mutual interdependence and collective survival.

The people of Sikkim have been aspiring for the reopening of this trade route for the sturdy resumption of both economic and cultural intercourse. Historically, this trade route emerged gradually to finally become one of the most viable and widely-used routes from across the Indian subcontinent. Though the concept of barter trade remained for long, it really picked up to become a trading system with all modern practices and amenities.

We have a huge depository of natural resources. We are one of the biodiversity hot spots. Therefore, there is an enormous scope for cooperation in sustainable management of natural resources. The global warming has tended to make the entire eastern Himalayan region vulnerable to climate change and hydel reconfiguration. The water resources which are our life line and a major source of livelihood remain threatened. This also calls for a constant monitoring and coordination of ecological variables on both sides of our borders.

Sikkim is a growing example of how the road map of sustainable development could be drawn and reaced at. Here nature and people have a harmonious cohabitation. It is in Sikkim, culture and trade traditionally complemented each other and continuity and change endlessly supplemented each other. Therefore, we would like to conduct the 21st century trade through Nathu La also in the broader framework of sustainable development.

We have the great vision of integrating trade and tourism. Because we think that we are the point of central tendency in the entire panorama of Buddhist circuit tourism among Bhutan, Nepal, Lhasa, Myanmar and Arunachal Pradesh, Bihar and Sikkim in India. This is undoubtedly going to be the most fascinating tourism hub and heritage sites in the world. We also have the great interest in making this route as the cultural highway that brings these cradles of ancient civilizations closer and closer. This is why we have in mind to propose a Sikkim-Lhasa bus service at an appropriate time.

At the same time, we also give top priority to regulate the entire trade so as to avoid any adverse impact on economic and socio-ecological systems on both sides. The reopening of this route would have been impossible had it not been for the farsightedness, vision and determination of the leadership of both India and China to bring about a steady warming up in the bilateral relations between these two neighbouring countries.

The people of Sikkim wish to express their heartfelt thanks and gratitude to our Prime Minister Dr. Manmohan Singh for extending all support and cooperation to make this happen. We express our deepest thanks and gratefulness to our former Prime Ministers late Rajiv Gandhi, late P.V. Narasimha Rao and Mr. Atal Behari Vajpayee for their epoch-making role in reopening this traditional trade route.

We also salute the efforts and commitment made by various constituents of the Union Government including Ministry of External Affairs, Ministry of Commerce, Ministry of Home Affairs, Ministry of Defence and

Ministry of Finance. We are very thankful to the army and other defence officials posted in Sikkim for so smoothly facilitating the process.

I am very thankful to our Governor Mr. V. Rama Rao for his constant support for this great cause. Let me also express my gratitude to all my colleagues in the Sikkim Legislative Assembly for their unstinted support and advice. Our very high appreciations and thanks are due to the members of the Nathu La Trade Study Group led by Prof. Mahendra P. Lama of Jawaharlal Nehru University, New Delhi and its National Advisory Board. Equally thankful we are to the Principal Secretary and all officials from Commerce and Industries and other related departments including Forests, Roads, Power and Communications for accomplishing this task of operationalizing the trade. I also thank all hoteliers, entrepreneurs, technocrats and other professionals for their crucial contributions.

I thank His Excellency Mr. Champa Phunstok, and the very distinguished delegates from the People's Republic of China and the Tibet Autonomous Region who have travelled a long distance to participate in this historic function. Your Excellency, you carry with you our warm greetings and thanks to your people for their support in this magnificient and far-reaching initiative.

Let me thank the people of our state and the country for their good wishes. My hearty thanks to all constituents of both local and national media for their vital role in sensitizing the people on the importance of this trade route.

Let Nathu La be what UNESCO project on Silk roads once called the "Roads of Dialogue".

Let this trade route further build trust, confidence and wisdom in the consolidation of ever flourishing relations between India and China. This event will mark the beginning of a new era in the relationship between the two economic powers.

This beginning, on all counts, has been made for the bigger things to come for people from both sides of the country. People from both the countries will stand to witness this event as the harbinger of flourishing trade, deeper understanding, wider cooperation and durable friendship between these two emerging world powers from Asia. Let us celebrate the beginning of this new era.

Let us greet and wish each other in the highest Sikkimese traditions for the fulfillment of all the humane goals that we have set forth in reopening this trade route. It is a win-win situation for all of us.

Thank you.

Jai Bharat.

Source: 5. Sikkim: Exploring the New Frontiers, Vol 3, *Information and Public Relations Department, Government of Sikkim, 2007: pp. 150-153.*

Inauguration of Trade Mart at Sherathang
(after the Reopening of Nathu La Trade Route)

Hon'ble Ministers, very distinguished officials of the Government of India, distinguished officials from the Government of Sikkim, respected media representatives both from India and abroad, members of the defence personnel, business and industry fraternity, ladies and gentlemen,

We have gathered here at Sherathang to witness a major historical event of the inauguration of trade mart for the trade between Tibet Autonomous Region of China and Sikkim state of India. I, on behalf of the Government of India and Government of Sikkim, extend our warm welcome to all of you to this memorable function.

This is the peak rainy season in our state where you may find the monsoon at its most beautiful attire and many a times at its most fearsome form. This is the season when our farmers sow the seeds of food security and sustenance. This is the time when the nature goes for regeneration. This is again the season when nature tests the grit of human capabilities to deal with hardships and calamities. In other words, this is the most auspicious time that represents nature and human combined-led prosperity. Therefore, we consider the Nathu La trade reopening as part of this most auspicious moment.

This event marks the beginning of a new era in the ever flourishing India-China relations. Let me recall how almost 133 years ago the real initiative began to formalize this trade route. John Ware Edgar, the then Deputy Commissioner of Darjeeling, was deputed in 1873 to enquire into the possibility of re-establishing Indian trade with the then *Tibet. This had* been in abeyance for nearly a century. He was mandated to submit to the government detailed information regarding the actual condition, extent, and prospects of trade. He wrote in his report:

"There was scarce a day during my stay in East Sikkim that I did not meet people either coming from, on their way to, Darjeeling with goods, the value of which at first sight seemed quite disproportioned to the labour that had to be undergone in taking them to market; but I have no doubt that the traffic pays them. These *murwa* sellers expected to get six rupees

---

Speech delivered on 6th July 2006 in Sherathang, Sikkim

for their *murwa* at Chhombi, and with this sum to be able to buy at Phari four maunds of salt, which they could sell in Darjeeling for Rs. 32, while the value of their *murwa* at Guntuck (Gangtok) was Rs. 4-8."

Since then a series of initiatives were put in place to give this route and the pattern of trade a proper institutional shape. As a result, the later half of the 1890s, witnessed a fairly good trade between British India with Tibet through Sikkim passes. This was highlighted by the then Political Officer for Sikkim. His diary extract of the 16th January 1898 mentions, "the trade for December are very good, amounting to Rs. 3,41,290. This includes a consignment of gold worth Rs. 16,800—the finest that has been sent in for some years."

The adventurous Younghusband Mission launched from Sikkim in 1903 accomplished its task of reaching Lhasa thereby leading to the 1904 Convention that firmed up the Anglo-Tibet trade. Since then this route remained a major point of exchange between the then Tibet and cities in the mainland India including Calcutta, Bombay and Madras.

Mention may be made here that regular trade between Tibet and British India was carried out on the basis of various conventions drawn between China and Great Britain from time to time in the distant past. There used to be altogether thirteen routes* operational from the Indian side for the trade: (i) From Ladakh, via Rudok, Mansarowar Lake, Mariamzla and Shigatse to Lhasa; (ii) From Srinagar, via Leh, Ladakh, Tashigong and Indus valley to Gartok; (iii) From Kulu and Lahul, via Shangrang la, and Chumurti to Gartok; (iv) From Simla, via Shipki to Gartok; (v) From Tehri Garhwal, via Nilang to Gartok; (vi) From Badrinath (British Garhwal) via, Mana la, and Toling (Totlingmath) to Gartok; (vii) From Almora, via Jashinath (British Garhwal), Niti la and Daba to Gartok; (viii) From Almora, via Milam and Uttadhaura to Gartok; (ix) From Almora, via Darma or Noe Pass and Gyanema to Gartok; (x) From Almora, via Lankpya, Lekh and Gyanema to Gartok; (xi) From Almora, via Lipu Lekh and Purang (Taklakot) to Gartok; (xii) From Siliguri, via Kalimpong, Jalep la and Chumbi to Gyantse; (xiii) From Siliguri, via Gangtok, Nathu La and Chumbi to Gyantse. Hence, the reopening of this route is like re-establishing the traditional bonds between the two countries.

The Memorandum signed between the Government of the Republic of India and the Government of the People's Republic of China Expanding Border Trade through Nathu La pass in Sikkim on 23rd June 2003 has striking positive dimensions. This local level economic exchange reflects the burgeoning and galloping economic relations between these two economic power houses. This is indicated by the massive increase in bilateral trade volume from a mere $ 49 million in 1990 to over $ 14 billion in 2005. Together they can be the forerunner in the making of "New Asianism" in the 21st century. India and China can together change the entire course of economic orientation and patterns of growth and development at the global level. We have a firm conviction that an arrangement like Nathu La trade route could be a solid support towards such direction.

The people of India and particularly of Sikkim and the neighbouring states of our country would like to really make use of this trade route as a major avenue for both economic growth and multi-faceted development. We need to steadily transform the present nascent level of infrastructure to a robust and modern system that could handle a major portion of bilateral trade between India and China. Besides the volume, we would also expect the composition of trade to undergo significant changes in the course of next few years. This means we shall have to constantly revise the list of tradable items that would pass through this shortest land route between India and China.

We would even think that this land route could be used for trade in services including in collaboration in areas like biotechnology, investment, and tourism and information technology. Sikkim and Tibet Autonomous region together constitute an unparallel variety of biodiversity. The Nathu La Trade Study Group in its report very clearly lists the investment opportunities and huge market size that are now available in whole of western China region. The starting of the railway line linking Lhasa with other major eastern cities of China adds an altogether a new dimension to the market access and investment opportunities.

For us in Sikkim, this is a major opportunity. So far we used to be handicapped by our land-lockedness. We were badly constrained in our market expansions and physical linkages. Today we have converted this disadvantage into an attractive opportunity. As people's representative, I always had this firm conviction in me that if we really pursue a public interest issue sincerely you can achieve. This is a result of a clear vision, consistent hard work and honest perseverance.

When I first mooted this proposal for trade route reopening, many shrugged off the view as something impossible. However, we incorporated this issue in our Election manifestos of 1994, 1999 and 2004. We worked hard with all the authorities at the Central Government and other stakeholders. Today we have succeeded in accomplishing this seemingly impossible task which has not only benefited Sikkim state but the entire country. Apart from resumption of trade, Sikkim has played the crucial role of bridging the two Asian powers both in terms of bringing the two countries closer and also economic cooperation. I would feel that this is one of the greatest contributions made by small state like Sikkim for the country.

Trade today has emerged as a powerful tool of growth and trade includes both imports and exports. In today's world, fair trade is not something which needs to be feared but should be looked upon as an opportunity for accelerating growth and ushering in prosperity.

Sikkim merged into the Indian Union on the basis of popular Referendum expressing the collective will of the people of Sikkim. And I find no other state with similar history to have merged into the mainstream. Today, Sikkim is the most peaceful state and one of the most progressive states in the country. Despite sharing international borders with neighbouring countries, Sikkim has remained peaceful and safe. This, in itself, is an exemplary in the context of whatever is happening in other parts of the country. Towards the country, this I feel is an exceptional contribution made by Sikkim and its people.

The Sherathang mart for the purpose of this trade is opened from today. Yet the Centre will have to continue to assist us for infrastructure development, construction of other amenities like guest house, hotel, parking places, expansion of roads etc. At this initial stage, infrastructure facilities are inadequate but whatever Nathu La requires is of national importance as the dignity and honour of the country would squarely reflect on the level of infrastructure including all other required facilities and services. Hence, it should not mean that this is only Sikkim's demand as such. All the distinguished officials from the Centre present today will have to act as our representatives at the Centre to voice our demand and fulfill them at an early date. You are all aware that we have not a single Minister at the Centre, no representative and officials at the Central Government. This is the unfortunate truth that the Sikkim Government has faced all these years.

We expect that this trade route will change the basic structure of the Sikkimese economy by refocusing on our comparative advantages like scientific harnessing of natural resources, emphasis on eco-tourism and other service-related activities. We also strongly feel that over the years, Sikkim could be a major trading zone like Singapore. We are, therefore, proposing to set up a Special Economic Zone where many of the small and medium enterprises from both India and abroad could be located.

We also consider this reopening of the Nathu La trade route as a beautiful peace dividend. We are the most peaceful state in the country by any indications and measurements. But we have not bought peace. We have earned it. We have built it brick by brick. We have nurtured it day and night. That is why peace is a sustainable phenomenon in Sikkim. In our notion of peace and stability we have strong elements of human and environmental security, social justice, respect for rights and freedom and communal harmony. We have been the strongest votary of rule of law. People-centric notion of governance is our mantra. People and peace, therefore, are central to our development philosophy, societal existence and political action. That is why despite situation of conflicts, violence and instability in our neighbouring states and countries we remain a citadel of peace and prosperity.

We would like to use Nathu La trade route as a means to achieve much greater heights. We would like to be a major actor in the building of modem India. We have already achieved some of the best indicators. Let me mention some of them.

We are one of the fastest growing states in the country. During the last three years of the 10th Plan (2002/03-2004/05) the state GDP has grown over 10 percent per annum at current prices. If this is maintained Sikkim would for the first time achieve a 2-digit growth rate.

The per capita net domestic product of Sikkim recorded over three-fold increase from Rs. 8457 in 1993-94 to Rs. 26,851 in 2004-2005. Today we have the 11th highest per capita income.

We were the third state in the country to publish Human Development Report and a Vision document.

We have one of most liberal investment policies. A number of investors from Europe and South East Asia are likely to invest in the state in the next couple of months.

We pioneered the concept of environmental security. I was voted as the "Greenest Chief Minister of India" in the nation-wide polls conducted by the reputed Centre for Science and Development in New Delhi.

We were the first state to ban use of plastic bags and possibly the only state where the forest cover has steadily increased from 45 percent in 2001 to 46 percent in 2003.

We have been declared as the third best state in the devolution and decentralization initiatives under the 73rd Amendment of the Constitution.

All our social indicators including the literacy rate, human development index, access to electricity, health facilities and drinking water, death rate, birth rate and infant mortality are in the top brackets in the country.

Within next one decade installed capacity of our hydel-power is likely to be over 1200 MW.

Before the trade route was closed down in 1962, this trade route provided hand some opportunities to the people of Sikkim. It provided them with a major source of livelihood. There is no record of any adverse fall out even after 80 years of this extensive trading. In fact the Government of Sikkim was so concerned that it appointed a committee to assess the negative fallout of the closing down of this route. The committee was supposed to provide alternative means of revenue generation for the state and livelihood for the people. Looking back we feel that if the trade had continued, Sikkim would have really undergone a massive economic transformation long time back.

Therefore, the debate and discussion should be more on the lines of how the people of Sikkim in particular can maximize the gains from this historic arrangement. We should strive for injecting the best of technologies, knowledge, human resources and institutions in order to optimally harness the benefits from this arrangement. We should devote a lot of time and resources to build capacities among the younger generation to durably internalize the gains from this trading arrangement.

The reopening of Nathu La trade route also augurs well for the entire North-East region of India. This is the way to realize the larger goals of India's 'Look East' policy and consolidate sub-regional groupings like South Asia Growth Quadrangle (SAGQ) and Bay of Bengal Initiative for Multi-Sectoral Techno-Economic Cooperation (BIMSTEC).

At the same time let me also emphasize that the trading community involved in this trade route has a onerous responsibility of doing only what is socio-economically correct. We do not want any irregularity. There is no place for fly-by-night operators. Our government will have zero tolerance on any anti-national activity.

We thank the farsighted Union leadership in Delhi, our very distinguished officials in various Union Ministries and the people of Sikkim and India at large for giving this unparallel honour to Sikkim to be a bridge between two oldest civilizations and the economic giants. Please be assured that this rare honour bestowed on us would be respected, maintained and operationalized in the best Indian tradition of keeping the national interest aloft for ever and ever.

Our very profuse thanks to all our distinguished guests who have come here to grace this nostalgic event.

Our very special thanks to all the media representatives for braving this rainy season. We salute all of you for your commitment to reach the message of peace and prosperity emanating from Nathu La to the entire global community.

Before I conclude, let me once again extend our heartiest welcome to all of you. I hope our arrangements and hospitality designed for this event will meet your expectations. And I also hope that your entire stay here face to face with Mount Kanchen-junga and serene rainy season will freshen the moods like freshly bloomed flowers in highlands of Sikkim.

Nathu La trade route is a thing of beauty. And let this remain a joy for ever.

Thank you.

Jai Bharat.

Source: 6. *Sikkim: Exploring the New Frontiers,* Vol 3, Information and Public Relations Department, Government of Sikkim, 2007: pp. 154-160.

International Tourism Bourse, Berlin

Distinguished participants, ladies and gentlemen

Let me first extend very warm greetings to all of you present here from the people of my state Sikkim and India. I am personally very delighted to be here in this very important, interesting and diverse gathering.

It had always been my dream to visit your great country, Germany and this magnificent city, Berlin, to see and learn from huge and deep development strides that have taken place here. We know the leading role Germany plays in influencing the global policies. We vividly remember the historic unification process in Germany in 1989. We remain deeply impressed with the ever-flourishing relations between our country and Germany.

My main objective to visit Berlin and Germany this time of course, is to attend and participate in this world-famous ITB in Berlin. We very keenly participate in the ITB because our state Sikkim is emerging as one of the most attractive tourism destinations in the country. We have very unique features in our entire tourism development and management.

We are deeply aware that there are several tourism-related practices in various parts of the world which are worth replicating in our state Sikkim and in India at large. There cannot be two opinions about the fact that the ITB brings together the world's best tourism practices to a single and very friendly forum. The ITB is also now a comprehensive meeting ground for professionals, businessmen, investors, policy-makers, development partners, media, tourists and other stakeholders.

At the same time, we also have quite a few things to offer to this great emergence of what I call "world tourism movement". Sikkim is dotted with pristine natural glory and magnificent varieties of resources. We have sustained peace and tranquility quite rarely found in many of the tourism destinations. Our concept of peace is not only absence of violence, instability and uncertainty, our peace is also individual-centric, society-wide and sustainably-built. We have unpolluted and plastic-less towns and villages.

We have scores of serene and calm lakes and waterfalls strewn around with an unparallel biodiversity. We are the link state for two greatest

---

Speech delivered on 9th March 2006 in Berlin, Germany

civilizations of India and China. We are the custodian of environmental security and the Buddhist relics in the entire Eastern Himalaya. This is why our state has bagged a large number of top national awards in India.

All these are there against the backdrop of the Mt. Kanchenjunga, the third highest peak in the world and the most beautiful gift of mother earth. Today the world tourism business is like a movement which brings gains, benefits, happiness, understanding and solidarity to the entire global societies. Every human being is touched directly and indirectly by this movement. Every region will get the benefits of the forward and backward linkages of tourism. The world is long hankering for peace. Tourism is one way to mobilize forces of peace and tranquility. Therefore, this 'world tourism movement' is the most beautiful aspect of ongoing globalization process.

Ladies and gentlemen, this is why we are here amongst all of you. To share, to learn and to disseminate the message of world tourism movement. We give a very high importance to our participation in the prestigious ITB. This is amply reflected in the composition of our Sikkimese delegation from India. I have with me a very high-level team consisting of hon'ble Minister of Tourism, hon'ble Minister of Agriculture, two senior lady hon'ble Members of the Sikkim Legislative Assembly and senior advisor and officials.

Let me confess, my visit to ITB, Berlin has been really an eye-opener. I remain deeply impressed by the great strides the tourism industry has made in the world. It is a serious business. In a way it is much more serious a business than dealing with commodities and products. Because in tourism business, we are mainly dealing with human beings and their likes and dislikes. We are talking about the movement of people from one place to another and giving them choices of their maximum utility. More importantly unlike the tradeable products, the varieties of people in the movement of tourists constantly change. They are dynamic in both demand and attitudes. In economics we call it maximization of utility. This maximization of satisfaction of tourists is a very formidable task. A massive challenge to the entire tourism industry.

Sikkim has a range of rich and magnificent cultural heritage. With over 4000 species of different plants and shrubs, around 700 species of rare orchids and rhododendrons, Sikkim's biodiversity is found to be unparallel in the country.

Sikkim is the gateway to India's 'Look East' policy. The new regionalism primarily triggered by globalization and flourishing people to people contact is fast influencing this 'Look East' policy. We are looking forward to play a crucial role in India's trade, tourism and other economic cooperation with countries in the eastern fringe including Bangladesh, Myanmar, Thailand, Malaysia, Singapore, China and even Japan.

The Nathu La pass trade route is being reopened. This trade route used to be a thriving link between India and China before it was closed down in 1962. This is the shortest viable land route to Tibet Autonomous Region of China from any of the South Asian countries. The reopening of this trade route is likely to bring about significant economic opportunities.

Against this backdrop and the background of India's effort to refocusing on European Union as a vital economic partner under the leadership of our intellectual-statesman hon'ble Prime Minister Dr. Manmohan Singh, I would like to put across two points before this very distinguished gathering.

Firstly, we would like to make Sikkim a very dear and friendly destination for the people of Germany and Europe. We do get a number of tourists, from the European countries. However, we want to attract more and more. We have everything an European tourist would like to take advantage of the warm and smiling people, trekking and mountaineering facilities, varieties of foods, traditional medicinal practices, hot springs and placid lakes. We have beautiful tourist cottages spread over in highly exotic areas and strewn with the sacred monasteries and temples. The holy seat of the Karmapa is located in Rumtek monastery in Sikkim. Our next door neighbour is the world-famous tea-producing region Darjeeling. We have very friendly tourism promotion and support systems. We have tourism all around the year in spring, summer, fall and winter. And most importantly we ensure absolute security.

Sikkim has the unparallel distinction of having bom rich practices of traditional medicines and availability of a rich variety of medicinal plants. The world today is enamoured by herbal charm. Sikkim is the most congenial place to cater to this huge and flourishing world herbal products market. Our hon'ble President Dr. A.P.J. Abdul Kalam has often mentioned about this unique strength of Sikkim.

Sikkim's track record in the reforms process both in economic system and governance and public management has been highly commended by both the governmental agencies and private sector. Our social sector indicators are one of the best in the country. We have managed our environment well. We remain the most peaceful and politically very stable state in the country today.

And secondly we would like to invite as many investors as possible from Germany and Europe. Sikkim is an investor-friendly state. We have designed very conducive investment policies. We have comprehensive enabling legal framework, environmental conditions and fiscal incentives. The labour laws in the state are most liberal. The State Government has now set up the Board of Investment under my Chairmanship to implement a Single Window Policy.

Sikkim was given the best state award among the 10 smaller states (including Delhi) for the most favourable investment climate by *India Today* media group in 2005. Sikkim has also been adjudged as an investor-friendly state by a leading national magazine *Business Today.* We have had a series of 'Investors Forum Meeting' in New Delhi and other cities of India where a large number of investors and business houses like CII and FICCI participated.

Government of India's industrial policy for the North-Eastern states provides ample provisions of fiscal and other relief and incentives to all new industries for at least ten years from the date of commencement of commercial production. The Union Government has also notified Sikkim for investment subsidy in infrastructural projects. The State Government has in turn declared some areas of the state as Industrial Belt. We have set up an Agricultural Export Zones (AEZ).

Sikkim already has the presence of eminent national and international public and private organizations including UNIDO, UNDP, World Bank, USAID, SIDA, Asian Development Bank and AusAid. Our greatest strengths are not the huge and gigantic factories to produce goods on mass scale but those products which are high value in content. Our biggest forte is biodiversity and other natural resources-based eco-commercial activities. This includes medicinal plants, horticulture, floriculture, agriculture and eco-tourism. We have tremendous potential in certain specific areas. For example, we are the highest producer of large-sized cardamom in the country. Our ginger, orange and orchids are all grown in organic conditions.

The hydel-power with a potential of 8000 MW and service-oriented sectors including health, education, tourism and information technology are our other strengths. By harnessing each bit of huge hydel-power potential, we aim at making Sikkim the "Clean Energy Capital of India".

We want the private sector to be a part of Sikkimese ethos, culture and development goals. We have very shining examples of Sikkim Distilleries, Sikkim Time Corporation, and Sikkim Jewels. They have been there for long, contributing immensely to the growth process.

Besides, we provide very distinct advantages for investors to invest in areas like educational, professional and technical institutions; organic farming; trading activities across the border; transport and communication; biotechnology; health; mountaineering and trekking; and small and medium enterprises.

The reopening of Nathu La trade route has in them the core economic and commercial contents of trade, investment and tourism activities. This is where we see a major role and opportunity for the German and European investors.

It would be a perfect match between the superb technology, quality finance and efficient management that Germany and Europe have so assiduously built, and ample natural resources, human capital and congenial investment environment we readily provide in Sikkim.

I am also very keen to utilize this visit of mine to reach an understanding with the potential investors, businessmen and development partners for their participation in Sikkim. Please do discuss all your interests with our officials and me.

Let us sign memorandum of understanding to initiate and concretize your interest in Sikkim and our commitment to host you. We have a very dynamic Embassy of our country here in Berlin led by Her Excellency Madame Meera Shankar who is one of our most experienced and knowledgeable diplomats.

Let me conclude by again extending our warm invitations to all of you to our state Sikkim in India. Let us work together to make Sikkim the eco-tourism destination for the very distinguished German and European tourists. Let me assure you of the highest comfort level and warmest hospitality.

Thank you.

Source: 7. Sikkim: Exploring the New Frontiers, Vol 3, Information and Public Relations Department, Government of Sikkim, 2007: pp. 167-171.

First anniversary of the reopening of Indo-China Border Trade through Nathu La

1st anniversary of the reopening of Indo-China Border Trade through Nathula was commemorated at Chintan Bhawan in Gangtok on July 5, 2007. It was organized by the Department of Commerce and Industries, Government of Sikkim, and Mr. D.D. Bhutia, Minister for UD & HD graced the occassion as the Chief Guest.

The Nathula Border Trade between Sikkim and the Tibet Autonomous Region (TAR) in China resumed on July 6 last year after a gap of 44 years. The resumption of trade has not only created history but also achieved an important opportunity to introduce Sikkim to the world. It may be mentioned here that this year the border trade started from May 1st, the value of items exported to TAR during the month was Rs. 3,43,000 while the import from TAR was nil.

Mr. D.D. Bhutia, Minister for UD & HD, speaking on the occasion, called upon the intellectuals to study the border trade in depth for further expansion. He stated that reopening of trade was a significant achievement of both Central and State government. It has generated tremendous amount of enthusiasm, a great expectation and a surge of interest to participate in the trade and other related activities, he added.

Mr. R.B. Subba, Minister for Commerce and Industries, said that it would take time for the trade to gain volume but most importantly, it has cemented the relationship between the two Asian giants, India and China. While commenting on the lists of items on the trade list, he informed that the matter had already been referred to the Union Government. The view of the Central government was to develop the infrastructure in a phased manner, which the state Government has implemented in a record time, he added.

Mr. S.P. Subba, Director, Commerce and Industries Department, presented a status report on Nathula Border Trade and informed that the Importer-Exporter Code Number (IEC) was not required for this border trade as the traders were authorized to trade in Indian Currency valuing up to Rs. 25000/- only. Following the traders demand to increase the value limit for exportable items, State Government had requested the Centre and the same has now been raised to Rs. 1,00,000/- per consignment per trader.

Source: 8. *Sikkim Today*, Vol. VII, No. 3 (July-Sept. 2007): p. 7.

SIKKIM 2007
INVESTORS MEET

With her stable economic conditions and favorable economic policies, today, India is the biggest market for the investors in the whole world. She has captured the imagination of the investors, who has been flocking in to take advantage of it. Sikkim. although a small State of this great nation, has been adjudged as the most investment friendly state.

With its proactive Industrial Policy, clear growth vision and also being the most peaceful and politically stable State, Sikkim has set its industrial progress in a fast forward mode. With a view to continue this tempo, Sikkim Investors Meet 2007 was held at Chintan Bhawan in Gangtok to develop a long term partnership with the private sectors.

Welcoming the enthusiastic investors, the Chief Minister, Mr. Pawan Chamling said that while taking full advantage of Sikkim's friendly and favorable industrial policy, investors should always give preference to locals when it comes to employment. "Be it an ordinary labour or skilled, preference should be given to the locals of the slate.Expressing his dissatisfaction, a visibly upset Chief Minister said that, unfortunately, the industrial units which had been set up in Sikkim, reap all the benefits under tax concessions and subsidies but failed to help the State Government in this respect.

Local youth should replace all those appointed from outside the State gradually and foreign labourers engaged in various projects should be withdrawn immediately and the local labourers should replace them, the Chief Minister stressed.

Mr. Chamling also released a booklet on New Industrial Policy and Other Concessions for the State of Sikkim (2007).

The Minister for Commerce and Industries, Mr. R.B Subba. who also addressed the gathering, said that it was due to the vision and the far-sighted policies of the Chief Minister that Sikkim became a potential target for the investors today.

An interactive session on matters relating to Power Projects, Tourism, Industrial Developments and hotels was participated by the Chief Engineer cum Secretary (Power), Mr. D.D Pradhan, Commissioner cum Secretary (Tourism), Mr. G.K. Upadhaya. Secretary (Industries), Mr. M.G. Kiran and Secretary (UD&HD), Mr. Tobjor Dorjee, respectively.

Earlier, the Secretary Commerce and Industries Department, welcomed the distinguished guests.

Source: 9. *Sikkim Today,* Vol. VII, No. 3 (July-Sept. 2007): p. 6.

ECONOMIC DEVELOPMENT

FACTS AND FIGURES SPEAK FOR THEMSELVES

- Sikkim has the 5th highest growth rate in the per capita NSDP.
- In per capita income it occupies the 10th highest rank in the country.
- It is 3rd in per capita plan expenditure.
- In literacy rate it ranks 16th highest in the country.
- In child mortality rate it ranks 13th when counted from below.
- In birth rate it ranks 12th when counted from below.
- In socio-economic infrastructure development index it ranks 9th position.
- In plan expenditure in social sector it ranks 4th position.
- In relation to Externally Aided Projects it occupies the 10th position.
- In total budget deficit it ranks 4th from below.
- Accordingto the fiscal policy of the central government VAT has been implemented in Sikkim.
- The state has currently achieved a 9% growth rate. It aims at achieving 10% growth rate at the end of the tenth five year plan.

Increase in State Revenue

Rs. in crores	1993-94	2005-06
• Tax Revenue	Rs.12.77	Rs 119.02
• Non Tax Revenue	Rs. 28.53	Rs.1013.22

- Tax GSDP ratio has increased significantly to 7%.
- Non Tax GSDP ratio has increased to 14%
- Fiscal Deficit has been drastically brought down from 11% to 4%

Decrease in BPL

- 1993-94 - 41.43%
- 1999-2000 - 36.55%
- 2006-2007 - 19.20%
- SDF Government has been successful in bringing more and more funds from the Centre. In 1994, the annual plan outlay was only Rs.120 crores but today it is Rs. 690 crores.
- When SDF Government came to power, State's internal revenue was only Rs. 41.30 crores. Today it is Rs. 300 crores approx.
- The Government has given priority to nature based economy. The strategy of development has identified water resources, natural beauty

of the state, its greenery, mountains, forest product, medicinal plants, minerals etc. Besides this horticulture, floriculture and human development have also been identified as important variables in development.

- Realising the importance of cooperatives and to encourage it, the government has formed cooperatives in most of the villages and also provides Rs.77,000/- support to every cooperative society.
- Today, there are 496 cooperative Samitis and 94 consumer cooperatives in the state which are being provided loan through SISCO Bank. Till now 1270 people and organizations have been benefited.
- For the management of the entire developmental activities of the state, a State Planning Commission has been formed.
- For formulation of developmental plans at the district level, District Planning Boards under the Zilla Panchayats have been formed in all the four district.
- Economic Survey of the State is now regularly published on an annual basis.
- Former Prime Minister of India, Shri Atal Behari Vajpayee during his visit to Sikkim announced an economic package of Rs.500 crores.

Industrial and Investment Activities

- After 1994 three big industries and 245 small scale industries have come up in the state. They are running successfully. Sick industries are also being divested, privatized or closed down.
- Under the Chairmanship of the Chief Minister, Government has set up a *Board of Investment.* This Board analyses all investment proposals proposed in the state and approves them at the highest level.
- Besides creating a friendly environment for the national and international investors and industrialists, the state has also framed policies to reduce the rising problem of unemployment.
- Beside providing land to industrial units, the government also provides capital investment subsidies to the tune of 25 % , 30 % and 15 % to small scale industries and export oriented industries which have been established by local industrialists and large and medium scale industries, respectively.
- To encourage the development of industries in the state, the Government has demarcated the following areas as Industrial Belts: Rangpo via Singtam to Ranipool; Melli via Jorethang to Legshep and from Rangpo to Rorathang.

- For tourism and industrial development workshops were held in Delhi and Kolkota with national and international investors and industrialists and non-governmental organizations. The first meeting of Sikkim *Investment forum* was held in Delhi on 22nd February 2001.
- To help industrialists who are interested in investing in Sikkim, the government has introduced the *single window* system in the state.
- To ensure the protection of the intellectual property and to deal with cases concerning the intellectual property rights, committees like Intellectual Patent Committee and State Intellectual Law Committee have been formed under the Chairmanship of the Chief Minister.
- The government is giving priority to those industries which are based on local raw materials available in the state and those industries which are environment friendly.
- A special scheme titled "Chief Minister's Self Employment Scheme" to educated and unemployed youth was launched to provide financial assistance for self-employment opportunities.
- Since a significant chunk of commodities coming from Nathu La Trade Route are likely to be raw materials, the government is exploring ways and means to process them in Sikkim and to make them fit for export. The government has plans to establish special industrial estate for this purpose.
- The Sikkim Industrial Development Corporation is regularly holding programmes and camps to encourage industrial activities in the state.
- After re-opening of the Nathu La Trade Route, a number of industrialists have already shown interest to set up industrial units in the state.

Source: 10. *Looking Back Twelve Years of the SDF Government* [1994-2006], Information and Public Relations Department, Government of Sikkim, 2007: pp. 25-28.

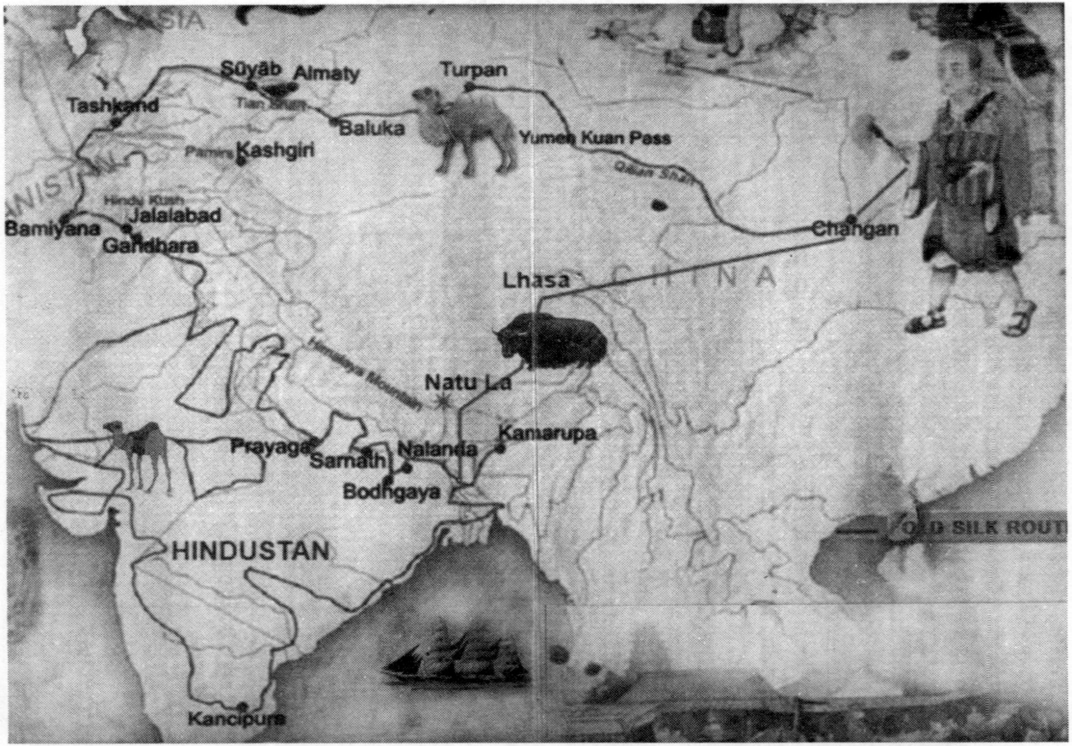

Sūyāb
Almaty
Turpan
Tashkand
Baluka
Yumen Kuan Pass
Kashgiri
Pamirs
Hindu Kush
Jalalabad
Bamiyana
Gandhara
Changan
Lhasa
CHINA
Natu La
Kamarupa
Prayaga
Samath
Nalanda
Bodhgaya
HINDUSTAN
OLD SILK ROUTE
Kancipura

Photographs

Old Silk Route. Photo courtesy: Department of Commerce & Industries, Government of Sikkim

Serathang Mart. Photo courtesy: Department of Commerce & Industries, Government of Sikkim

India-China Border at Nathu La. Photo courtesy: Department of Commerce & Industries, Government of Sikkim

Approach to Nathu La. Photo courtesy: Department of Commerce & Industries, Government of Sikkim

Main Bazaar of Gangtok in 1952. Photo courtesy: P.D. Rai

Main Bazaar of Gangtok in 2005. Photo courtesy: P.D. Rai

List of Contributors

Amiya Kumar Chaudhuri is a Fellow at Maulana Abul Kalam Azad Institute of Asian Studies, Kolkata.

P.D. Rai, an entrepreneur and eco-tourism specialist, is a member of the Advisory Council, Centre for North East Studies and Policy Research, New Delhi and an Executive Member of the Ecotourism and Conservation Society of Sikkim, Gangtok.

M.G. Kiran is the Secretary, Trade & Commerce, Government of Sikkim.

K. Elumalai is an Associate Fellow at the National Council of Applied Economic Research (NCAER), New Delhi.

Binoda K. Mishra is a Fellow at Maulana Abul Kalam Azad Institute of Asian Studies, Kolkata.

Renzino Lepcha is Executive Secretary of Ecotourism and Conservation Society of Sikkim, Gangtok.

Shubhrajeet Konwer teaches International Politics in Gauhati University.

Jyoti P. Tamang is the Consulting Fellow-cum-Coordinator (Academic), Sikkim Central University, Gangtok, and Scientific Advisor to the International Foundation for Science, Sweden.

Sohel Firdos is a Fellow at the Development Studies, Centre for Studies in Social Sciences, Kolkata.

Index